DAVID McCONNELL

IMPLEMENTING
Computer Supported
COOPERATIVE LEARNING

2ND EDITION

**KOGAN
PAGE**

For Martin

First published in 1994
Second edition 2000

Kogan Page Limited
120 Pentonville Road
London
N1 9JN
UK

Stylus Publishing Inc.
22883 Quicksilver Drive
Sterling
VA 20166-2012
USA

© David McConnell, 1994, 2000

British Library Cataloguing in Publication Data

A CIP record for this book is available from the British Library.

ISBN 0 7494 3135 0

Typeset by Jean Cussons Typesetting, Diss, Norfolk
Printed and bound in Great Britain by Clays Ltd, St Ives plc

Contents

Contents

Acknowledgements

This book is the outcome of many years of collaboration with friends and colleagues in researching and designing learning events. I would like to thank them all, especially: Mark Bryson, John Burgoyne, Ginny Hardy, Vivien Hodgson, Sarah Mann, Bob Lewis, Michael Reynolds and participants on the various intakes of the computer mediated MA in Management Learning at Lancaster University. They have all contributed in one way or another to the ideas in this book. Finally, I want to give special thanks to Martin Middleton who commented on drafts of the book and offered me constant support while writing it.

Part of the research for, and writing of, this book was supported by a UK Economic and Social Research Council grant (number R000234531).

Some sections of the book are derived from previously published work. Parts of Chapter 2 are from Hardy, V, Hodgson, V, McConnell, D and Reynolds, M (1991) *Computer Mediated Communication for Management Training and Development: A research report*, CSML, Lancaster University, Lancaster, UK, and from Hodgson, V and McConnell, D (1991) 'Online education and development', in Prior, JK (ed.) (1991) *Gower handbook of Training and Development*, Gower, Aldershot. Chapter 4 derives from McConnell, D (1997) 'Interaction patterns in mixed sex groups in educational computer conferences', *Gender and Education*, 9 (3). Parts of Chapter 6 are from McConnell, D (1992) 'Computer mediated communication for management learning', in Kaye, AR (ed.) *Collaborative Learning through Computer Conferencing*, Springer-Verlag, Berlin. Part of Chapter 7 is from Hodgson, V, Lewis, R and McConnell, D (1989) *Information Technology-based Open Learning: A study report*, Occasional Paper, InTER/12/89, Lancaster University, UK.

Introduction

This book is about the use of computers to facilitate cooperative learning amongst groups of people in formal learning situations such as university and college settings and organisational training situations. On the whole, the people I have in mind are those who are geographically isolated from each other. But this isolation may take many forms: members of the groups may be literally miles from each other, in the same country or in different countries. They may be in the same building, separated by nothing more than bricks and mortar. They may be on a college campus or be part of an organisation, separated more by the conventions of their everyday work-lives than by any major physical barrier. No matter how distant each member is, they all have a need to work together on some aspect of their learning, and do this through the use of computers. I call this form of cooperative learning *computer supported cooperative learning* – CSCL.

The book is not about what we *could* do with computers, if we had all the time and money available. It is about the use of existing, readily accessible, affordable and readily usable technologies which we can use *today* to support cooperative learning. Although new technologies which can support cooperative learning such as multimedia and video-teleconferencing, and new communications media such as ISDN (integrated systems digital networks) and optic fibre, are mentioned, they are not the technologies that will largely be at most teachers' and trainers' disposal, nor within their usual budgets. So the focus is largely on the use of widely available technologies which we know can support groups working together, and which are affordable in most circumstances. These technologies include personal computers, communications software, modems, mainframe computers, telephone lines, the Internet, the World Wide Web and the like. All learning and training institutions will have these technologies, to varying degrees. And, although by no means universal, many learners these days have their own personal computer, which with a modem and communications software can be turned into a vehicle for group communication.

The other aspect of CSCL is of course the learning that takes place via the technology. The major message of this book is that people learn best when they have the opportunity to work with other people, through processes of cooperation and collaboration. This may take many forms, such as working on a project together, eg producing a joint paper or report; or working on an action learning problem related to their particular learning context. They may be involved in supporting each other in carrying out their own, personal learning tasks, eg helping each other define what they want to learn, how to go about it and how to evaluate it when completed. CSCL can be a combination of learning and working together, and learning and working by yourself with support from others.

What is central to the idea of CSCL in this book is the benefit to learners of taking part in discussions about their learning. Discussion makes us aware of our own learning and that of others. It forces us to articulate our thoughts and ideas, and makes them available as a resource for the group to use and learn from. Discussion can also lead to changes in our ideas, ways of thinking, and eventually our ways of doing; it is therefore highly developmental. It is also the basis of our democratic social system, and in computer supported cooperative learning the democratic process is a central concern, working towards supporting and empowering the differences that each learner brings to their work in the group.

In CSCL, discussions largely take place asynchronously and not in real-time. This is a major benefit to learners. In asynchronous discussions learners have the time to participate as and when they like. They are not tied down to particular times and places, as they are in face-to-face discussions. They also have time to reflect on what is being discussed since there is no pressure to contribute immediately. Generally speaking, the kind of CSCL discussed in this book facilitates flexible, open, cooperative learning.

In some ways, this book is more about what computer supported cooperative learning could be, rather than what it is. The concept of CSCL is so new that we are faced with using a term that has no widely accepted meaning as yet, and may never have. It is described as a new paradigm (Koschman, 1996). CSCL is an idea that helps surface questions about the role of technology in learning, and about the nature and purpose of learning itself. The book is therefore tentative. But it is grounded in research, experiences and understandings of cooperative and collaborative learning methods and designs, some in CSCL-type environments, some in face-to-face contexts.

In the book I try to bring together a variety of diverse issues to do with the nature, purposes, outcomes and ways of promoting cooperative learning. The primary focus is on people working in cooperative learning groups where there is a strong social element to their work. This socio-cultural perspective on learning is becoming widely appreciated and acknowledged in the practice and research of many educationalists today. The book is also concerned with the use of communication and distributed advanced learning technologies in supporting this form of cooperative group learning; the book is a distillation of ideas and thoughts about CSCL.

Who the Book is For

This book is intended for reflective practitioners involved in the processes of learning and training who have an interest in working with cooperative groups using computers. It will be of special interest to those involved in distance learning and those using the Internet and World Wide Web, be they administrators or practitioners. The book should be of interest to those involved in developing new strategies and methods of teaching and learning, such as staff development officers in universities, colleges and organisational training departments; those involved in researching cooperative learning, and to students of education and training interested in recent developments in thinking about group work, and how that might be carried out via computers.

Overview of the Book

The book is divided into three sections. Part I considers what cooperative learning is, what technologies there are for supporting cooperative learning and ends with a comparison between tutoring and learning in CSCL and face-to-face environments. In Part II, I look at design issues to do with CSCL and present a case study of a long-running CSCL programme. Part III deals with new advanced learning technologies which could be used for cooperative learning, and finishes with some ideas on ways in which we could carry out research into CSCL.

In Chapter 1 I consider what is meant by the term 'cooperative learning'. The benefits of cooperative learning groups are discussed, and research into cooperative learning is examined. This chapter indicates that in many cases, cooperative learning produces greater benefit to the learner than traditional, individual learning. In Chapter 2 I move on to a discussion of technologies currently commonly used to support cooperative learning, and pay special attention to technologies designed to support the work of groups. In Chapter 3 I indicate some differences between tutoring and learning in CSCL groups and in face-to-face groups. Particular attention is given to the use of time in CSCL group work. Chapter 4 looks in some depth at the dynamics of these groups, with particular reference to gender differences in participation.

Chapter 5 looks at designing learning and training events for CSCL. This chapter is based on personal experience of running CSCL programmes. I offer some thoughts on six design features used to promote and support cooperative learning. These are: openness in the educational process (the learning community); self-determination in learning; having a real purpose in the cooperative process; a supportive learning environment; collaborative assessment of learning; and assessment and evaluation of the ongoing learning process. I also present a specific CSCL design which has been successfully implemented in a higher education setting. Chapter 6 continues with a discussion of design issues by presenting a case study of CSCL in action. The focus here is on the design and management of CSCL in open learning contexts, where learners and tutors cooperate in the design and running of the programme. Issues to do with using computer supported cooperative learning in such contexts are discussed, as is the nature of professional practice in these environments.

In Chapter 7 I take a slightly broader perspective, and consider some recent developments in advanced learning technologies which could be used for cooperative learning, looking in particular at recent innovations in America and in Europe. The final chapter – Chapter 8 – considers ways of researching group work in CSCL environments. A major focus here is on researching CSCL in ways that are compatible with the purposes of CSCL itself, using collaborative methodologies which attempt to involve learners, tutors and researchers in an exploration of the meaning and experience of working in this new group medium.

1 | What is Cooperative Learning?

Introduction

'Cooperative learning' is a fairly new concept, certainly as a way of thinking about and conducting the educational process. Cooperation in learning is not in itself new, but the idea of 'cooperative learning' as a particular system of learning is. But what do people mean when they talk of cooperative learning? And what are the outcomes and benefits to the learner of cooperating with other learners?

In this chapter my aim is to provide a general overview of the meaning of cooperative learning, its benefits to learners, and some of the issues surrounding the use of cooperative learning methods. I will look at the nature of cooperation and what it means to cooperate in learning. I will also consider what educationalists mean when they talk about cooperative learning, and will look at some of the research that has been conducted into cooperative learning.

In later chapters, I will relate these understandings of cooperative learning to the particular concern of this book, ie *computer supported cooperative learning* (CSCL).

The Nature of Cooperation

The act of cooperation is something which is deeply embedded in western societies. It seems to be a fundamental aspect of our everyday lives that people cooperate, although we do make choices about when to cooperate and with whom. The nature of cooperation is something which social scientists are interested in analysing and researching. Argyle (1991, p.15) defines it as, 'acting together, in a coordinated way at work, or in social relationships, in the pursuit of shared goals, the enjoyment of the joint activity, or simply furthering the relationship'. This is a fairly wide ranging definition that can be useful in thinking about the nature of cooperation in learning situations. It emphasises the role of groups of people in cooperative acts and points to the wider social dimension of cooperation. Cooperation is seen as central to our everyday lives.

Why cooperate? Argyle (1991, p.20) suggests three possible reasons, or motivations for people to cooperate: for external rewards; in order to form and further relationships; and in order to share the activities they are involved in. If we view learning situations as part of the wider social context in which we live, then it is not difficult to relate to this. The educational system may not be particularly concerned with fostering cooperation in learning (indeed, as we know, there is often a concern to ensure that learners do not cooperate), but informally learners do work together and share their learning to some degree, depending on the particular context. Why do they do this? Because they know that it is beneficial for themselves and for others to share their learning.

Formalising what happens informally is one of the purposes of cooperative learning. By building on our knowledge that learners do cooperate in order to achieve external rewards (grades, diplomas and degrees, amongst other things), to develop and sustain friendships and to share in what they are doing, we can show that cooperative learning offers a view of learning which is socially based. Those interested in cooperative learning in its broadest forms do not view the learning process as a purely individual pursuit concerned largely with accumulating intellectual knowledge; rather they see it as part of the wider social context in which we live, a point to which I will return throughout this book.

A Theory of Cooperation

The social science view of cooperation focuses on the intrinsic aspects of cooperation in society, and relates these to ideas about survival and evolution. Another view comes from political science and emphasises the self-interest associated with cooperation.

The political scientist Robert Axelrod suggests a theory of cooperation based on mutual reciprocity. This theory combines the realisation that there is always an element (at least) of self-interest in any cooperative effort, as well as a concern for others, or a concern for the welfare of the group as a whole. Altruism (which can be described as a sense of social responsibility, a sense of community, a sense of group-interest (Margolis, 1982)), it is suggested, is never a self-less pursuit. 'True' altruism is cooperation as ideology.

The theory of cooperation derives from analysis of the Prisoners' Dilemma Game, where players have two choices: to cooperative or to defect. The dilemma is that if both defect, they will do worse than if they had cooperated. The theory suggests that cooperation always benefits both players. The Prisoners' Dilemma Game, where players work on a tit-for-tat basis, suggests that you should cooperate if the other player does, but also cheat if they do over a long period of time. Everyone wins if they cooperate. For example, even if you don't like the other learner, cooperation based on reciprocity can develop, and you both benefit from that.

The traditional educational system can be viewed as one set up to encourage envy. There are those who can, and those who can't. The advice of Axelrod's theory is, don't be envious. Envy leads to trying to win, which leads to defection. In most educational systems, students are required to do the same piece of work (an essay or some other assignment) which they know will be assessed according to a set of well-defined criteria. Often there is a limited number of high grades being offered, and the students know this. This encourages competition. The students compete on a zero-sum basis; whatever one person wins, the other loses. Cooperation theory suggests that if they were to cooperate, they could all do well (this of course requires an unlimited number of high grades to be on offer). If not, then some will inevitably do better, which will lead to everyone competing. In non zero-sum learning situations, all learners can do equally well if they cooperate.

> The main results of Cooperation Theory are encouraging. They show that cooperation can get started by even a small cluster of individuals *who are prepared to reciprocate cooperation* even in a world where no one else will cooperate. The analysis also shows that the two key requisites for cooperation to thrive are that the cooperation be based on reciprocity, and that the shadow of the future is important enough to make reciprocity stable. But once cooperation based on reciprocity is established in a population, it can protect itself from invasion by uncooperative strategies (Axelrod, 1990, p.173).

The emphasis in the above quotation is mine. I think it indicates a wider aspect of cooperative learning which is important, and that is that individual learners must wish to cooperate, and must be willing to act in cooperative ways in order for that to succeed. We shall see below some of the differences between cooperative learning situations where learners are asked by someone else (usually a teacher) to cooperate, and are rewarded by that person for doing so; and cooperative learning situations where learners themselves choose to cooperate with no external rewards or policing by a teacher. The design of the cooperative events may appear similar, but the relationship of the learner to the modifers, and the motivation of the learner to cooperate will be different.

How can Axelrod's theory help in thinking about cooperative learning? Behind this theorising is the assumption that the world is largely made up of egoists. He asks if cooperation can occur in these circumstances without a central authority. In most (if not all) learning contexts, there is always a central authority, usually a teacher or tutor whose job it is (amongst other things) to ensure that students learn the material put in front of them. We shall see below how this works in many cooperative learning situations. Axelrod's theory poses the question: what would happen if there were no such central authority, if learners were not policed? We shall also look at such situations in a later chapter which examines a specific CSCL programme.

Cooperation in Learning

In the very broadest sense, cooperative learning involves working together on some task or issue in a way that promotes individual learning through processes of collaboration in groups. It is:

> the opportunity to learn through the expression and exploration of diverse ideas and experiences in cooperative company… it is not about competing with fellow members of the group and winning, but about using the diverse resources available in the group to deepen understanding, sharpen judgement and extend knowledge (Cowie and Rudduck, 1988, p.13).

A distinction is sometimes made between cooperative and collaborative learning. Collaborative learning is sometimes associated specifically with helping students become members of a knowledge community. At other times it refers to situations where students engage in solving problems together (Koschman, 1996). Although the distinction is sometimes helpful, I will use the term 'cooperative learning' throughout this book to refer to both forms of learning.

Cooperative learning is process-driven, ie those involved engage in a social process and have to pay attention to that process in order for them to achieve their desired end point. It usually involves people working in groups (ie, at least two people are involved, usually more). There may be group 'products' towards which the learners are working; cooperative learning can give rise to 'products' which are not easily achievable by people learning on their own. And there may be individual 'products' which are achieved through the people in the group helping each other deal with their own individual learning concerns. Because cooperative learning has a large social dimension to it, it is usually enjoyable and developmental: it gives rise to outcomes which are not usually considered academic, such as increased competence in working with others, self-assurance, personal insight and so on, as well as academic outcomes.

Socially Oriented Theories of Learning

The recent interest in socially oriented theories of learning (as opposed to purely psychological theories) has been highly influential in promoting a new perspective on learning within the CSCL movement. Koschmann (1996, p.11–12) describes three movements that have contributed to these new understandings:

1. *Constructivism.* The role of peer interaction in cognitive development (emerging from the work of Piaget and his followers) has been influential in new conceptions of learning. Knowledge is actively constructed, connected to the individual's cognitive repertoire and to a broader, often team-based and interdisciplinary, context in which learning activities take place (Salomon, 1997).

    Cognitive scientists are interested in the cognitive processes relevant to cooperative learning. They have been highly influential in helping to define the learning benefits of cooperative learning, from a cognitive process perspective. Terms such as 'collaborative knowledge construction', 'co-construction of knowledge' and 'reciprocal sense making' are terms they often apply to this field.

    Social constructivism is particularly influential in many areas of learning and teaching, especially in the field of continuing professional development. Knowledge is seen as something that is constructed in social groups. The view of knowledge taken is that it is fallible and non-absolute. Meaning is arrived at by negotiation (Greeno, 1997).

2. *Soviet socio-cultural theory.* From the work of the Soviet scientist Vygotsky, the construct 'zone of proximal development' (Vygotsky, 1978) has been hypothesised. This suggests that a learner's ability is enhanced when they work closely with someone who is more skilled. Their potential development working alone is less than what they can achieve when working under adult guidance or in collaboration with more capable peers (Wood and Wood, 1996).

3. *Situated cognition.* Situated cognition and situated learning suggest a way of reconceptualising educational practice. Communities of practice have embedded in them knowledge about practice, and learning is seen as the process of entry into that community. 'Learning is a process that takes place in a participation framework, not in an individual mind' (Lave and Wenger, 1991, p.15). Participation in the community is referred to as 'legitimate peripheral participation', a form of apprenticeship in which the learner

performs several different roles implying different forms of responsi-bility, relations and interactive involvement. Wenger (1998) suggests that learning in these communities of practice involves processes of 'reification', through which the members share and learn from each other's experience. Practice is captured and made visible and share-able, and it is argued this helps it to persist over time. Scardamalia (1999) makes similar claims in the knowledge society concept that underpins the use of the CSILE system (now called Knowledge Forum), and Goodyear and Steeples (1998) write about the creation of shareable representations of practice. Other authors develop addi-tional views on situated learning and cognitive apprenticeship (eg Singleton, 1998). The design of spaces for collaborative knowledge work is an accompanying theme in the learning technology perspec-tive on situated cognition (see eg Gailson and Thompson, 1999; Goodyear, 1995).

These influences point to a fundamental shift in our perception and understanding of learning, which in turn influences and helps to define our pedagogical methods and approaches. CSCL as an emerging new paradigm of learning draws on these movements to help construct its epistemological stance.

Other authors have attempted to situate these emerging ideas and theories within the existing cognitive psychology approaches to learning (Salomon and Perkins, 1998). The focus is on the debate around learning as something that takes place in the individual's mind, where knowledge and skill are acquired as discrete, transferable entities and learning that occurs in collective, participatory settings of 'active knowledge construc-tion emphasising context, interaction, and situatedness' (Salomon and Perkins, 1998, p.2). Four meanings of what can be termed 'social learning' are elaborated:

1. *Social mediation.* Here a person or a group helps an individual to learn. A teacher may help a student with a particular learning problem. A group may help a member deal with an aspect of their own, individual learning.
2. *Social mediation as participatory knowledge construction.* Here the focus is on participation in the social process of knowledge construc-tion. 'Social mediation of learning and the individual involved are seen as an integrated and highly situated system in which interaction serves as the socially shared vehicles of thought.'
3. *Social mediation by cultural scaffolding.* Here the emphasis is on the

use of tools (necessarily socially constructed) in mediating learning. Tools and artefacts such as computers and books 'embody shared cultural understandings'.

4. *The social entity as a learning system.* The focus here is on learning that occurs in groups, teams and other collectives, eg the 'learning company'. The learning that takes place in collectives concerns the development of that collective, bringing about changes in its underlying values, beliefs, culture and norms.

These four perspectives form the basis for a critique of a socio-cultural perspective on learning, and of how the individual and social might relate. By focusing on the situated versus the cognitive, and the social versus the individual dimensions of learning, Salomon and Perkins ask how individual and social learning relate to one another. They make three propositions. The first is that 'individual learning can be less or more socially mediated learning', a position that acknowledges that all learning is to some degree social, but the degree varies from situation to situation. The second proposition is that learning can be distributed throughout a group or collective, with individuals participating *as individuals.* Individuals in teams may learn by themselves, but they also acquire skills and knowledge that benefits the group as a whole. The third proposition is that these two aspects of learning (individual and social) develop in 'spiral reciprocities' where the one influences and supports the other.

As we shall see in later chapters, individuals and groups in CSCL environments seem to exhibit characteristics that support these propositions. We can see individual students bringing their particular individual learning issues, concerns and problems to the group and contracting with the group to work cooperatively in addressing them. At another level, we can see the group posing problems and raising interesting questions and working collaboratively in trying to address them. Learning is always situated in the life of the group and the particular, formal learning context in which it functions. It always has a social dimension. But individuals are learning by themselves as well as the group learning by itself. The individual and the social aspects of learning occur side by side.

This can have profound implications for how we perceive the meaning of learning:

It is not enough to learn how to direct one's own learning as an individual learner abetted by artefacts such as textbooks. Learning to learn in an expanded sense fundamentally involves learning to learn from others, learning to learn with others, learning to draw the most from cultural artefacts other than books, learning to mediate others' learning not only for their sake but for what that will teach oneself, and learning to contribute to the learning of a collective. (Salomon and Perkins, 1998, p.21).

We shall see later in an examination of a CSCL course how this translates into practice.

Making Learning Public

Unlike traditional, curriculum-based learning where learners work for themselves, do not share their learning in a public forum, and work largely in isolation, the form of cooperative learning which I shall largely be focusing on in this book (cooperative learning where individuals work closely with others on their own learning) engages learners in thinking about why they are learning, and for whose purposes they are learning. For example, working cooperatively in a group involves me in thinking about what I am trying to achieve through my learning and engages me with the other group members in thinking this through. The group helps me with my learning, and by the same measure I help the others in the group with their learning. Additionally, there will be times when all members of the group work on something collectively, such as the process aspects of the group work, eg pursuing questions about how we are working together; where the power and authority currently lie within the group, and why; the 'roles' we are adopting within the group and how this happens to come about, and so on.

Cooperative learning makes public our own learning, the learning of others and the learning of the group. This 'making public' works as a central process in cooperative learning and confirms its social and democratic nature. It can be thought of along several dimensions: our learning is public when it is known to others and to ourselves; it is blind when it is known to others but not to ourselves; it is hidden when it is known to ourselves but not to others; and it is unconscious when it is not known to ourselves or to others (see Figure 1.1).[1]

Working cooperatively with others helps raise the public awareness of our learning so that those aspects of learning which are blind, hidden and unconscious become clear, open and conscious. We become aware of our learning by working with others and by focusing on the processes of working cooperatively. We reduce the hidden and blind areas and open the public areas through the group's cooperative work.

This of course requires commitment to working cooperatively, and agreement on how the cooperative group will function. If a group has

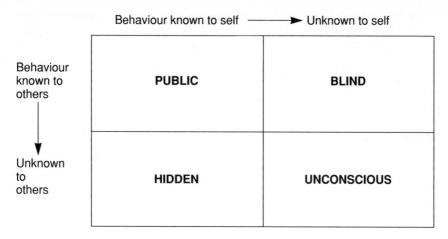

Figure 1.1   *The public–private/conscious–unconscious dimensions of cooperative learning*

people in it who are not willing to cooperate then it is unlikely that they will engage in making their learning public. Similarly, if the group does not address its own learning and come to some initial, and over time ongoing, agreement about itself then it is likely to fragment and the members will essentially end up learning in isolation. It is of course the case that people who wish to work cooperatively are not always willing, or able, to be public about their learning. This raises the issue of choice within cooperative learning, and is an issue for the group to address. People will vary in the degree to which they wish to be public and at different times they will vary in the degree to which they wish to be confronted with those aspects of their learning that are blind, hidden or unconscious. Within the kinds of computer supported cooperative learning groups which I shall be discussing later in this book, these issues and concerns are dealt with by the individuals in the groups as part of the learning process itself.

At this point, it will be useful to say something about groups, as they are central to learning cooperatively.

Defining 'Group'

In its simplest sense, a group exists when there are two or more people together. But in educational terms, what more can we expect from a definition of a group? When people come together to work in educational settings, they usually have a purpose for doing so; they have something in mind that they are trying to achieve or work towards; they have a notion of who they are as a group, ie who the members of the group are; they often have an idea of how they are going to work together, or at least they often address this issue once they are working together.

In arriving at a usable definition of a group, we can 'imagine' groups from various perspectives. For example, sociologists will generally think of groups in terms of what they can observe of the external life of the group. Psychologists will be more concerned with the internal life of the group. This difference of viewpoint – 'societies as (composed) of groups' – sociological viewpoint; and 'groups as societies' – psychological viewpoint (McCollom and Gillette, 1990) provides two different ways of thinking about, working with, and examining groups.

Neither of these perspectives is however sufficiently useful on its own for people in education and training who are working with groups. A viewpoint that encompasses both disciplines, and is indeed interdisciplinary, is probably more useful. Consider the following definition:

A human group is a collection of individuals

(1) who have significantly interdependent relations with each other
(2) who perceive themselves as a group, reliably distinguishing members from non-members
(3) whose group identity is recognised by non-members
(4) who, as group members acting alone or in concert, have significantly interdependent relations with other groups, and
(5) whose roles in the group are therefore a function of expectations from themselves, from other group members, and from non-group members (Alderfer, 1984, quoted in Gillette and McCollom, 1990).

This seems to me to be a more useful definition of a group. It comes from Organisational Behaviour (OB), an interdisciplinary field which looks at human relations at various levels, and applies its findings to places of work, including education and training organisations. According to McCollom and Gillette (1990):

OB writers describing groups, for example, acknowledge the individual group member's experience, the group process and output, and the environmental context of the group all as important components of group theory (p.5).

In discussing Alderfer's definition of a group, they state that:

A group is defined here by individual members' experience, by the relationships among members, and by members' relations with non-members. The 'new tradition' we describe here requires maintaining a complex view of the simultaneous influences on group dynamics created at different levels of the social system in which the group exists (p.5).

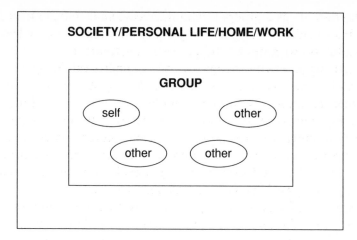

Figure 1.2   *The learning group in its wider context*

The view of groups taken in this book has much in common with the OB perspective. People working cooperatively in CSCL environments do work in groups. These groups work in complex ways, in open learning situations where there are many different simultaneous influences on the group. Because members of CSCL groups will usually work in different locations and are therefore dispersed, or in virtual (Wexelblat, 1993) groups, there are influences from beyond the social structure of the group itself, such as influences from their personal and home lives (see Figure 1.2). In later chapters, I will discuss what we mean by the dispersed environments in which CSCL groups work.

In thinking about groups in CSCL environments, we therefore have to keep in mind not only the nature of the group vis-à-vis its members and their purposes for working together, but also the wider contexts in which they function. When learners work cooperatively in CSCL groups, they will be viewing the work of the group from their own perspective and from that of the other learners. Additionally, their work in the group will be influenced by what is happening around them in their social and other work lives, and they will be bringing these experiences and perceptions into the group.

Ways of Thinking About, and Carrying Out, Cooperative Learning

The term 'cooperative learning' has particular meaning for many practitioners and researchers within the United States and Israel where it is most commonly practised as a system of education. In the UK and else-where, cooperative learning has perhaps less specific meaning, and encompasses a wide range of activities and methods, most of which are based on group work where the emphasis is on discussion.

The US perspective on cooperative learning is particularly interesting and influential, and unlike the UK scene, in the United States there has been considerable research conducted into cooperative learning. I will therefore largely discuss the US perspective here and examine the research which has been conducted into such cooperative learning situations. In a later chapter on designing for computer supported cooperative learning, I will widen the definition of cooperative learning somewhat, and offer some alternative ways of thinking about cooperation in learning.

Two Views of Cooperative Learning

At this stage, I would like to summarise what I see as two views of coop-erative learning. In doing this I will necessarily pose them as belonging to different ends of a spectrum in order to make my point. In practice, however, they are more likely to share much more in common than might be suggested here.

There are a series of dimensions of cooperative learning which help to illuminate these two views. For example, when considering cooperative learning we have to think of such things as the degree to which the teacher imposes a structure on the learning events; the amount and kind of control over the learning that the teacher takes; whether the learners are working from internal motivation which arises from their interest and engagement with their learning, or from external motivation which is controlled by some external force, such as the award of grades or certifi-cates or other externally held rewards (see Figure 1.3). The practice of cooperative learning can vary along these dimensions, depending on the views of the teacher in relation to each dimension, and the context in which the teacher and learners are working.

This indicates that there can be no one view of cooperative learning, but rather a variety of views. Cooperative learning is a rich and diverse concept.

View 1

The first view is dominant in the cooperative learning movement in compulsory school education in the United States and Israel. It is curriculum-based and applies a broad behaviouristic approach to learning.

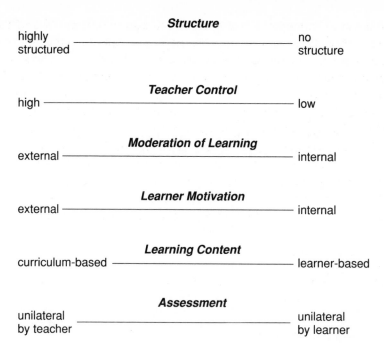

Figure 1.3 *Dimensions of cooperative learning*

Cooperative learning tasks are part of an overall curriculum which students have to work through. Cooperation is structured and policed by a teacher. Motivation to learn is largely by rewards allocated by an external moderator (teacher). It is criterion-referenced with external assessment of learning (usually unilateral by the teacher). Learning goals are defined largely by the teacher.

Although this form of cooperative learning has its origins in compulsory school education, it is now also being applied in higher education with apparent success. It is however important to bear in mind that much of the research conducted so far into cooperative learning in the United States has been carried out in schools, and much of that in experimental, research settings. Researchers are now beginning to carry out studies in cooperative learning in higher education, and are claiming similar successes to those now widely accepted within the compulsory education sector (for examples, see the journal *Cooperative Learning and College Teaching*).

The issue of rewards is an important (though, as we shall see, controversial) one. The design of cooperative learning events usually means that students work in teams or groups. Teams often vie for rewards which are held by the teacher who polices their activities and controls the allocation of the awards. For example, in describing a cooperative method called Team Assisted Individualization (TAI), Slavin (1990) comments that:

> Each week, teachers total the number of units completed by all team members and give certificates or other *team awards* to teams that exceed a criterion score based on the number of final tests passed, with extra points for perfect papers and completed homework (p.5, emphasis in the original).

and later, in describing the Jigsaw cooperative learning method:

> students take individual quizzes, which result in team scores based on the improvement score system.... Teams that meet preset standards may earn certificates (p.10).

and in describing the Learning Together method:

> students work in four- or five-member heterogeneous groups on assignment sheets. The groups hand in a single sheet, and receive praise and rewards based on the group product (p.12).

This suggests the possibility for a large element of competition in these cooperative classes.

Many researchers and practitioners believe that students working in cooperative groups need some external incentive to cooperate. Knight and Bohlmeyer (1990) quote the work of Slavin who suggests that cooperative incentive methods and structures can take one of three basic formats:

a. a cooperative incentive for *individual* learning within the group, eg each person's performance is used to arrive at an average mark or grade or other reward for the group as a whole
b. a cooperative incentive for *group* learning where the group reward is based, for example, on a group product
c. an individualistic incentive for individual learning, where individuals are rewarded for individual performance, but within a cooperative working environment.

View 2

My second view of cooperative learning is a somewhat looser one which emanates from practice in liberal school education and adult education, as well as from the practice of group work generally. Within the compulsory school education sector, this view is perhaps more prevalent in the UK (Topping, 1992).

It is a form of open, negotiated learning. Within post-compulsory education, it has a history in the humanistic approach to education (eg, Rogers, 1969) and in the self-directed approach to learning (Knowles, 1975). This approach emphasises internal moderation by learners themselves. It is problem- or issue-based. Learners learn largely through intrinsic motivation, and rewards are largely intrinsic. There is little if any 'policing' by a teacher or tutor. There is much choice by learners in decision making and in group processing. There is often internal assessment of learning, which may involve self, peer and tutor collaborative assessment. The learning goals are largely defined by the learners themselves. I will discuss this form of cooperative learning in some detail in Chapter 4, on designing for computer supported cooperative learning.

The Outcomes of Cooperative Learning

Measuring Achievement

In their work into the relative impact on achievement of competitive, individualistic and cooperative learning efforts, Johnson and Johnson (1990) looked at 323 studies conducted over the last 90 years. Their conclusions indicate that cooperative methods lead to higher achievement than competitive or individualistic ones when measured by a variety of possible indices. They used four indices of achievement:

1. *Mastery and retention of material.*   Students in cooperative learning environments perform at a higher level than those working in competitive or individualistic environments. When achievement in 'pure' cooperative groups is compared with achievement in groups using a mixture of cooperative, competitive and individualistic learning methods, the results show that the 'pure' methods consistently produce significantly higher achievements.
2. *Quality of reasoning strategies*
    *   Individuals working in cooperative groups use focusing strategies more often than those working competitively or individualistically. Learning problems are therefore solved faster.
    *   Those involved in cooperative work use elaboration and metacognition strategies (such as showing an awareness, and self-control of learning) more often than those working in competitive and individualistic situations.

- Higher-level reasoning is promoted by cooperative learning.
- When comparisons are made between students using cooperative, competitive and individualistic learning strategies for tasks requiring higher- or lower-level reasoning strategies to solve them, students in cooperative groups discovered and used more higher-level strategy methods.

3. *Process gains.* Process gains such as new ideas and solutions are generated through group interaction that are not generated when people are working on their own.

4. *Transference of learning.* There is a high degree of group-to-individual transference after working in cooperative groups, ie when individuals have worked in a cooperative environment, their learning is transferred to situations where they have to work on their own.

Johnson and Johnson conclude that:

> On the basis of the research conducted to date (which is considerable), it may be concluded that generally achievement is higher in cooperative situations than in competitive or individualistic ones and that cooperative efforts result in more frequent use of higher-level reasoning strategies, more frequent process gain, and higher performance on subsequent tests taken individually (group-to-individual transfer) than do competitive or individualistic efforts (p.26).

Slavin (1990) suggests that in addition to these academic outcomes, cooperative learning has positive effects on social, motivational and attitudinal outcomes also. He suggests that:

- Cooperative learning works positively in promoting intergroup relations, such as cross-cultural relations.
- It can help to overcome barriers to friendship, interaction and achievement of academically less able students, and can increase self-esteem in students since they work in situations where they are more likely to be liked by their peers, which in itself has positive effects on achievement.
- Cooperative learning creates norms in groups that support high achievement. Typically, students feel that their peers want them to do their best. This is supported by the work of Deutsch (1949) who carried out laboratory experiments which suggested that students who discuss human relations issues with each other under cooperative conditions, a) felt more pressure from their peers to achieve; b) felt more of an obligation to their group mates; and c) had a stronger desire to win their peers' respect. Students in competitive learning settings do not exhibit these traits.

- Cooperative learning leads to success, which in turn leads to students thinking that they can succeed.
- It increases time on task, ie the time actually spent doing work out of the total non-instructional time. Time on task is increased by improvements in the students' motivation to learn and by engaging their attention.
- Students in cooperative learning situations enjoy being in those classes.
- Cooperative learning increases the positive effect of classrooms. Students like their classmates and are liked by them.
- Students working cooperatively become more cooperative; they learn pro-social behaviours such as how to get along with others, how to listen and so on.

Other researchers (Sharan, 1990) suggest that cooperative learning fosters knowledge about the learning process, and therefore encourages a spirit of learning to learn. It also informs students about the construction of understanding and knowledge. These two suggested attributes of cooperative learning are highly developmental outcomes. We will look at how cooperative learning can encourage a spirit of learning and an understanding of the nature of knowledge in a later case study.

It has to be noted that the educational situations that Johnson and Johnson and Slavin and other workers in this field are referring to are school contexts where the teacher has ultimate power and control, and where the teacher assesses and rewards individual groups through the use of grade-points and other such devices. The role of the teacher is central to cooperative learning in these studies. He/she largely chooses the topics to be covered and the particular cooperative method to be used. The teacher functions in what might be termed a policing role, acting as arbitrator, ultimate decision maker, power controller and rewarder. Additionally, there seems to be the assumption that the social interaction, personal purposes and goals of the learners are predictable and amenable to teacher control.

Experience in working with older or more 'adult' learners in post-compulsory education settings suggests that their behaviours are less predictable than those of children (I leave aside the question of whether children's behaviour is indeed more predictable), and less amenable to the sorts of control that appear to be used in the studies reported. I will discuss in a later chapter what might happen when groups of learners work in situations where there is little if any external policing carried out on their behalf, and where the control is by the learners themselves.

Explaining High Achievement Outcomes

The effects of cooperative learning on achievement are positive. Why do students do so well in cooperative learning groups? Slavin (1990) suggests two theoretical models which can be used to throw light on this.

The first model – *motivational theory* – suggests that the motivation of each student working in cooperative learning groups is high. The reward or goal structures of cooperative learning groups are said to increase students' motivation to achieve. It is the effect of cooperating with others within a defined and well-planned learning environment where each student knows the goals to be achieved, which motivates students to cooperate and do as well as they can. Learning goal structures can take at least three forms:

> cooperative – where each individual's goals contribute to those of other individuals
>
> competitive – where the goals of one individual frustrate those of others
>
> individualistic – where the goals of one individual have no effect on those of others.

In the cooperative goal structure, the only way to achieve your own goals is through working with others. Group work of this kind becomes self-reinforcing. The group provides the necessary praise and reward for the positive effort of each member. To work in this way requires each member to try their hardest, to be a regular attendee of the group and to help others. We will see later how this works in cooperative groups learning in electronic environments.

The other explanation for the high achievement of learners in cooperative groups – *cognitive or learning theory* – relates to the cognitive processes occurring during cooperative learning. Cooperative learning involves dialogue between learners, and a great degree of inter-action generally. This increases the learner's grasp of conceptual material. In developmental terms, students who work closely with their peers will be exposed to situations where their own conceptual skills are stretched by the interactions with their peers. The gap between their actual developmental level and their potential developmental level is narrowed by the interactions they engage in with peers of greater capability. This is called the zone of proximal development (Vygotsky, 1978, p.86).

Slavin (1990) notes that Piaget has also suggested something similar:

Students will learn from one another because in their discussion of content, cognitive conflicts will arise, inadequate reasoning will be exposed and higher quality understanding will emerge (p.16).

There is an obvious difference between the work of Piaget and Vygotsky: Piaget largely views development from an individualistic perspective whereas Vygotsky views it from a social, communicative perspective (Jones and Mercer, 1993). It might be proposed therefore that the work of Vygotsky may have more to offer those interested in cooperative learning.

Talk in Learning

Other researchers such as Douglas Barnes in the UK (Barnes and Todd, 1977) have indicated the importance of talk in learning. They have shown that this form of cooperation can benefit all learners, especially those from lower-middle-class homes who will conduct high-level discussions of academic subject matter when in group-discussion situations. But it should not be assumed that it is a case of the 'brighter' students always helping the less bright ones, as seems to be the suggestion in the interpretation of Vygotsky's work. The social interaction in cooperative groups produces superior problem solving in all the students involved. The 'better' students do not merely supply answers to the less able ones (Sharan and Shachar, 1988, p.4). and the talk indulged in need not be formal or structured for learning to occur. Informal talk, or chat, can help many learners make the link between their present understanding of a topic or issue, and a more meaningful understanding:

> Children learn by talking and listening and should be given more opportunity to talk. Children talking in small groups are taking a more active part in all their work. Tentative and inexplicit talk in small groups is the bridge from partial understanding to confident meaningful statement. Present talking is future thinking (Barnes *et al.*, 1969, p.126).

This view is supported by other researchers such as Rosen (in Barnes *et al.*, 1969), Phillips (quoted in Graddol, 1989) and Graddol and Swann, 1989.

In my experience, the role and importance of talk is also true for students in post-compulsory education, and is a central aspect of the design of CSCL environments. Cooperative learners should be encouraged and supported in all kinds of talk: informal and tentative, and formal too. Talk is central to cooperative learning groups and we can predict that working in this way will improve the learning of all members of the group.

What are the functions of talk and conversation in learning situations? Barnes and Todd (1977) suggest several functions of both a social and cognitive nature:

LEVEL ONE
1. Discussion Moves – such as initiating, extending, eliciting, responding.
2. Logical Processes – such as proposing causes and results; advancing evidence; evaluating; suggesting ways forward.

LEVEL TWO
3. Social Skills – such as progressing through task; competition and conflict; supportive behaviour.
4. Cognitive Strategies – such as constructing questions; raising new issues; setting hypotheses; using evidence; expressing feelings.
5. Reflexivity – such as monitoring your own speech; evaluating your own and others' performance; being aware of strategies.

In their research into communication and learning in small groups, they applied these categories to the analysis of talk in small learning groups. They also suggest that this system may be of use to those wishing to get a better understanding of the usefulness of talk in learning situations.

Teachers and tutors can develop their understanding of talk by analysing group discussions using these categories, and they are sometimes surprised by the level and content of discussions taking place in these small groups.

When Barnes and Todd played back to teachers recordings of groups talking, the teachers were impressed:

> When we played back the recordings to the teachers, their reactions were commonly of surprise and delight. They were surprised because the quality of the children's discussions typically far exceeded the calibre of their contributions in class; and were pleased to hear the children manifesting unexpected skills and competencies (Barnes and Todd, 1977, p.ix).

Motivation – Extrinsic and Intrinsic

The question of what motivates students to work cooperatively is of particular importance and raises some interesting questions about our views of learning. Studies focusing on motivation have used various reward systems or incentive structures such as group or individual rewards and intergroup competition to try to illuminate the issue. Some researchers feel that extrinsic rewards are needed in order to motivate students in cooperative learning groups (eg, Slavin, 1990). Others suggest that the intrinsic motivation afforded by the personal involvement of students in cooperative tasks is sufficient to produce high achievement (Sharan and Shachar, 1988, p.120). What is at issue here seems to be a matter of personal educational philosophy, as much as anything else. For example, the US educational system seems to be built around extrinsic rewards. Students studying in most situations seem to require the presence of an extrinsic reward to motivate them; no less so perhaps in cooperative learning groups.

In other countries and other educational systems, this may not be the case. For example, Sharan and Shachar report on a series of experiments into cooperative learning in Israel. They explain that teachers there had voiced concern about rewarding students for learning. Their particular cooperative learning methods took this into account and emphasised the intrinsic nature of learning such as the degree of involvement, interest and attention which is evident in cooperative learning:

> the Group-Investigation approach to instruction [a particular type of cooperative learning] is based on theoretical principles that emphasise the importance of 'intrinsic motivation', of arousing students' involvement by structuring the learning situation to maximize their initiative and responsibility for their learning, both individually and collectively (Sharan and Shachar, 1988, p.119).

They note, in support of their belief, that students chose to remain in the class and continue with the cooperative work rather than take the usual break in-between classes. There was no 'reward' to continue other than the sense of achievement gained from working with others. The intrinsic motivation was sufficient. In forming a conclusion about the relative worthwhileness and appropriateness of extrinsic and intrinsic motivation, they offer the following hypothesis:

> Indeed, we are inclined to speculate that the kind of motivation stimulated by external rewards, and the kind fostered by the social-intellectual environment created by the Group-Investigation approach, may very well be two completely different kinds of motivation whose differences are not fully captured by the terms 'extrinsic' and 'intrinsic' (Sharan and Shachar, 1988, p.120).

In a later chapter, we shall look at a computer supported cooperative learning programme which emphasises a community of learners in which the philosophy of cooperative learning is one largely based on intrinsic motivation.

Before closing this chapter, a word on the role of the teacher or tutor or facilitator in cooperative learning is perhaps needed. The role of the teacher or tutor in cooperative learning is to provide a supportive context for the cooperative group to work. In some situations, the tutor will wish to provide a fairly structured context where he or she will assign work to the learners and provide roles for them within the group. The tutor will set up group processes and ensure that they are followed through, and will make decisions about the learning and its assessment, and how it should be carried out.

In other situations, tutors will wish to provide more open contexts for the groups to work in, which rely less on external structure. They will minimise their own role and influence in the work of the group. This does not mean that they will not be active in the work of the group, but they will be conscious of their special role as tutor and will work towards a situation where they will not over-police the activities of the group. These issues concerning the role of the teacher or tutor in cooperative learning are discussed in more depth in later chapters.

Conclusion

This chapter has looked at what cooperative learning is and how it benefits learners, both individually and collectively. Although the label 'cooperative learning' is used to describe a variety of seemingly diverse activities, and has perhaps different meanings and purposes in different contexts and cultures, there is a common belief that it is a highly beneficial form of learning.

In summary, we can say that cooperative learning:

- helps clarify ideas and concepts through discussion
- develops critical thinking
- provides opportunities for learners to share information and ideas
- develops communication skills
- provides a context where the learners can take control of their own learning in a social context
- provides validation of individuals' ideas and ways of thinking through conversation (verbalising); multiple perspectives (cognitive restructuring); and argument (conceptual conflict resolution).

Note

1. This is called the 'Johari Window' which is a common part of the T-group agenda (Smith, 1980; Luft, 1963).

2 | Technologies for CSCL

Introduction

Having said something about the nature of cooperative learning in Chapter 1, I now want to move onto a discussion of technologies for supporting cooperative learning, paying particular attention to technologies that are designed to support the work of groups in formal learning contexts, which is the central theme of this book.

The focus of this chapter is on those technologies that are widely available, relatively cheap, and readily usable today. Most of them make use of narrow data bandwidths (eg, for transmitting text), or medium bandwidths (eg, for transmitting audio, text and audio, and still images).

Wide bandwidths (such as ISDN, fibre optics, direct broadcast by satellite, etc), which allow full moving images and audio, are still too expensive for general use. In a recent survey of video-conferencing technology in education in North America, no examples of actual applications of the use of ISDN and compression technology for use in multi-media two-way communications were identified (Bates, 1993).

Hardware costs are falling, making workstations relatively affordable; transmission costs are still high, but falling; but the most expensive costs are in:

- developing new pedagogic approaches
- preparing teaching materials
- training the teaching staff, and possibly students as well
- facility costs, such as codecs and building conversions
- network management (scheduling etc) (Bates, 1993).

High cost technologies such as multi-media, the use of ISDN and other broadband technologies are therefore less likely to be immediately usable by most teachers and institutions, other than perhaps as demonstrators of what will be available in the near future. The shared virtual realities of today – information spaces that allow learners to meet across networks – are those based mainly on narrow and medium data bands, using relatively low-level technologies. Multi-media technologies are still stand-alone. Shared multi-media virtual realities will only be possible when current stand-alone multi-media technologies are developed to be used across distributed network environments (Hodges and Sasnett, 1993, p.266). Some demonstrator projects along these lines are being tested (see Hodges and Sasnett, 1993; Paquette *et al.*, 1993) but by and large it will be some time before such systems are widely available for general use. Indeed, current

> issues and technical underpinnings of broadband network computing may suggest that distributed multi-media services will not be in common use for quite some time. This is indeed the case; the first tentative models addressing some of these issues are only now beginning to appear in research laboratories (Hodges and Sasnett, 1993, p.266).

The proceedings of an international conference on Teleteaching (Davies and Samways, 1993) also support this view, although there are several interesting wide bandwidths and multi-media prototypes which point to possible future scenarios.

Classifying Cooperative Systems

Computer systems designed to support the work of groups can be classified according to several criteria. The terminology applied to these systems is diverse: 'groupware' and 'computer supported cooperative work' (CSCW: eg Beaudouin-Lafon, 1998; Greif, 1988) systems are terms often used to mean much the same thing, although it might be argued that CSCW subsumes groupware.

Rodden (1991) suggests a classification of CSCW systems which is useful when considering computer supported cooperative learning (CSCL). The classification is based on two major characteristics common to all cooperative systems: the form of interaction and the geographical location of the users. Cooperative work can occur in synchronous and asynchronous interactions, and users can be remotely placed, or located in the same room (co-located). These dimensions provide a matrix for describing four classes of cooperative systems (Figure 2.1).

Rodden's classification however omits another dimension of CSCW systems, and that is the degree to which they are structured or unstructured. This distinction is important in CSCL environments, where open learning is the predominant method and where, it might be argued, unstructured groupware is more effective.

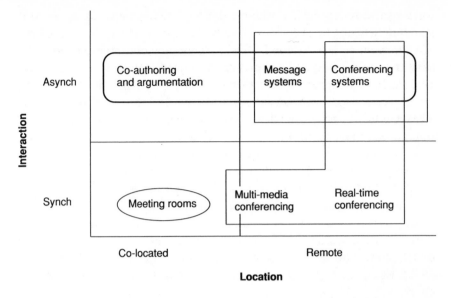

Figure 2.1 *Classification space for CSCW systems*
(After Rodden, T, 1991. By permission of the publishers, Butterworth-Heinemann Ltd.)

CSCW and Groupware

Although the term 'groupware' is applied to any piece of software designed to support group work and communication, a distinction can be made between structured groupware, designed to provide, more or less, a pre-defined structure for a group to work in; and groupware which is relatively unstructured, providing little in the way of pre-defined structure. (A new generation of groupware is appearing which is tailorable, permitting users to define their own structures for group work). These two forms of groupware should not be seen as alternatives, but as complementary. Whichever one is used will depend on the needs, aims and purposes of the users.

In the following I will consider both structured and unstructured groupware, give some examples of each and the ways in which they are used, and consider their potential uses in CSCL.

Structured Groupware

CSCW systems
Most structured groupware is designed to provide structure and support

29

for people electronically working together. This form of group work is generally referred to as computer supported cooperative work (CSCW).

The target audiences for CSCW systems are organisations, and the primary aim for their use is the improvement of organisational effectiveness. System designers try to bring an understanding of the ways in which groups in organisations work to the design of CSCW systems. They try to integrate knowledge and expertise of both computer technology and human communication and collaboration. Group roles, tasks, purposes, aims, procedures, outcomes and so on are mirrored in the design of groupware. Built into CSCW systems are intentional group processes and procedures to achieve specific purposes, together with software tools designed to support and facilitate the groups' work. CSCW deals with the study and development of systems that encourage organisational collaboration. The 'human system' and the 'tool system' are equally important in the design of groupware (Engelbart and Lehtman, 1988). Some uses of groupware can be categorised as follows (Opper, 1988).

Document editing systems automate the editing procedures associated with multiple reviewers commenting on a document. Users are assigned particular roles by the system, eg, main author; co-author; reviewer; editor; and their work on the system is confined to these roles. Reviewers can see and add to each other's remarks without altering the original document (the main author has this priority). All comments are initialised and can be printed.

Team (or group) development systems assess and give feedback to groups on the way in which individuals work in a group, and on team makeup. They can be used when the correct formation of a group is important. Members of the proposed team(s) complete electronic sociograms, and the system provides feedback on the nature of these sociograms. These can then be used to determine in advance how people are likely to function in a group. Use of the system is reported to have reduced the time required to form a group (by interviews) from four days to 30 minutes, giving similar results to the traditional method, but in more detail.

Workgroup communication management systems allow groups to have electronic discussions, coordinate group calendars, schedule meetings, keep track of communal projects and follow up on plans and associated work. Desk accessories such as calculators, notepads and telephone diallers are often included. Some systems have artificial intelligence techniques built into them and can act as 'assistants' to the group, dealing with incoming information, processing it and distributing it to everyone;

scheduling meetings on the basis of information in the communal diary, and so on. Some systems also allow e-mail to be sent directly to 'outsiders' by facsimile.

Some examples

It is beyond the scope of this chapter to review all existing CSCW systems (see Rodden, 1991; Malm, 1993; Beaudouin-Lafon, 1998; Kanselaar, Veerman and Andriessen, 1999; and the Groupware Central website at www.cba.uga.edu/groupware/ for reviews). However, in order to provide an understanding of the purpose and scope of structured groupware, it will be useful to describe a few important systems currently in use.

The Coordinator is designed on the principle that computers are action machines. Language leads to action, and the Coordinator is an action-coordination system based on speech-action theory (Winograd, 1988).

The Coordinator organises information exchange between members of an electronic group. It helps the sender and receiver organise and keep track of exchanges (called 'conversations for action').

> A conversation can be viewed as a kind of dance, in which particular linguistic steps move toward completion: if an action was requested of you, you promise or decline; if you promise to complete the action, you report completion, or revoke your promise; if you requested an action, you cancel your request, ask for a progress report, or declare that your conditions have been fulfilled and the action completed (Winograd, 1988).

This set of procedures is the basis for communication in the Coordinator. The history of each conversation for action is recorded and can be viewed as and when required, forming the basis of the management support mechanism of the Coordinator. The purpose of this 'people-centred system' is the clarification and simplification of human action.

Both Information Lens and *Object Lens* use artificial intelligence research to enhance e-mail in the support of group work. E-mail can be filtered, sorted, prioritised and automatically processed.

Object Lens 'provides a user interface that integrates many of the capabilities of electronic messaging, rule based "intelligent" agents, object oriented databases, and hypertext' (Crowston and Malone, 1988).

The object database may, for example, contain person objects with fields for a name, phone number, job description and so on. These can be searched, and the text of them can be linked to other frames as in hyper-text (hypertext allows you to link parts of a document to other parts, so allowing non-linear navigation through the document). For example,

OBJECTS   **OBJECTS**

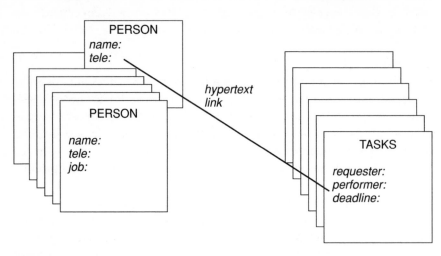

Figure 2.2   *Hypertext links*

hypertext allows you to find the telephone number of a Performer by linking the Performer field in the Task Object to the Telephone field in the Person Object (see Figure 2.2). The 'intelligent' agents can perform a variety of tasks, such as sorting e-mail, running a query in the object-oriented database, scheduling meetings for the group, and so on.

Object Lens can be used for task managing. For example, a manager could display the status of all tasks being done by people in his or her group. Tasks can be sorted by name, deadline, costs, etc. Information about the status of tasks is in-put by the system on the basis of 'action requests' and 'commitment' messages (similar to Coordinator, above).

Cosmos is a British, Alvey-funded human interface project. Its aim is to provide an electronically supported environment for business meetings, company procedures, project work and so on.

> Every organisation has dozens of... activities, suffering from problems like too much paperwork, lack of coordination, individuals not doing their bit on time, lack of control, unclear objectives, lack of flexibility and straightforward lack of organisation. Cosmos will tackle these problems head on by first enabling users to specify their activities, then keeping track of what is going on, notifying individuals of their expected next step, and carrying out all the incidental clerical work (Cosmos Information Brochure).

Cosmos uses a special user-oriented language called Structure Definition Language which allows users to define the structure of their work environment, after which messages and objects can be exchanged according to the rules of the structure. Cosmos was developed to run initially on SUN machines, and later on PC compatibles (Young, 1988).

Conclusion

The provision of a structure for group decision making, and software tools to support the management of group tasks, are seen as the strengths of CSCW systems. However, groupware fails if it doesn't allow for errors and differing ideas and opinions of what is appropriate and worthwhile. Built-in 'typical procedures' may be misleading and constraining. Strict adherence to set procedures is usually the exception in real situations. Decision makers rely heavily on intuition, and this is difficult to accommodate in structured CSCW environments (Grudin, 1988).

Groupware of the kind described here is at a relatively early stage of development and use. Most of the products mentioned above have been around for only three or four years, some less. It is difficult to evaluate their potential use in the CSCL environments since none of them has been extensively evaluated for general organisational use, let alone for use in an educational environment. They do, however, represent the state of the art in CSCW and may well be tailorable to the needs of the CSCL system users.

Unstructured Groupware

CSCL systems

Unstructured groupware generally encompasses the electronic messaging system, ie electronic mail systems, bulletin board systems and computer conferencing systems. These are termed 'unstructured' here because they do not have any pre-defined structure which tries to model an observed 'real' situation. They are essentially electronic 'spaces' into which users place textual communications, and impose their *own* structures (in as much as the software permits this).

CSCL systems exploit the store, process and retrieval capabilities of the computer for teaching, learning and training. Users of CSCL utilise the computer to structure and facilitate human communications. The objective is 'collective intelligence' (Turoff, 1987) and knowledge building (Scardamalia, 1999).

The term 'CSCL' can be used to cover any form of cooperative learning communication that occurs over a network of computers. In Rodden's terminology, CSCL spans the asynchronous–remote spectrum and the asynchronous–co-located spectrum. CSCL primarily involves the use of computers to send and receive textual communications. The text is usually held in a mainframe computer where it can be retrieved at any time by those wishing to read or use it.

CSCL allows for a variety of types of communication, each of which can be used for cooperative group correspondence. Existing facilities include e-mail, bulletin boards and computer conferencing.

E-mail

Conventional e-mail primarily supports communication between individuals. Users can send and receive personal messages, which are logged by the system on a 'store and retrieve' principle. Most e-mail systems allow users to reply to messages with attached copies of the original message sent back to the originator, thus allowing the path of the correspondence to be displayed.

In addition, group communications are possible by the use of distribution lists which allow the same message to be sent to large groups, with replies from individuals circulated to all group members too. But this becomes a cumbersome method of group work if used constantly. Nevertheless, the combination of a 'reply' facility and distribution lists does permit some form of limited group communications in ordinary e-mail systems.

It is now also possible to attach graphics and other files to e-mail and to computer conferences; voice annotation may soon be available.

Bulletin boards

Bulletin boards (bboards) take group communications one step further by allowing any user to 'pin' messages on to a communal message space so that all users can read them. Any correspondence between the group can take place via the bboard so that everyone can share in the communication.

Although many bboards allow users to manipulate the entries, for example by searching message headers and text for keywords, a bboard is essentially only a method of display and is not structured for high levels of *interactive* group work.

Computer conferencing

Computer conferencing (CC) allows for communal *interactive* group communications. Messages are entered on to a communal message space and users can attach new messages or responses to existing ones in a way that allows a conversation to develop. A record of the proceedings of the group communications is kept permanently on the mainframe and can be read linearly (equivalent to following a discussion from start to finish) or can be searched in a variety of ways depending on what information a user is looking for (equivalent to using it as a database).

Communications via CSCL usually occur asynchronously, although occasionally users do coordinate times when they are 'online' together. But the asynchronous nature of these systems is often cited as a positive benefit to busy workers and learners who prefer the flexibility of communicating whenever it suits them. The nature of electronic meetings – the social presence, process and outcomes – differs from face-to-face meetings (McConnell, 1990) and possibly requires new ways of thinking about the meaning of group work when it is mediated via computers.

In CSCL, textual learning material can be stored on the computer for retrieval by learners, both on-site and off-site. Such material might include course outlines, aims and objectives, independent study material, lecture/seminar notes, academic papers on the subject being studied, study guides, self-assessment material, databases of associated learning material, and so on.

The communications system, in conjunction with the stored course files material, provides an electronic interactive teaching and learning environment where students and tutors have equal access to the learning resources and are able to communicate with one another via the same system. Knowledge building by the co-construction of information, ideas and resources is possible.

CSCL should be seen as a new medium, allowing us to do new things in new ways. The challenge is to design courses and learning situations which will exploit this new medium.

What's Needed?

In order to participate in CSCL, each learner and tutor will require a workstation, and there will have to be a host computer for the CSCL software.

The basic set-up requires a host computer where the CSCL software is held, and computer terminals or personal computers capable of connecting with the host to allow users to interact with the CSCL software. If there are large numbers of users and if access is needed by several users at the same time, then the host computer will usually be a mainframe computer, although mini and PC computers are now being used to host communication software.

Users can access the CSCL software by a variety of methods, using a variety of equipment. Four basic scenarios are suggested in Figure 2.3.

Direct PSTN Link

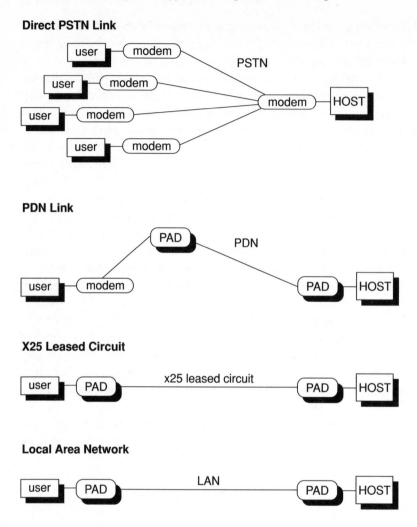

PDN Link

X25 Leased Circuit

Local Area Network

Figure 2.3 *Four possible routes to the host computer*

Direct PSTN link

Accessing the host using the public switched telephone network (PSTN) requires each user to have a personal computer with word-processing software, communications software, a modem (modulator-demodulator – a piece of equipment that changes the digital signals from your computer to analogue signals which can be transmitted down the telephone line) and an appropriate telephone point. The telephone need not be dedicated for teleconferencing; it can be used for ordinary 'voice' calls as well.

The user simply directs the communications software to connect their computer with the host via the modem and the public telephone lines. The cost of connecting in this way is the same as the cost of an ordinary telephone connection to the location where the host is held (this of course varies depending on the time of the day and the location of the host). The quality of the connection varies enormously with the quality of the PSTN, and data are sometimes corrupted due to 'noise' on the line. Transmission of data can be rather slow via this method.

PDN link
The public data network (PDN) provides a better quality connection to the host than PSTN often does. Most Internet service providers offer this route.

With this method, access is gained by dialling the local PDN node via any ordinary telephone line and connecting to their PAD (packet assembler disassembler – a device for sending and receiving 'packets' of data. PDNs use packet switching to send 'packets' or parts of a message rather than the complete message; the packets are reassembled at the other end into the complete message). The user then has access to the completely digital data network to connect to the host. These services provide error correction and various other supports which make data transmission quality very high. Speed of transmission is also higher using PDN, ranging from 2,400 bits per second using standard modems, to 48,000 bits per second (and more) with higher quality modems.

Leased circuit
Where volume of use from one location is high (eg, many users in the same buildings accessing a distant host) and quality and speed of data transmission are important it may be preferable to lease a digital line. Leased circuits provide permanent connections to the host, and users may access the host from a terminal connected to the line, or via a personal computer connected to it. No modems or telephone points are required. The costs of a leased line vary depending on the distance between the two points being connected, and on the data transmission speeds required. Additionally, there would be the cost of buying and installing the in-house cabling and PAD. This configuration would allow at least 16 simultaneous users to access the host.

A leased line is clearly not feasible for single users, but may be beneficial where there are many users in close proximity. The higher bandwidth of a leased line enables large volumes of data to be transmitted.

Private local area network

Many organisations have private local area networks (LANs) which function in a similar way to a leased line. LANs are usually installed within a building (several LANs in different buildings may be connected together) and would connect the users to a host computer also situated within the same building.

It is of course possible to combine any of these data networks with any of the others, eg PSTN and PDN can be linked together, and public leased lines can be combined with private LANs, and so on.

Working with CSCL Technology

Computer supported cooperative learning systems include e-mail, computer conferencing, bulletin boards and online databases. For clarity and convenience, I will limit the discussion here to the use of computer conferencing (CC) since that is the most profitable medium for carrying out group work in training and learning contexts. I will draw on examples from the Caucus CC system to illustrate what is possible.

Members of a computer conference are able to carry out the following basic operations:

- read the text of the conference
- add their own items (ie, freestanding textual communications) to the conference
- add responses to other people's conference items (or indeed to their own items)
- send private messages to any number of individual conference members.

Thus members of a computer conference can have both one-to-one communication via the conference system and one-to-group communication. They are able to link into the conference at any time and on any day of the week. Whenever they do link into the conference they are told what new activity has taken place in the conference since they were last online. That is, they are informed of how many new items have been added to the conference, the number of new responses that have been added to items and how many new personal messages they have received.

Conference items and responses are a way of organising, ordering and structuring inputs into a computer conferencing system.

```
JOIN which conference? hilltops
You have 3 new message(s).

        New          Items with       Total new      Conference
        Items       new responses     responses      ----------
         2               5                8           bianca
         4               3               16           champers
         0               4                3           chiang_rai
         0               1                3           etna_maml
         6               6                5           genesis
         0               4                7           hilltops
         0               2                3           jitol_project
         1               4               10           spectrum
         0               4                4           speedwell
```

```
        *****************************************
        *                                       *
        *          WELCOME TO HILLTOPS          *
        *      THIS IS THE MEETING PLACE FOR    *
        *            Greg, Sandra, Steve        *
        *              Daniel and Mary          *
        *                                       *
        *****************************************
```

```
ITEMS IN THE CONFERENCE ARE:
 1  Decisions about this conference
 2  CHATTING
 5  SEMINAR PAPER 1
 6  HOLIDAYS AND OTHER LAZY PERIODS
 7  HOW WE PLAN TO WORK AS A SET
 8  mary - CHAT/WORK
 9  greg - Chat hotline
10  Sandra's Item
11  CRITERIA AND ASSESSMENT - THOUGHTS ON
12  Daniel's PAPER
13  EVALUATING FEEDBACK ON ESSAYS
14  Feedback on Greg's S.P.
15  GENERAL DISCUSSIONS ON PROJECT ESSAYS
16  DANIEL'S PROJECT ESSAY WORKSHEET
17  MARY'S PROJECT ESSAY
18  Sandra's Item for P.E.
19  Project and Evaluation Chris R
20  HOW HAVE WE BEEN WORKING AS A SET?
21  CONTRACT ITEM
22  DANIEL'S ASSESSMENT AND FEEDBACK FOR PROJECT
23  Sandra's item for assessment and feedback
24  MARY'S P.E.
**********************************************************************

The CANCEL key is Control-C
New responses on items:
    1   2   5   6
There are no polls in this conference.
AND NOW?
```

Figure 2.4 *Joining a caucus conference*

Levels of Organisation

Conferences

A conference is the most general level of order or organisation. Any group of CSCL users may set up as many conferences as they require. For example, on the CSCL MA programme in Management Learning at Lancaster University (described in Chapters 4 and 5), there are at least three main types of conferences: general, tutor group, and specific.

Everyone contributes to and participates in the general conference as a way of keeping the whole group in touch with each other. Substantive management learning issues are discussed collectively, and individuals can inform each other of developments in other conferences or activities occurring elsewhere. This conference also acts as a noticeboard for the programme as a whole.

Each member is also joined to a cooperative tutorial group conference. These have smaller numbers of participants and are primarily concerned with discussions around the assessed work on the course and personal development issues.

The specific conferences are meeting places to discuss such things as the design of residential workshops, to share information about books and papers that participants have read, and to place resources (bibliographies, research papers and so on) to share with others.

Items

The next level or organisation is an item within a conference. Items are basically sub-topics of the general conference theme or purpose. Any member of a conference can add an item, and there can be as many items as are required by participants.

Responses

The final level of order is that of a response. For each item added by a conference member, others can add responses to that item, so that a discussion emerges around the item topic. Responses are added either until the discussion concludes, or until a decision is made that the discussion has moved sufficiently far from the original topic focus that it would be more profitable to start a new item in order to acknowledge the change of focus and start a fresh dialogue around the new emerging ideas.

Thus the metaphor of the conference being the meeting place to discuss a general theme, the items being the sub-themes or sub-topics and the responses being the group dialogue, provides a way of helping us to understand the nature (process and product) of an electronic meeting. It is helpful to apply a useful title to each conference to help orientate group members to the purposes of that conference each time they join it. In these ways you can provide a 'living' electronic learning environment which has meaning for the participants, and which embodies an aura of belonging and support. Figure 2.5 is taken from one of the CSCL MA computer conferences. Names have been changed to ensure anonymity.

Logical Structure of Conferences

The logical structure of a CC system may largely determine the ways in which it is used. By structure I mean the way in which the computer software handles the various different discussion topics in a conference, eg the way it displays entries and the way it handles the presentation and manipulation of information. In a computer conference, users enter a textual piece of information that can be read and commented on by other users. A user can enter a 'free-standing' piece of information, which essentially forms the beginning of a sub-topic in a conference. Other users can respond to (or 'comment on') this, and so develops the electronic equivalent of a face-to-face conversation.

Different computer conferencing systems have different architecture. They mainly fall into one of two basic designs: the grapevine, tree or branching design; and the book design.

Grapevine, Tree or Branching Design

Examples	CoSy; Participate
User metaphors	tangled mass of spaghetti, wall of ivy
Underlying logic	computer programming logic

In a branching system, users can attach responses to previous entries at any point after reading an individual's entry. They are not forced to read all the entries in the sub-topic, or item, before entering their own response. This arrangement has the advantage of allowing free ranging responses to whatever entry one likes without having to read all the responses to the original entry before responding. This can have the effect of 'spraying' the responses, as shown in Figure 2.6.

Item 9   26 JUN-90   9:45   Geraldine Crosbie
Assessment on MAML programmes

This is my account of a discussion held during CSML's work week. It is about
assessment on MAML programmes. I thought you might be interested – here goes.

During our work week at Borwick, a session about assessment within MAMLs was
led by Robin Snell. He was discussing whether there should be a move from a
system of marks to one of a simple pass/fail. Within CSML there were different
views about this and as a result he agreed to do some research into the issues for a
session at work week.

Robin conducted a questionnaire survey of past MAML participants and about a third
replied. Of these, just over a half were in favour of a move to the pass/fail option.
Many of the opponents of the marking system emphasised the pain and anxiety
experienced, the absurdity of haggling over 1 or 2 marks and the contradiction
between the student-centred/humanist leanings of the programme.

Pro-markers emphasised the need for the feedback that marks gave and also the
motivation. Some felt that the whole issue of marks was relatively trivial when
compared with some of the other controversial issues such as tutor role and power in
general, admission to the programme, the awarding of a degree.

(item cut here for brevity)

4 Discussion responses
9:1) Charles Rayburn   27-JUN-90   14:26
Hi Geraldine
Very interesting.
I'm a pass/fail with comments, person myself.
Love
Charles!
- - - - - - -
9:2) Ian Fleming   30-JUN-90   14:48
Hi geraldine thanks for putting this on. It certainly appears to polarise the debate on
assessment. I know from my own experience that I found grading particularly
difficult but I also realise that I would be unlikely to fail my own work no matter
how bad it was but I would be prepared to mark or grade myself accurately e.g. see
gradings in K.g.B conference. So as you can see most people come down firmly on
one side or the other although I could see occasions where I would edge my bets.
What a fence sitter I could become on this issue.
What do others think.?
See you soon
- - - - - - -
9:3) Daniel McBride   02-JUL-90   23:00
Very interesting. I agree with Ian's point that you'd be unlikely to submit a piece of
work which you saw as a fail, but that having to give it a mark does, however
uncomfortably, focus you to evaluate it more finely. I've found the very process of
grappling with how you will mark yourself quite self revealing. Maybe I'll get bored
with it by the end of the course!
- - - - - - -
9:4) Zoe Cunnigham   03-JUL-90   16:29
This must be short cos I am getting cramp from one and a half hours typing! well it
wasn't all typing! Anyway at the level of taking part broadly in the debate I thought
Geraldine's summary was v. good. I guess I am a pro currently for the very reasons
that Ian and Daniel suggest. Also I think it gives a better indicator of movement and
progress as one travels through the programme! Zoe.

Figure 2.5   *Edited text from a caucus computer conference*

Branching Design: 'spraying'

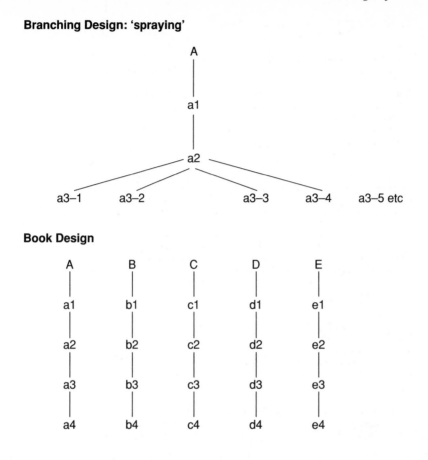

Book Design

Figure 2.6 *Architecture of conferences*

The drawback of this flexibility is that the conversations can become unwieldy and difficult to track through. There is also considerable redundancy because users often have to read entry a3 before reading a4(1), and then again before reading a4(2), and before reading a4(3). The underlying logic of these systems is sometimes compared to the logic used by computer programmers who plan software systems with multiple branching threads so as to acknowledge the various sub-routines needed in much computer software. From the non-computer programmer perspective, these conferencing systems can appear messy to use and taxing to weave through. Their structure is sometimes compared with masses of tangled spaghetti – thick and interwoven with lots of cross links.

Book Design

Examples	Caucus, Confer
User Metaphors	chapters in a book, transcript of a live conversation
Underlying Logic	reader logic, social science logic

In the book computer conference design, each user can start a new sub-topic ('item') within a conference; these are similar to chapters in a book. Users can only add an entry at the end of the transcript of responses already attached to the original entry (or 'item'). Users are therefore forced to read all the previous responses before entering their own. This has the effect of producing a linear sequence of entries.

The logic behind this is that in face-to-face conversations we usually listen first, then respond. So a transcript of a 'book' conference would look much like a transcript of a live conversation. This design produces less redundancy and no 'spray' conversations; conversations are relatively coherent and easier to follow than in branching systems. It is argued that these systems appeal more to ordinary (non-computer) users since the 'chapters in a book' or 'turn-taking in a live conversation' metaphors have immediate currency and appeal.

The Architecture of Computer Conferences, Groupware and Course Authoring Systems

There is a wide variety of systems available for supporting online education generally, and cooperative learning specifically. They include: computer conferencing systems designed largely to support electronic communications; groupware systems designed to support the work of groups of collaborative learners; and systems that have been specifically developed to support the construction of learning material as well as electronic communications – these systems have powerful authoring capabilities. Some of the systems work synchronously. They are all based on similar basic designs though they do have different properties.

Some of these new systems have an underlying purpose of 'instructional delivery', a rather teacher-centred approach to the technology. However, others support forms of education that are concerned more with 'knowledge construction'. 'In these learning environments facilities are systematically embedded to support learning interaction between students, sharing of cognitive achievements and interaction between students and teachers. Students are encouraged to take responsibility for their own learning. Widening local networks offers the opportunity of breaking the boundaries of the classroom and communication among different learning communities' (Simons, 1999).

There are many reviews of these systems on the World Wide Web, and what follows is a selected composition of some of those reviews, along with reviews from other paper-based sources. In particular, I draw on reviews developed as part of a project on collaborative learning that I and my colleagues Nicholas Bowskill, Jonathan Foster and Vic Lally are currently running at the University of Sheffield (www.collabo-rate.shef.ac.uk). Those reviews drawing on the information on the site are marked thus: *. I would like to acknowledge the work of Nicholas and Jonathan in creating the site. Our Web site also provides online reviews of some major systems, comparisons between the systems and examples of their use in education.

Asynchronous Systems

Caucus

The system which is referred to most in this book is Caucus.
Caucus features:

- e-mail
- conferencing structured as 'conferences', then 'items', then 'responses'
- external Web links possible from within a message
- graphics can be included in messages
- files can be attached to messages
- notebook – where you can gather pages from the conference and store them in folders
- search – this allows you to search a conference for people.

Caucus is a 'book' design system. Each unique conference can be compared with a book since it has its own particular purpose and intention and has its own readership (members). Each conference is set up by a conference organiser (in other systems the organiser may be called a moderator or SYSOP). The organiser has certain privileges and powers and can:

- Define the purpose and focus of the conference.
- Say who its members are, and whether they have full participation rights (to start new items, enter responses, delete their previous

responses and so on) or reduced rights (only to respond to, but not initiate, items; only to read what is in the conference but not actually enter comments).

- Bar existing members from further participation.
- Delete any other user's entry in the conference.
- Pass on the role of organiser to another conference member.

Each conference has its own title and 'greeting' (written by the organiser) which users see every time they join the conference.

Depending on the above possible constraints, each member of a conference can start new discussion topics (items) around the general theme of the conference; any other user can participate in these new discussions. Each item is initiated by a command and has a unique structure that distinguishes it from any other entry (response) in the conference. An item has a title, which is displayed each time a user reads any of the responses attached to it.

Each item is automatically added to the conference list of items so that a user can ask to see the existing list of items like the contents list of a book.

Users can manage the growing conversations in the conference using various tools available in Caucus. For example, each time they join a conference, they can ask to be shown all new items and responses entered since their last visit. They can search the whole conference or particular items for specific words or phrases, just as they would use an index in a book. They are told in which items and responses the word or phrase appears. They can ask who the members of the conference are, and when they last visited it. They can ask the system to 'forget' any items they do not wish to read; they will then only see activity in those items they wish to actively participate in. They can choose to read backwards through the responses in an item, from the most recent to the 'oldest' response. They can select particular responses from the body of the item without having to read through any others before or after it. They can ask to be shown which items any other user has read, the number of responses any user has entered and so on. These are probably amongst the most useful and frequently used tools available within a conference; there are others that more sophisticated users might wish to use.

In addition, Caucus provides the user with tools to manage information about the system as a whole. For example, users can list all the conferences on the system, check the activity in the conferences they belong to, check which conferences they belong to and who the organisers are, and so on.

As well as the conferencing system, Caucus also has its own electronic mail system (e-mail on Caucus is referred to as 'messages'). Users can send personal e-mail messages to any other Caucus users. The system automatically keeps a record of all e-mail received; this can be listed in various ways and deleted when no longer required. The system does not automatically keep a record of all outgoing e-mail; users have to send themselves a copy of outgoing e-mail if they wish to keep a record of it. Users can elect to automatically receive a receipt when e-mail is opened by the receiver.

Web site: screenporch.com

CLARE
The CLARE-system is a structured argumentation and critical thinking tool. It has been developed to 'facilitate meaningful learning through collaborative knowledge construction' (Kanselaar, Veerman and Andriessen, 1999). Students are taken through two main phases in their collaborative work: an exploration phase and a consolidation phase. The teacher enters a text into the CLARE system, which is presented to the students as a hypertext document. The students then have to work together on tasks requiring them to summarise and evaluate sections of the text. Students can add comments and critiques to each other's summaries. Information on summaries, evaluations, comments, disagreements and conclusions are made available to all those participating.

*COW (Conferencing On the Web)**
The COW software is shareware. As such, it is relatively inexpensive to implement. No client software is needed and there is an easy Web interface.

The conferences are divided into 'items' that in turn are made up of several 'conversations'. Within any conversation there are various messages.

COW allows attachments to messages, offers a preview of messages before being submitted and offers an option to customise messages with HTML. COW can include graphics within messages.

Web site: thecity.sfsu.edu/COW2

*First Class**
This is a very popular conferencing system accessible through a browser. For full use of the many features, client software is required. The

software is available for both Apple and Windows users and the client software is free and downloadable from the company Web site. This software presents the user with a series of folders and icons as a way of organising documents and discussion areas.

Its features include (text taken from vendor's site) 'software [that] is quite a rich environment that offers both real-time (synchronous) facilities and delayed time (asynchronous) resources.' They include:

- Graphical user interface – clicking on folders and icons.
- Chat is available for real-time discussions and they can be logged for review.
- Shared documents can be created and edited amongst a group of people.
- Bulletin Board facility available.
- Mail: personal e-mail is available as Internet integration.
- Conferences and discussion groups are available and can be made private or public.
- Possible to e-mail to a conference or input through the browser.
- Discussions are threaded.
- Fully functional Web server.
- Can work offline and upload later.
- Possible to edit any message or document after you have posted it.
- Supports connections via AppleTalk, IPX, TCP/IP, Telnet or modem.
- Runs on Macintosh, Windows, DOS, and UNIX Client logins.

First Class Collaborative Classroom

There is free client software and Web interface to this Intranet server software. The software is structured in folders within which are the various conferences. One key feature of First Class is that resources can be almost any format including audio and video. There is also a private and public chat system for real-time discussions built into the system.

FCCC installs on virtually any Windows or Macintosh computer on your network and supports connections via AppleTalk, IPX, TCP/IP, Telnet or modem. Its features include:

- complete e-mail and messaging
- advanced workgroup communications
- fully integrated Internet mail
- full featured Web serving
- easy html publishing
- true multi-platform support

- seamless remote access
- access to mail and conferences via common Web browsers and Internet mail clients.

Web site of supplier: www.softarc.com
Web site for FCCC: www.education.softarc.com/product/fccc/demo/index

CSILE/Knowledge Forum
Knowledge Forum has been developed from CSILE (Computer Supported Intentional Learning Environment). CSILE was developed by a team of cognitive research scientists in Toronto and teachers across Canada (Scardamalia *et al.*, 1989).

> At the system's core is a community database, constructed by the users. Items in CSILE's shared work space are called notes. Notes may include text, graphics and links to other media. All notes can be read by all users, but edited only according to set rules. Users create notes or comment on another note, in which case the original author is notified and can immediately view the comments and respond to them. Participants can link notes to any organisational framework created with the CSILE graphics program, thus producing high level visualisations of work on a particular problem or issue. They can also create special-purpose discussions or conference notes. (Scardamalia, 1999)

Typical notes in Knowledge Forum include a question, a problem, a graphic illustration, a research plan or a summary of information found from resource material (Simons, 1999). The difference between Knowledge Forum and other database systems is that files in Knowledge Forum are placed in a common, accessible area rather than in segregated areas for each student. This offers an open learning system where students and teachers can share their knowledge and work collaboratively in building new knowledge notes. Each database is open to all Knowledge Forum users. This model of learning supports a constructivist approach to knowledge (Scardamalia, 1999). The form of communication encouraged here is not point-to-point, but rather a 'knowledge society' where participants collectively build and contribute.

Web site: www.csile.oise.on.ca

Lotus Notes, Learning Space and Domino
Lotus Notes consists of three separate but integrated modes: a shared database system that can be designed in a flexible manner; a communications system similar to other conferencing systems; and a programming

language for automating common tasks. Domino is a Web-based version of Notes. Learning space is a course authoring environment which can be used either on the Web or with client software.

One of the strengths of Lotus Notes is that it is already multi-platform: Mac, Windows, OS2, UNIX client, Sun SPARC and the IBM AIX, HP-UX and SCO-ODT platforms, using Motif as the user interface.

Features for users include (text taken from the vendor's Web site):

- Enterprise calendaring and scheduling. Lotus Notes clients now include a rich set of easy-to-use tools for creating mail, managing time and setting up appointments and meetings. Users gain secure and real-time access to colleagues' calendar information.
- Direct access to the Internet. The Personal Web Navigator gives you access to the Internet right from within Notes. Share key information with other members of your team.
- The one for the road. When you're mobile, make just one call to replicate and synchronise information from multiple servers, thanks to the new server Pass thru feature. Save time by replicating only the information you need.
- Three-pane interface. Navigate through volumes of information quickly and easily. See views, folders, document relationships and preview documents all on the same screen. Each pane can be resized to meet your needs.
- Agent builder. A simple three-step interface with point and click access lets users automate tasks.
- Hierarchical folders. Create your own folders to store documents and messages. Let Notes Agents automatically organise information for you.
- Enhanced linking. Create links to Notes databases, documents, OLE-compliant applications and Web pages. Save time by previewing linked documents before opening.
- Navigators. Navigators provide you with a graphical way to find documents or take actions without having to manoeuvre through multiple views or find menu commands.
- Hotspots. Just click on graphical or text hotspots to go to a related Notes document, view or database.
- Permanent pen. Designate your own personal signature (font, size and colour) for editing Notes documents.

Notes databases are free-format and can contain different types of document in the same database and different types of data in the same document. Hypertext-style links can be created between documents both within and between databases.

To add non-Notes information to Notes documents, you can:

- Use your operating system's Clipboard.
- Use the Notes File Import command.
- Link or embed objects on the PC or Subscribe on the Macintosh.
- Use Notes file-attachments.

Notes database designs can be done centrally and distributed on disc or (after appropriate treatment) by e-mail – or better still by Notes itself (in this case including version control, etc). Even if everyone didn't call a central system themselves, a single archive could still be maintained.

Notes data can be imported from and exported to a range of graphic, word-processor and spreadsheet formats on all platforms. A Notes client licence costs no more than any full-blown, multi-platform database system and can cost quite a bit less, depending on the number of licences bought (Bryson, 1994).

Behind all of this is a communications system that the user is largely unaware of. Unlike most stand alone communications software packages which require considerable writing of procedures for automation (see Hardy *et al.*, 1991 for details of the most commonly available communications software), Notes has all the necessary communications architecture built in. Users are presented with a relatively easy-to-use database system that can be updated automatically by logging into the server.

Notes requires a dedicated server, and a system administrator who is given some powerful tools for coordinating the databases and the activity of the users. Notes differs from conventional conferencing systems in that the metaphor is that of an existing office, classroom or organisation. Anything that already exists on paper should be converted into Notes databases. And just as these paper files are easily available in the office or classroom, so they are similarly available at a distance, through electronic communications. Access to each database is assigned by the administrator: manager, designer, editor, author, reader, depositor and no access.

Groups communicate using a sophisticated conferencing and e-mail system. Documents such as spreadsheets, text processed files, graphics and sound can be attached to any personal or group communication.

Notes is heavily dependent on the ability of the administrator to programme. Although different tasks can be accomplished easily using the 120 or so provided icons, specific needs of groups require new icons which have to be programmed, eg for users to easily access their favourite applications from within Notes.

For some users, Notes may appear rather daunting. It is very sophisticated and although it is easy to accomplish the basics fairly quickly, going beyond that requires perseverance, a willingness to learn about the system, and lots of time. But the benefits could be enormous to cooperative learning groups.

Lotus Learning Space

Learning Space is a course-authoring environment for Web-based teaching and learning. It includes both synchronous and asynchronous facilities as well as group and individual spaces.

This system has many different facilities and can also contain documents in many different formats (video etc). Links to other parts of the course environment and beyond are also easily included. This is known as the Schedule facility. Lotus Learning Space has a range of facilities for authoring and structuring course materials. Its features include:

- CourseRoom. A conferencing space where students and tutors can collaborate around a discussion or a document.
- Schedule. This is where participants can view things like the timetable, syllabus, assignments, etc.
- MediaCenter. This is the resource warehouse that can be in various formats (video, audio, etc.).
- Profiles. This is similar to an electronic pigeonhole or personal filing cabinet that can also be used to display personal information (like a student's home page).
- AssessmentManager. A space where tests, exams and other forms of assessment can be offered to an individual.
- Learning Server. For synchronous collaboration, including audio and video as well as shared whiteboards and other tools.

Web site: www.lotus.com
Learning Space: www.lotus.com/home.nsf/tabs/learnspace

Top Class

According to the vendor's Web site, Top Class has the following features:

- Web-based training using Top Class engages learners in a way that allows them to work at their own pace, in their own time, and in a location of their choosing.

- The Top Class Server architecture provides simple, zero effort and cost-effective courseware distribution.
- The Top Class server significantly reduces the burden of administering a class and helps to change the paradigm from a situation where the instructor manages and teaches a class to one where the instructor is free to concentrate on teaching and facilitating students.
- Top Class is a powerful, flexible and secure system to handle all aspects of collaboration, content and class management.
- Top Class is in use by thousands of education and corporate institutions around the world, including SUNY; a 64-campus, 400,000-student institution; and many blue chip enterprises around the world.

Web site: www.wbtsystems.com

Virtual-U

According to the vendor's Web site, Virtual-U offers the following features:

- a proven infrastructure tool for delivering Internet learning and collaboration
- a standard environment to support a department or institution which needs to deliver multiple courses over the Internet
- a browser-based tool for instructors and students to access and organise course materials without using html, or server protocols.

The educational strengths of Virtual-U are:

- a flexible framework for different teaching approaches
- instructional tools and support based on pedagogical principles for instructors designing online courses
- asynchronous communication support, using the principles of active learning, collaboration, and knowledge building
- a multilingual environment (English and French included; Portuguese soon to be available)
- has already been used to teach over 3,000 students
- used in ongoing research into effective online learning.

The technical strengths of Virtual-U are:

- single security model (one password) allows students and instructors access to all of their own courses and related resources

- browser-based, so students and instructors can use many different computing environments (Windows, Macintosh, UNIX)
- Virtual-U Server is platform independent – supporting both UNIX and NT server environments
- allows any type of file to be uploaded from the Web browser (security model does not allow .cgi or .exe files to be uploaded).

VGroups Conferencing System

This supports group communication and collaboration in a secure news-group-style setting. Instructors can easily set up collaborative groups and define structures, tasks and objectives. Any user can learn to moderate conferences and sub-conferences. Users can easily sort messages in different ways to follow conversational threads and view as a list of message titles or view the whole message. Messages can easily include links to refer to any course materials or anything on the Internet.

Course Structuring Tools

These enable instructors to organise course resources into a flexible online course syllabus without programming knowledge. These resources can include downloadable files, course texts, relevant Web links, assignments, and any type of multimedia file. The tool automatically places the course syllabus on the World Wide Web for access by all students enrolled in that course. The instructors do not need to manage the class list, or student passwords, as the Virtual-U administrator manages these tasks for all courses.

Assignment Submissions

This tool enables instructors to request, receive and comment on course activity and assignment files which are submitted by students in a Virtual-U course. Instructors can set open and closing times for file submission. Students can submit their file from within their Web browser.

GradeBook

This is a tool for instructors to grade activities for each course delivered with Virtual-U, and post the results online. The GradeBook provides:

- areas for multiple evaluation systems (including numerical grades, letter grades, P/F, etc) and confidential comments
- either a graphical or textual view for students of their own grades and relative position in the class

- simple statistics for graded activities, and tools for the instructor to set and re-define grade ranges
- support for cooperative grading among instructors of the same course.

System Administration Tools

These assist the system administrators in installing and maintaining Virtual-U. They include functions such as creating and maintaining student accounts, defining access privileges and establishing courses on the system. Administrators can also perform batch imports of class lists from existing registrar data.

Web site: www.vlei.com

WebBoard*

This is a system designed for Windows users only at present. This is a Web-based system that can run as its own server. Discussions are structured into Forums and threads. It is quite inexpensive.

Again this system does not require any client software and can be accessed through any browser. To post a message to a conference you simply fill in a box. The conferencing system is both cheap and effective. Amongst the various facilities in WebBoard there is a chat facility integrated into a split screen.

Features of this technology include:

- chat facility for real-time discussion
- conferencing facility for threaded discussions amongst a group
- runs on Windows 95/98/NT
- attach files to messages
- Web server functionality.

Web site: webboard.ora.com

WebCT*

WebCT is a Web-based course authoring and electronic communications system developed at the University of British Columbia.

Within WebCT there is a bulletin board system which allows users to discuss matters of interest and post information to each other. The environment is structured in 'forums'. Within a given forum, people can post messages called 'articles'.

Course tutors using WebCT are also afforded a view of the level of activity and participation from their students. They are able to see who has logged in and which pages they have looked at as well as anything they have posted and when they have been in the course space.

Within the course environment Web pages can be offered in a structured way which offers the user an overview of various documents in the course. This is achieved using the Path Editor, which is just one part of the authoring environment; it requires very little technical skill to achieve some success.

WebCT offers a number of features including:

- Web-based tools for authoring pages of text, graphics, etc
- chat for real-time discussions that can be logged
- e-mail facilities for individuals as well as group mailing list facilities
- conferencing facilities for threaded discussions.

According to the Vendors WebCT offers:

- Widespread use. In the first 16 months WebCT has been in business (to February 1, 1999), over 1200 licences have been sold to institutions in over 33 countries.
- Publishers. WebCT has been chosen by many of the largest higher education publishers as their tool to build Web-based courses to complement their course textbooks.
- Low cost. Having begun as a university-based project, the charge is kept at a level that is just enough to provide support, maintenance and continued development. WebCT is free to download, install and create courses.
- Support. The support team responds to questions in a friendly and prompt manner.
- Very active users' group. WebCT has dedicated users who contribute regularly to the 'WebCT-users' mailing list.
- Very broad and deep feature set. This is best evaluated by using WebCT, though some of the comparative evaluations attempt to detail this.
- Origin. WebCT is a tool built by instructors for instructors. It was built by educators at the University of British Columbia as a tool to allow other educators without a lot of time, resources or technical expertise to build sophisticated Web-based learning environments.
- High renewal rate. Nearly all (roughly 90 per cent) of licensees have chosen to renew their licences once expired and most have renewed for a larger number of users.

- Language Translations. WebCT's student interface is available in many languages, including English, Spanish, French, Dutch and Finnish, and more translations are planned.
- IMS conformance. WebCT is a member of the Instructional Management System Project (IMS), is tracking the standards effort closely and is implementing those standards.
- Easy to get started. WebCT can be tried out on the Web site. Additionally, the WebCT software can be downloaded immediately for installation on a local server.

Web site of supplier: www.ualberta.ca/WEBCT
See also: www.webct.com

'4 windows'
'4 windows' is an integrated, multimedia environment which has a novel ('4 windows') interface (see Figure 2.7). Each window has a specific function:

- The north-west window holds an evolving group knowledge base.
- The north-east window gives access to the groups' conferencing system.

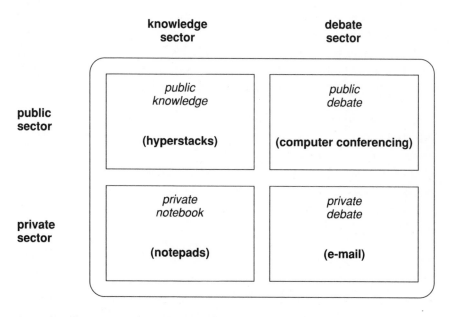

Figure 2.7 *The '4 windows' model*

- The south-west window is a personal notebook application.
- The south-east window gives access to e-mail.

The north sections are for public use – public database and public knowledge; the south ones are for private use – private debate and private knowledge. The west sections are for knowledge (public and private); the east sections for communications (public discussions and private discussions) (Gardiol, Boder and Peraya, 1993).

The '4-windows' interface provides an easily understandable set of metaphors for the user and gives them pointers about where to carry out what activities. The underlying database and communications architecture are hidden from view. A user works offline examining databases, reading and writing discussion points, and adding to the groups' evolving knowledge base. The system automatically updates their own personal and public discussions and database by communicating with the server, so that the '4 windows' becomes their local version of the groups' collective work to date.

Synchronous Systems

BelvEdEre
The BelvEdEre system (Learning Research and Development Center, 1996) is designed to support the construction of argumentative, online diagrams with groups of students. Students use specific problem statements to organise their arguments, and this is believed to be a useful learning activity during the planning phase of ill structured problem solving tasks (Kanselaar, Veerman and Andriessen, 1999).

Conference MOOs
MOOs are Multiple Object-Oriented systems which are text based. Many users can link into a MOO and communicate at the same time, using text dialogue boxes divided into classrooms, hallways and other virtual meeting places. Like many chat systems, users can prepare their text in a window without others seeing it before sending it. Once sent, it appears in the shared chat history. Students can also carry out other actions, such as waving, smiling and so on, through recognised non-verbal gestures. MOOs are sometimes used to support decision making and other tasks that benefit from synchronous communication.

Diversity University MOO is one of the most well-known of these environments tailored for educational purposes. It is organised around a campus metaphor.

Its features are:

- writing tools
- communication tools
- exploration commands
- manipulation commands
- bulletin board
- videoconferencing handler
- VRML view
- ghost view
- MOO map.

Web site: moo.du.org:8888 (Telnet access: moo.du.org 8888)

CTP
The Collaborative Text Processing (CTP) (Andriessen *et al.*, 1996) is a semi-structured system consisting of a shared word processor, a chatting tool and private information resources. It is restricted to use by pairs of students and can be used to help students collaboratively write argumentative texts at a distance. Arguments can be presented as text or pictures, and students are free to enter text into a shared text window, but turn taking is controlled.

Dialab
Dialab is a highly structured system and uses a strict logic-based dialogue system to support argument and critical thinking skills. Pairs of students use Dialab. Rules from a dialogue game are used, defining allowable moves, a set of commitment rules and a set of dialogue rules (Kanselaar, Veerman and Andriessen, 1999).

*WebChat Broadcasting System**
The WebChat system allows the user to communicate in real-time with other users via text-based messages. Recent versions of the application also support the uploading of images during chat. In addition to supporting chat, the home Web site incorporates a number of other features which support the community orientation of its service, including: the ability to search the profiles of those currently online; setting up your own homepage; a news stand; instructions on establishing a Net Circle; and an electronic mail account. Since its arrival in 1993 WebChat has attracted over 3 million users. In 1998 WebChat was acquired by the Internet service Infoseek.

Features include:

- browser-based
- organised into topic forums
- real-time discussion
- different chat modes: streaming chat, frames, no frames
- allows uploading of images during chat
- allows private chat.

Web site: pages.wbs.net

Internet Relay Chat*
Single chat servers can be networked. This allows the user to chat simultaneously across a number of different servers or channels within a specific network. This has come to be known as Internet Relay Chat (IRC). The IRC Helpsite provides a general introduction to this technology and a tutorial at the same site is also available. To link to an IRC network you will need to install a client, for example mIRC, which is a windows-based client. For Macintosh users see for example Mac IRC Clients and for Unix users ircII.

Its features include:

- text-based communication in real time
- topic-oriented 'channels'
- keyword searching of channels lists
- provision on some networks to establish own channel.

Web site (List of IRC Networks and Server Lists): www.irchelp.org/irchelp/networks
Liszt's IRC Chat Directory: www.liszt.com/chat/intro

CU-SeeMe: Internet Videoconferencing*
This desktop videoconferencing software which can be run over the Internet supports group (and one-to-one) conferencing. The technology also supports 'videochat' and an electronic whiteboard as a collaboration tool to support the sharing of documents and graphics. Its relatively low cost makes use of this technology a real possibility for interested academics.

Its features include:

- contact list

- simultaneous viewing of video images
- whiteboard facility
- chat facility
- caller ID
- directory services for locating other CU-SeeMe users
- operable with other conferencing software e.g. Microsoft NetMeeting
- available for Windows 95/98, Windows NT, and Mac OS.

Web site: cu-seeme.cornell.edu
Manufacturer's Web site: www.wpine.com/products/CU-SeeMe/index

Microsoft NetMeeting*
Windows-based collaboration tool incorporating data, audio and video conferencing in one package.
Its features include:

- collaboration through windows-based applications
- data conferencing
- electronic whiteboard
- file transfer
- text-based chat
- audioconferencing
- videoconferencing
- ability to share data with audio/video in real-time
- supports communication with users using compatible products.

Web site: www.microsoft.com/netmeeting

Netscape Conference*
This is a real-time communications and collaboration tool. It features:

- real-time audioconferencing
- chat
- whiteboard
- collaborative browsing
- file exchange
- supports communication with other tools and phones through open standards
- integration with other Communicator 4.0 components.

Web site: www14.netscape.com/communicator/conference/v4.0/index

Computer Skills Required

There are three levels of computing operations ideally required for CSCL technologies:

- word-processing skill
- telecommunications skill
- conferencing skill.

Word-processing Skill

To use CSCL most effectively it is best to prepare the text of items, responses and personal messages before going into a conference. This is perhaps less important if you are working from a terminal with a permanent link to the host; you can then use the online conferencing editor to prepare text, although the text editors on most conferencing systems are so primitive that the experience can often be excruciating! For those linking into the host by PSTN or PDN it is usually preferable to prepare the text in advance using ordinary word-processing software, save it on the personal computer and 'upload' it to the host when connected. Some systems, such as Lotus Notes, allow you to work offline and then upload to the server.

Telecommunications Skill

Communications software is used to link the personal computer to the host computer through one of the methods described above. Although simple enough in theory, this part of the process is often the most bewildering, confusing and frustrating aspect of teleconferencing. It is an application of computers that is little understood, and where so much can go wrong, that even so-called computer experts fail to offer corrective guidance when called in to give advice.

The procedure involves the user setting the PC communications software to match those required by the host, instructing the PC to dial into the PSTN or PDN and connect to the host. After logging into the host (by providing a user identity and unique password), the PC keyboard is used to instruct the host computer to run the conferencing software. In systems such as Lotus Notes, all of this is done automatically.

Everything that the user does now originates from their own keyboard; all instructions to the host are sent from the PC down the line (which may be a few miles long or several hundred or thousand miles long). Users typically join the conferences of interest to them and download (ie, receive on their own PC) conference text and personal messages; they upload similar text into conferences and send personal messages to other users; they often also type-in text while in a conference, and move in and out of the conference system and their own PC text-processing system.

Conferencing Skill

When joined to a computer conferencing system, a user needs at the most basic level to be able to:

- read new items and responses as required
- read items and responses that they have previously read
- add new items
- add new responses
- send personal (e-mail) messages.

There are many other operations that the more sophisticated user of any particular conferencing system is able to carry out and which enhance the potential of the medium. Some of the more obvious ones are:

- list all the conferences on the system
- list all the items (briefly or in detail) in a conference
- check which conferences they are a member of and the number of new items and responses that have been added since their last visit
- check which members of a conference have visited the conference recently
- search a conference for key words or phrases
- set up a new conference, customise its users and 'design' the nature of the meeting that will take place in the conference.

The Role of the Conference Organiser

As with most educational and training situations, the person organising and running a computer conference (the trainer, tutor, facilitator or whatever term you prefer) is crucial to the success of the venture. Their role is to set up the conference (which is usually a fairly straightforward set of procedures) and help prepare the participants for the event. Once the conference is under way, the organiser (or moderator as she/he is often called) has a similar role to the professional trainer or facilitator. They have to have skill in working with people, in creating a positive and supportive group culture online and in allowing participants to use the medium in ways that they think appropriate. CSCL will only be successful if the process emphasises *group* learning. Additionally, the moderator has certain 'privileged' controls over the meeting, eg they can delete messages and they can control entry to the meeting (meetings can be open or closed).

Perhaps most importantly, the moderator has to ensure that there is a real meeting of minds online – not just unassociated pieces of text. The role of the moderator of an online conference is as complex as that of any teacher or trainer in a face-to-face situation. Issues of educational philosophy, relationships with learners, power and control, the nature of knowledge and learning and so on are as important and problematic in CSCL as they are in face-to-face meetings. (Some authors have written about the role of moderators; for example, Feenberg, 1986; Kerr, 1986; Collins and Berge, 1998). The role of the moderator is discussed in Chapter 5.

Some Characteristics of CSCL

Computer supported cooperative learning and training is clearly different to learning and training events held face to face. Some of the more significant differences are:

- people from geographically distant sites are able to 'meet' without physically travelling to one location
- there are savings on time and travel (and therefore financial savings, although there will be initial capital set-up costs, and recurring costs)
- meetings are continuous in nature – a CSCL meeting can take place over a defined time span (eg, a week or a month), or can continue indefinitely (for months or years)
- interactions (responses to contributions etc) are not instantaneous or immediate
- people can contribute to the groups' work whenever they feel they want to, ie without waiting their turn or interrupting others
- contributions can be made at any time of the day or night, seven days a week
- a user can contribute from any geographic position, eg people who have to travel in their work can link in from almost any location
- communication usually (but not necessarily) happens in a slower, more sporadic fashion

- there is a permanent record of the groups' work and of everyone's contribution to it (this can be manipulated like a database)
- participants can access electronic resources and databases other than those used for the particular programme
- social presence, process and product of CSCL meetings often differ from face-to-face meetings
- the opportunity to work cooperatively in groups is enhanced – CSCL technologies can support cooperative learning and group processes in ways that may be difficult to achieve in face-to-face meetings.

As yet, CSCL is a relatively new medium in education and training and very little research has been carried out into its relevance and effectiveness. There is a growing body of opinion however, which is substantiated by initial research into the medium, that one of the important aspects of CSCL as an educational medium is the opportunity it offers for the democratisation of educational exchanges. This is believed to be associated with not having to interrupt others or talk over people in order to say what you want to say within a conference. All users have the same access to the dialogue. In addition, visual cues which can be used to denote status and power are eliminated. Thus CSCL potentially offers the possibility for what Roger Boshier identified as Habermas' 'ideal discourse', which Boshier claims should be 'free from coercion or distorting self-deception, is open to other perspectives and points of view, is accepting of others as equal participants' (Boshier, 1990).

Some General Uses of CSCL

It is possible to discuss at least four possible uses of computer conferencing within education and training (see Mason, 1998 and Collis, 1995 for other classifications). Computer conferencing may be used as a *complete replacement* for face-to-face meetings, as an *adjunct* to them, as a *multi-media approach* to teaching and learning and as a *fully integrated approach*.

Complete Replacement

Computer conferencing may be used to replace conventional face-to-face meetings, either by offering these meetings electronically at a distance for geographically isolated learners, or by offering them as a viable alternative to in-house courses.

Computer conferencing is being used in North America in the direct provision of online courses. The Connected Education programme at the New School for Social Research in Manhattan offers entire courses via this technology. The conventional college environment is mirrored in these electronic courses: the classes are conducted by computer conferences where the main interactive teaching and learning occurs. There are also conferences to create the 'electronic campus' – a 'cafe' for students and staff; a 'student lounge'; a 'tutor lounge'; an electronic library and newsletter. Connected Education attracts students from the Western USA, Tokyo, Singapore and the UK, as well as from the New York area itself.

Computer conferencing is also being used in the provision of continuing education courses for industry and commerce, and for teacher inservice education work. It is also used in undergraduate degree courses at the New Jersey Institute of Technology where over 60 staff use the system for tutoring both internal and external students. Subjects taught by CSCL include anthropology, management practices, maths, computer science and introductory sociology (Hiltz, 1986a).

Adjunct Method

The technology of electronic communication is also suitable as an adjunct to face-to-face meetings. Electronic seminars and tutorials can add a useful and interesting focus to on-campus and in-house courses. Material covered in lectures can be added to and completed in a computer conference. Students can question the lecturer or trainer about the course, request additional information or indeed add their own information to the conference for the benefit of the class as a whole. Face-to-face sessions can also be extended into asynchronous meetings for continued discussion of points raised or items which were unable to be discussed face to face. Alternatively, education and training offered solely via computer conferencing can be conducted throughout the year, with learners and tutors participating in them as and when they like. This has the benefit of allowing participants time to consider substantive topics over longer than usual periods of time (for example, see McConnell, 1990).

Multi-media Approach

The multi-media approach is perhaps exemplified by resource-based learning which emphasises a variety of different media and approaches to teaching and learning. An example of this approach is an Open University course in information technology. In addition to all the usual packaged learning materials provided as part of the course (course text units; audio-cassettes; broadcast television; a course reader; supplementary readings; course guides, and so on) students are also given access to computer conferences for such activities as course information and updating, course tutoring and self-help groups. Here, computer conferencing is only one of several alternative ways of learning on the course. The variety of media available can begin to meet the varying learning needs of the students (Mason and Kaye, 1989; Mason, 1989).

Fully Integrated Approach

New designs for educational and training programmes that fully integrate CSCL are now feasible. At Lancaster University, we experimented with the design of a part-time MA in Management Learning which involved two distinct but highly complementary learning environments. Over a two-year period, participants attend five residential workshops where they examine relevant research and theory. In between these workshops they join the 'electronic learning environment' where they continue discussing issues raised in the workshop, plan their assignments and assess them, work in action learning sets and so on. The electronic meetings are an important and integral part of the whole programme, not just an added extra. This programme is discussed in detail in Chapters 4 and 5.

Conclusion

Several factors may now lead towards a wider use of CSCL within education and training:

- personal computer prices are continuing to fall, making them within the grasp of many people taking a course of learning or training. PCs are increasingly being used at home and work and are becoming an integral part of many people's professional lives
- text processing and communications software is becoming more sophisticated and at the same time easier to use
- networks for computer supported cooperative learning and training are widely available – users can access CSCL systems via ordinary telephone lines, via data lines or through private local area networks

- the Web and the Internet are becoming part of many people's daily lives. Places of education are utilising these technologies to offer alternative methods to face-to-face, campus-based education.

The introduction of CSCL into post-compulsory education and training offers an alternative to conventional face-to-face work. The exploration of the possible benefits to teaching and learning offered by the new CSCL technologies is challenging, especially when the technology offers the hope of bringing people together who might otherwise never have the opportunity to meet, discuss and cooperate on educational and training issues.

3 | Tutoring and Learning in CSCL and Face-to-face Environments

Introduction

The two previous chapters have laid the foundation for a consideration of computer supported cooperative learning. The major focus of this chapter and Chapter 4 is the ways in which people in online, cooperative learning groups work together. Working in groups is a social process, as well as one having a product. We know a great deal about working in face-to-face groups, but we know very little about the experience of working in groups online.

In this chapter I will indicate some differences in the way people work in cooperative online groups, and focus specifically on some issues to do with the effects on time and group dynamics. The chapter is based on research carried out over the past few years into the perceptions and experiences of staff and students on a CSCL programme at Lancaster University, and on desk research into the educational potential of CSCL generally. Chapter 4 will consider the dynamics of mixed-sex groups of online learners.

Online Groups

The groups I am referring to here are small ones made up of five, six or seven participants and a tutor. The members are all participants on the computer mediated MA in Management Learning, offered by Lancaster University Management School. Members are all professional management trainers and developers. The programme is part-time and is designed around five residential workshops over a two-year period, with substantial periods of 'online' group work in between, lasting from between three and seven months. The Caucus computer conferencing system was used. Participants log on using a modem and communications software at their home or place of work. Staff log on from the University or from their home.

A major concern on the programme is with the social aspects of learning via CSCL media. Our starting point is not the technology: we see that as a tool, a means to an end. Rather, we are concerned to establish and maintain a supportive learning environment where participants and staff are involved in actively constructing meaningful learning relationships that are acceptable to them all. We use the term 'learning community' to emphasise the social and learning relationships that are encouraged online and in the workshops. The programme is concerned as much with participants' self- and professional development as with their academic learning. The design of the programme and an analysis of it appear in Chapters 5 and 6.

Cooperative Group-work Online

What kinds of activities are the members of these cooperative online learning groups involved in?

Individuals carry out their own work and are supported by each other in achieving personal aims. This might include members working on issues to do with each other's personal development, or discussing their interests in learning and the different meanings and models that can be attributed to the term, and so on.

People work at developing the social aspects of the group. By the social aspects I mean all those activities and issues to do with building and developing a sense of 'group' online. We consider it vital that we address the social contracts that are necessary for any group to work and survive successfully, just as one would in a face-to-face setting. These are what McGrath (1990) calls the 'member support and group well being functions' which are so important in successful technology mediated group work, yet which are often neglected, or worse still, never considered. Like us on our computer mediated MA, McGrath believes technology mediated group work requires:

> the deliberate creation of the very kind of social norms that apparently arise spontaneously in natural face-to-face groups, and that are very powerful and effective devices for regulating face-to-face communication in these groups (McGrath, 1990).

People initiate discussion about 'problems' in their work and life, and invite others to share in those discussions and offer feedback and ideas which will help take them forward.

People work on their current, self-chosen, piece of work for assessment for the MA. This involves:

- personal choice in what to work on
- sharing this with others
- engaging in dialogue about the piece of work
- testing ideas against members' experience and knowledge
- offering semi-drafts of the work for comment.

Group members are also involved in receiving each other's completed piece of work and in offering feedback on it and engaging in dialogue about the substantive issues of each paper. Collaborative assessment of each member's piece of work is carried out, involving assessment by self, peers and tutor.

There is very little consensus reaching activity in these groups. There is no exact problem or issue to be solved. But, some consensus is needed over:

- How the group is going to work together online, eg how often they will use the online system each week; how they will deal with each other's responses; how they will 'look after' the group. Sometimes discussion of these issues is formalised at the beginning of the online period; sometimes an issue emerges as they work together and is then discussed amongst the members of a group.
- How to develop criteria for assessment. The process for determining criteria for the assessment of each participant's current piece of work is a major aspect of the group's agenda. Sometimes the group develops criteria which can be applied across everyone's piece of work; sometimes criteria are specific to each individual's piece of work.
- Pacing of the group work, eg deadlines for deciding when to stop discussions; when to submit members' assessed pieces of work to each other; when to start giving feedback; when to assess; when to close the group, and so on.

The work of the group is characterised by the importance of the social interactions that take them forward. The climate of each group is non-competitive. The forms of cooperation in these groups require a high order of involvement, a high willingness to share, and a belief that individual development is enhanced by working with others around issues of mutual interest. The collaborative work of the groups is unusual given

71

the formal educational environment in which we find ourselves. It is not the accepted tradition for students to collaborate in these ways on an MA programme. What happens on the programme is perhaps more akin to the sort of teamwork that is sometimes found in public and private sector organisations.

The Experience of Group-work Online

We tend to take for granted most of the experiences of working in face-to-face groups. Most of us have worked in such groups so often that, even though the experience is complex and at times unpredictable, we tend to approach it with a certain degree of familiarity. Working with others in online environments is so unusual that we may have to approach it as if it is a completely new experience. Relying on well-born strategies, and working from common assumptions about how groups work in face-to-face environments, is not always the best orientation to take.

Over the past nine or ten years I have been working with groups in cooperative educational settings using computer conferences. I have used this medium for learning that involves cooperation, such as in seminar work, problem solving, discussions and indeed most activities that any of us involved in the educational process would normally engage in.

The MA is run using face-to-face workshops and electronic computer conferences (see Chapters 5 and 6 for details). This programme runs alongside a 'conventional' part-time MA which does not employ computer conferencing. Working on both programmes has given me the opportunity to compare the experiences, and to consider what some of the differences are in working with groups in these two environments.

Some of the differences between face-to-face and online groupwork are presented in Table 3.1. Clearly, some are more tentative than others and may be seen as working hypotheses worthy of future research. Some may be regarded as 'positive' aspects of CSCL, some as 'negative'. I will not discuss all these differences here, but will focus on a few that I find to be particularly interesting and important. These are the issues of 'time', and gender differences in group dynamics (the topic of the next chapter).

'Time' is important because it is a central issue in any of our professional lives. Working online poses questions about the nature of time as we have come to experience it in face-to-face meetings, and what that might mean for us working in a more open, and arguably 'timeless' environment such as computer conferencing. Group dynamics, and gender differences in these, is one of *the* central issues in cooperative learning, and deserves some special attention.

Table 3.1 *Some differences between teaching and learning in CSCL groups and face-to-face groups*

	CSCL	**Face-to-face**
Tutor's sense of control	Less sense of tutor control Easier for participants to ignore tutor	More sense of leadership from tutor Not so easy to ignore tutor
Scheduling meetings	No dates are scheduled nor needed, but 'contracts' for how often people come online usually established Unlimited contact possible	Dates are scheduled and punctuate the working life of the group Contact limited to set dates
Conditions of meeting	No waiting for participants to arrive No late comers or early leavers, etc.	Often have to wait for others to arrive People leave during the meeting, etc.
Mode	Discussions through text only; can be: structured; dense; permanent; limited; stark	Verbal discussions: a more common mode, but impermamant
Physical context	Don't meet in a room; no shared physical context (other than text)	Meet in a room; strong physical context
Time	Group meets continuously Concept of 'to meet' is different since no scheduled date and time and location Time less important and doesn't limit group – at least span of time is greater No sense of leaving the meeting Less controllable Sometimes deadlines are not adhered to since it is possible to extend beyond deadline to next period of online work	Group meets in 'stop and start' fashion Strong sense of when group meets – all those involved attend at same time, date, etc. Time important and is a limiter People leave during meeting for other meetings Controllable Deadlines usually adhered to since the expectation to complete on time is high, and it is not really possible to continue into next period of time

Table 3.1 *Continued*

	CSCL	Face-to-face
Work/discussion focus	Work on multiple issues at the same time	Usually work on one issue at a time and advance through agenda item by item
	Work not condensed–fluid and interweaved with other activities	Work is condensed and focused
	Group contact continually maintained	Little group contact in-between meetings
	Depth of analysis often increased online	Analysis varies, often dependent on time available
	Discussion often stops for periods of time, then is picked up and restarted	Discussions usually completed during meeting
	Members sometimes lose sense of where they are in the discussions over long periods of time (information overload)	Discussions occur within a set time frame, therefore less likely that members will lose sense of where they are
	Level of reflection high	Often little time for reflection during meetings
	Able to reshape conversations on basis of ongoing understandings and reflection	Less likelihood of conversations being reshaped during meeting
Group dynamics	Group dynamics not same as face-to-face; participants have to learn how to interpret them online	Dynamics 'understandable' to most participants because they have experienced them before
	Less sense of anxiety	Anxiety at beginning/ during meetings
	More equal participation, especially for females; participants can take control of this	Participation unequal and often dominated by males, but group may try to share time equally among members
	Less hierarchies, etc.	More chance of hierarchies
	Dynamics are 'hidden' but traceable	Dynamics evident but lost after the event
	No breaks – constantly in the meeting	Breaks between meetings
	Can be active listening without participation	Listening without participation may be frowned upon

Table 3.1   *Continued*

	CSCL	**Face-to-face**
	Medium (technology) has an impact on dynamics	Medium (room) may have less impact
	Different expectations about participation?	Certain 'accepted' expectations about participation?
	Slower – time delays in interactions/discussions	Quicker – immediacy of interactions/discussions
Accessing other groups	Can access other groups easily	Never have access to other groups
	Can see who is working in other groups	Can't participate in other groups
	Can participate in other groups easily	Can't see what is happening to others in groups
Effects of medium	Effects of group software	Effects of room/location?
	Effects of technology	
Absence and rejoining	Psychological/emotional stress of rejoining is high	Stress of rejoining not so high
Giving feedback on people's work	Feedback on each individual's piece of work very detailed and focused	Less likely to cover as much detail, often more general discussion
	Whole group can see and read each other's feedback	Group hears feedback
	Textual feedback only	Verbal/visual feedback
	No one can 'hide' and not give feedback	Possible to 'free-ride' and avoid giving feedback
	Permanent record of feedback obtained by all	No permanent record of feedback
	Delayed reactions to feedback	Immediate reactions to feedback possible
	Sometimes little discussion after feedback	Usually some discussion after feedback – looking at wider issues
	Group looks at all participants' work at same time	Group looks at one participant's work at a time
Total effort of group	Greater using CSCL	Less than CSCL

Table 3.1 *Continued*

	CSCL	Face-to-face
Divergence/choice level	Loose-bound nature encourages divergent talk and adventitious learning, since it is an open system regarding time, place, source and recipient	More tightly bound, requiring adherence to accepted group protocols
	Medium frees the 'sender' but may restrict the other participants (receivers) by increasing their uncertainty	Uncertainty less likely due to common understandings about how to take part in discussions

Time

In conventional face-to-face meetings there is a strong sense of when the group meets. All those involved attend at the same time and each meeting has a time limit. Time is important and is a limiter – people need to leave for other meetings or carry out other activities at certain times during the meeting or after it. So we can talk of the meeting beginning and ending according to hours in the day. The meeting is controllable. At a different level, the work of the group is punctuated by periods of time when members work together, and periods of time when they are apart. There is a loss of relationship between the group members in the periods in-between meetings, and some effort has to be put into rebuilding those relationships when members next meet. During the meetings time can be used for concentrated effort, to focus in-depth on issues and problems. Quick banter between participants, with immediate feedback and solution of problems, is possible. The sense of immediacy is perhaps one of the most important aspects of face-to-face meetings.

Figure 3.1 *Face-to-face groups*

In online groups, meetings are continuous; there are no breaks between one meeting and the next. The concept 'to meet' is different because there are no scheduled dates and times and locations. There is no sense of leaving one location to travel to another for the meeting. Time is less important and doesn't necessarily limit the group. At least, the span of limited time is greater. In a sense, you have less control over the time given to the meeting since the meeting is 'there' all the time and constantly beckons you to participate. There is little if any sense of loss of relationship between participants working cooperatively in online groups since they are constantly relating to one another. Discussions are often prolonged, and participants can use the time to dig deep into issues, exploring many different avenues of thought at the same time. This can lead to diverse results and outcomes. Participants can reshape conversations on the basis of their ongoing understandings and reflections. They can revisit 'old' conversations and restart them. The possibility to reflect on conversations is perhaps one of the most important aspects of online meetings.

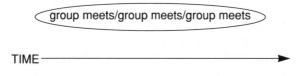

Figure 3.2   *Online groups*

Time therefore has different meanings and different consequences for learning in face-to-face and in online groups. Equal time may be allocated to each type of meeting, but the possibility for different locations, times of day and week in online groups can be advantageous. For example, on our MA programme we may allocate six hours to a one-day face-to-face meeting on the 'conventional' part-time programme. In the online programme, this same period of time may be scattered over several weeks. There is the same duration of time, but different possibilities for working together. The productivity value of the same period of time is not equivalent.

What effect does all of this have on members of online groups? It can have positive and negative impact on group members. Participants in online groups can experience the use of time in different ways. For some, the continuous nature of the online group-work means that it is constantly part of their life. It never goes away. It is absorbed into their lives:

> I don't feel I've been on a part-time programme because the programme is what I've been doing all the time I've been on it over the past two years. My fantasy is that the other programme (the conventional part-time one) would have been something that would have featured in my diary as 'lumps', and those lumps of time would have had more of a sense of something to fit into my life rather than *doing* my life... which from time to time would have erupted into a paper which I'd have to send to someone to read. And I wouldn't have wanted this (computer mediated programme) to be different (participant group member).[1]

That sense of 'living' the programme comes largely from the way in which cooperative groups work online. The medium allows constant contact with group members. Each group has to spend time developing a social contract for working together to which the members are personally committed. The sense of ownership concerning the purposes, processes and outcomes of the group is therefore high. Members view their relationships with each other in a professional way. There is little sense of a 'tutor' having to structure the way in which the group should work. The tutor's role is in many ways no different to that of any other participant. He or she is a 'tutor participant', bringing those skills and insights to the learning process that any professional tutor could bring, but always with an eye to being aware of the possibility that they might be using their authority inappropriately within the context of a cooperative learning environment.

The various activities of each group are not discrete in the way they often are in a face-to-face group. Members work on multiple issues at the same time. And because the issues are introduced by the participants themselves and are about important concerns and interests they have in relation to the work of the group, there is a different quality to the group members' relationship with the issues than might be the case if they were introduced as 'tasks' or topics by, say, a tutor. So, members' perceptions of 'time' can be governed by their relationship to the issues they are working on, and who introduced them.

The permanent nature of the group and its work over lengthy periods of time, and the way in which members are able to 'rejoin' at any time, means that participants can seem to carry the work of the group with them in their everyday lives:

> For me it's not just the being online; the reading, the writing – but I have these constant interventions in my life. I go online; I get some information. I read it there and then or I print it out. I sit down and read it. I think about it; I think about it a bit more. I think about what I am going to say to that. I think, well I could ignore it. I think 'Oh god, I've got to say something good about that because that was something pretty good she put there'. It's become my whole life. I'm driving along thinking 'What can I say to that?' or 'I don't know what to say to that'. I'm feeling I can't say anything to that! You know, its just sort of eaten into my whole life (participant).

Although this participant experiences her online work as a great source of enjoyment, it does also have serious implications for the amount of time needed by her to participate in a way that she felt she wanted to in order to support others in the group, and benefit from them working together:

> In terms of time when I started the programme, I had no idea... I thought I understood it... but I didn't have any idea of the amount of time this programme has actually taken out of my life. I thought I knew, but I wouldn't like to go back now and add up the amount of hours. And I'm sure the other MAML programme (the 'conventional' part-time one), if I were to equate the two... there is this huge discrepancy.

This is not to suggest that she is unhappy with this situation, because when asked the question, 'Is it worth it?', she replied 'Oh yes. It has to be worth it. I chose it for the cm (computer mediated) part. It does attract me and it does suit my life style, but takes a lot of time'. But she is willing to give that time because it is reciprocated by the other group members. If it wasn't, she would not be so inclined to cooperate as much as she does. Infrequent interactions online mean that people are less likely to respond or interact if each member only responds infrequently themselves. Interactions have to be kept relatively high for everyone to feel they are getting sufficient cooperation from the group members. Axelrod (1990) points to the need for frequent interactions to keep cooperative groups functioning.

This participant's statement about the time taken in all of this accords with current research which suggests that not only is individual effort increased in online group-work, but the total effort of groups is increased when they work in these environments (Pinsonneault and Kraemer, 1990).

These extended periods of time working online produce very positive outcomes for the groups. On the whole, interpersonal processes are a major concern of the groups and are worked at assiduously. This in turn creates a climate in which it is enjoyable and challenging to work on the 'tasks' of the group, and the conversations and outcomes are usually of a very high quality.

McGrath (1990) points to this as an important aspect of the work of groups. Groups given short, tight time periods in which to accomplish tasks work at a fast pace but with low quality, and their interaction patterns are highly task-focused. Those given extended periods of time, often free of a deadline, usually work slower, produce high quality outcomes and are concerned with the interpersonal relationships of the group. But the important aspect of this is that both kinds of groups continue to work to the same patterns when the time periods are changed. When more time is given to the first group, they still work in the same way. When time is restricted in the second group, they also continue to work in the same way. This suggests that setting an appropriate learning culture in an online group is important to the success and well-being of the group.

The use of time to create a climate in which the online group looks after itself and its members, and as a consequence produces good quality outcomes, may seem like a 'taken for granted'. But groups working via technology can often make the mistake of thinking that the technology itself will 'look after the group': after all, the groupware has been designed to do just that. Experience suggests that the social processes and relationships of the groups has to be worked at by the group members, just as they would do if meeting face-to-face. This takes time, but it is time well invested.

The fluidity of time in electronic environments often allows groups to view their work and tasks in innovative ways. Conventionally, each group on our computer mediated MA forms for a period of two to three months in order to carry out the work of that period, and then all members on the programme re-form into new groups for the next period and so on. This methodology gives a sense of pacing within each group over the period of time and helps the group structure its time in order to carry out the various tasks within the given period. Within the electronic environment, it is possible for groups to continue indefinitely, while at the same time the members can re-form into new groups. This allows participants to extend work in 'old' groups for as long as they find it useful. For example, this can support the continuation of discussion around feedback and assessment of members' individual pieces of work. Instead of having to bring such discussions to a close, often with members feeling they have not had sufficient time to explore each other's pieces of work, such discussions continue into new periods of time. Many members value the extension of their group-work in this way and like being in multiple groups. It feels like a quality experience for them. For staff though, there are drawbacks. The psychological energy needed to maintain contact with discussions around each member's piece of work and engage in work in new groups at the same time, can be very demanding. Discussions become too spread out, and the depth of analysis that members engage in sometimes means that tutors can't always fully remember previous discussions. But the educational benefit to group members is perceived by them to be enormous.

Some Possible Drawbacks of CSCL

Working in CSCL environments affords certain advantages over working in face-to-face settings. But there are of course some drawbacks which have to be mentioned.

Mode of Communication

The first is the mode of communication. Communication face to face involves both verbal and non-verbal exchanges and provides a rich source of information for us to understand and interpret. Communicating via CSCL strips our exchanges of the non-verbal mode. Some researchers suggest that most of our exchanges occur through the non-verbal mode; Mehrabian (1981, quoted in Chesebro and Bonsall, 1989) suggests that 93 per cent of social meaning is accounted for by non-verbal communication. In an attempt to deal with this, users of CSCL sometimes use simple signs online to stimulate non-verbal facial reactions, called emoticons. Some of these include:

:)   – I'm happy
:(– I'm sad
:s   – I have mixed feelings
8)   – I'm wide awake
:o   – I'm surprised
(:o – I'm very surprised
:p   – Pfftt! (sticking out the tongue)
:9   – Yummy
:/   – Human
:v   – I'm chatting
B)   – I'm wearing my shades

(P H Lewis, 1986, quoted in Chesebro and Bonsall, 1989).

Information Overload

Another potential drawback is the possibility of CSCL users becoming overloaded with information. When users are participating frequently this is less likely to occur. But when there are periods of absence from the groups' work, then it is often the case that large amounts of information accumulate and are presented to the member on their return. This can have several effects: the member may feel overwhelmed by the amount of communications to be read, and they may either choose to ignore it all (thus missing out on the groups' actions); try to read and digest it (which can be extremely time-consuming), or skim over it in an attempt to get a rough understanding of what has been happening during their absence.

Even when users are participating frequently, there are times when the groups' activities are so involving that the amount of information piles up daily. This can be exciting and challenging for members of the groups, and if they feel connected to the interactions the high level of activity does not become a problem of information overload. But of course there are always times when it is just not possible to read everything, and users sift through the material using online tools. This phenomenon is considered to be like coping in high social density environments, where some 'screening' is useful:

> Screeners... effectively reduce the stress of numerous inputs by constructing a priority-based pattern of attention to information (ie by disregarding low-priority inputs). [They] cope with the high rate of social interaction in the environment in a deliberate and organized manner... Nonscreeners are more likely to become overaroused in situations characterised by high rates of information and are prone to fatigue and psychosomatic components in such settings (Mehrabian, 1977, quoted in Hiltz and Turoff, 1985).

Group members self-organise the amount of information they encounter online, just as they would in face-to-face groups. Choices are made on the basis of their present relationship to the group, the time they have to hand for dealing with communications, their purpose at any time for attending to the group, their relationships with other members, and so on. In CSCL environments, information overload has two components: first, there are too many communications presented to the user, by too many people. The possibility to work with more people than you would normally in face-to-face meeting is huge; this in turn means that the possibility of receiving communications from more people is also increased. Second, new messages are not always organised sufficiently well for you to see their relationship with previous ones. This can be referred to as 'information entropy' (Hiltz and Turoff, 1985). The user response to both these conditions might involve them in:

1. failing to respond to certain inputs
2. responding less accurately than they would otherwise
3. responding incorrectly
4. storing inputs and then responding to them as time permits
5. systematically ignoring (or filtering) some features of input
6. recoding the inputs in a more compact or effective form, or
7. quitting (in extreme cases).

(Sherridan and Ferrill, 1974, quoted in Hiltz and Turoff, 1985.)

The above list does not, however, take into account that in CSCL environments such as computer conferences, there is a high degree of structuring imposed by the architecture of the system which essentially directs users to put messages into meaningful locations (such as items within the Caucus system), and helps users find their way round the conference. This routing of information is one of the features that differentiates computer conferences from e-mail and bulletin boards, and which makes them particularly useful for group work.

CSCL systems offer users various tools with which to structure the information; additionally, groups can devise processes to help overcome information overload and manage their interactions. (There are various guidelines for supporting communication processes on the Internet. This is called 'netiquette'. See eg www.fau.edu/netiquette/net/index.) Some of the more common processes and tools include:

Processes:
- length limitations – group members agree that information should be presented in single-screen size pieces. Long inputs of more than a screen are discouraged (and in practice are often ignored in any case unless there is a good reason offered for including them)
- advance organisers – users alert other users to the length and type of information in the first line of response
- conference organiser presents a list of all items as part of the introductory conference greeting. Additional information can be added to the greeting in order to inform users of something new in the conference
- personal items – each user has a personal item for their own particular use which is recognised as such by other users
- each item is managed by one person – this shares out the work of managing the conference as a whole
- items where a specific type of communication is required have limited or very specific members. For example, items dealing with assessment in cooperative learning may only have triads of assessee, peer assessor(s) and tutor
- different conferences for different purposes.

Tools for:
- asking to see who the other group members are
- asking to see which inputs other group members have made, and reading a selection of those
- searching for key words and phrases, and only reading those items/responses where the words and phrases appear

- moving backwards through the communications, either chronologically or by some other system
- selecting individual responses which are presented in isolation from the rest of the material
- listing all items – either as a brief overview, or with details of who set the item up and when
- making some items 'read only' items, (ie no one can enter new material into them)
- giving each item a title to reflect content/processes acceptable in it
- freezing items, ie closing items from further entries
- making items 'disappear' – you are not aware of activity in them after doing this.

Written Dialogue

Working in these kinds of CSCL environments means that all communications are made via a keyboard, in textual form. Research suggests that typing skills are not important for the success of online group communications (Hiltz, 1984; McConnell, 1988). Nevertheless, when asked if they ever felt constrained in the type of contributions they could make, many students do say that they feel constrained at *some* time (McConnell, 1988a). It could well be that, for some at least, having to present their thoughts publicly in typewritten form acts as a barrier to full participation. However, most students say they are usually able to express their views during the online meetings.

Reluctant Tutors and Students

The open nature of CSCL, with its emphasis on cooperative learning strategies, may not suit every tutor or student. Although, as we have seen in Chapter 1, there is considerable evidence to support the educational benefits of cooperative learning, and even though many people prefer cooperative methods irrespective of whether there are wider educational benefits, some tutors and students will not wish to participate in cooperative learning through CSCL.

This is to be expected, and should be accepted. Some tutors may prefer situations where they have more control over the learning process; they may wish to be more directive than is sometimes possible, or desirable, in CSCL. Similarly with some students, who may have a high need for external structure and direction in their learning. The open learning environment of CSCL demands a certain kind of openness in the communications of those involved. You can see everything that any group member enters into the system. This might prove rather threatening to some tutors and students.

The method chosen by any of us for tutoring or for learning may be related to our values and beliefs. In very simplistic terms there may be two extremes here. Some of us may value more highly those activities which are based on cooperative methods and ideas, where students and tutor try to act as equals in a process aimed at democratising the generation of knowledge. Others may prefer situations where individualisation is more important, where there are well-defined roles and expectations relating to the work of tutors and students.

These 'systems' are not necessarily mutually exclusive, and involvement in one system at one time does not necessarily exclude involvement in the other at another time. Whether one system has greater value than the other may be an issue for debate. Both systems can suit different purposes at different times.

Conclusions

In this chapter I have relied on field research interviews, group reviews with tutors and participants on a computer mediated MA programme, analysis of online group dynamics and my own personal reflections and experiences of working with cooperative groups in online environments, to say something about the nature of group work in educational computer conferences. Specifically, I have considered the issue of 'time' as it affects online groups. In the next chapter I will consider in some depth some aspects of gender differences in the dynamics of mixed-sex groups.

Notes

1. Quotations in this section are taken from the MA programme reviews. As part of the face-to-face workshops, we are involved with participants in reviewing the programme to date, especially the online work. These reviews are open-ended discussions which often lead to redesigning certain aspects of the programme, such as our online group work.
2. These quotations are taken from a series of in-depth interviews with participants on the computer mediated MA programme. The interviews were free-flowing, focusing largely on participants' and tutors' experiences of working in online groups. This research is reported in Hardy *et al.*, (1991).

4 | The Dynamics of Group Work

Introduction

The dynamics of groups – the ways in which people relate and work together – is an important area of study generally. This is no less so in educational and training settings where the role of group work is seen as important in achieving many goals.

Cooperative learning technologies are designed around the concept that learning in groups is worthwhile. It is often cited that cooperative learning environments like computer conferences are also more democratic media for educational exchanges than conventional learning environments (such as face-to-face meetings). If this is the case, then we could imagine that the dynamics of these electronic meetings should be different from face-to-face meetings.

There is an increasing interest in gender online generally (see eg Lally and Barrett, 1999; Light *et al.*, 1997; Spender, 1995; Turkle, 1995; Yates 1997, 1999) and in the dynamics of mixed-sex groups in online environments in particular, especially the experiences of males and females in these environments. One example of this is the ways in which males and females participate in groups online: there appear to be some differences in the ways in which males and females participate in group work. This research field is still very exploratory, but our experiences are sufficient to suggest that there is a gender difference, in some aspects at least.

Interaction Patterns

Although, as we shall see, there has been considerable general interest in researching patterns of interactions in face-to-face mixed-sex groups, the examination of such gender differences in electronic learning environments is rare.

In this chapter, I will report on a study concerned primarily with establishing, from empirical data, differences in the interaction patterns between females and males in mixed-sex educational computer conferences. Additional supporting data from field observations, interviews and group reviews is also provided. Although the major focus of the chapter is on groups of management trainers and developers working in post graduate settings, the findings will no doubt have relevance to mixed-sex learning groups in general.

Establishing patterns of interaction is important because it informs us of issues such as turn taking, duration of speech (ie typed contributions) and control of direction of conversations in mixed-sex groups. It tells us something of the power dynamics of learning groups. On its own, however, it is not enough. We also need to go beyond the empirical work of looking at patterns of interaction to an examination and interpretation of dialogues between male and female participants in these electronically mediated groups. Although important, I will not be covering that aspect here.

Examining Gender Differences in Mixed-sex Groups

Four major approaches to studying gender differences in mixed-sex groups from an empirical viewpoint have been established. These are:

- Allocation of speech turns. The emphasis here is on who takes most turns at talking. Turn taking involves one person talking and then giving way to another.
- Patterns of interruption. Interruptions are part of the movement from one speaker to another, ie gaining the floor.
- Choice and development of conversational topics, ie who chooses the topics for conversation. Are conversations differentially supported depending on the gender of the initiator?
- Length of exchanges. Who talks the longest?

Previous studies broadly fall into one of two categories: those carried out in educational settings with the intention of analysing differences between female and male students in learning contexts (see eg Aries, 1976; Eakins and Eakins, 1978; Brooks, 1982; French and French, 1984; Josefowitz, 1984; Swann and Graddol, 1988; Graddol and Swann, 1989; Kelly, 1991; Holden, 1993) and those carried out in non-educational settings with the aim of assessing interactions in everyday conversational settings (see eg Thorne and Henley, 1975; Zimmerman and West, 1975; Haas, 1979; Jones, 1980; Michard and Viollet, 1991; Wheelan and Verdi, 1992; Bischoping, 1993).

The different purposes, settings and methodologies of these studies make global statements about the findings somewhat problematical (for reviews and summaries see Thorne and Henley, 1975; Graddol and Swann, 1989; Michard and Viollet, 1991; Wheelan and Verdi, 1992; Bischoping, 1993). Nevertheless, although by no means conclusive, the outcomes of these studies seem to be fairly consistent in suggesting that males tend to dominate conversations in mixed-sex groups. The findings suggest that:

- Male speakers talk more than females (Eakins and Eakins, 1978; Brooks, 1982; Josefowitz, 1984).
- Males take more of the available time per turn ie they talk longer than females (Eakins and Eakins, 1978; Brooks, 1982).
- Males initiate more interruptions than females (Eakins and Eakins, 1978).
- Male speakers control the choice of themes in conversations (Michard and Viollet, 1991; Zimmerman and West, 1975).
- Female speakers develop others' themes more than males do (Michard and Viollet, 1991).
- When women are talking, males and females will talk simultaneously; when males are talking simultaneous speech occurs less (Graddol and Swann, 1989).
- Females raise more topics than males; but fewer of their topics 'succeed' in being established in the conversations than those of males (Graddol and Swann, 1989).
- Females support conversations throughout the whole period of the conversation; males tend to support at the end of the conversation (Haas, 1979; Graddol and Swann, 1989).
- Females talk about people and relationships, males talk more about work and money (Haas, 1979; Bischoping, 1993).

All of the above are from studies looking at male–female interaction and conversation in face-to-face settings. It should be pointed out that it is important to differentiate between actual speech and contributions which occur during computer conferences, as in the present study.

Why Look at CSCL?

There are several reasons for studying gender differences in this medium.

- CSCL, and electronic communications generally, is becoming an established environment for post graduate courses, and for management learning and development courses in particular.[1] We need to understand how female and male participants in these electronic groups relate and work together.

● Some researchers claim the use of the medium can afford a more democratic regime than face-to-face meetings for peer discussions. It is said to allow each individual equal opportunity to take part in conversations without all the difficulties associated with talk in face-to-face meetings (see eg Harasim,1987; McConnell, 1988). However, the medium is not intrinsically apt to support democratic participation (Mantovani, 1994).

● As indicated above, much research into gender differences in mixed-sex face-to-face groups suggests that female participants are at a disadvantage in discussions and that males tend to dominate the proceedings. It would seem important to determine if online environments might allow more equality between the sexes in terms of their participation in conversations. For example, previous research into management trainers' and developers' personal experiences of working in online environments suggests that there are differences in the way people participate according to gender. For example, some female participants experience male participants as dominating conversations. (Hardy *et al.*, 1991). Again, it would seem important to have an empirical assessment of these claims.

This Study

This study looks at patterns of textual interaction of post graduate students in mixed-sex groups in asynchronous computer tele-conferences. The actual system used was the Caucus computer conferencing system. The medium is often referred to as an 'online' medium, and is an example of a more generic type commonly referred to as computer mediated communications (CMC), groupware, computer supported cooperative learning (see Chapter 2) or computer supported cooperative work (CSCW) media (Greif, 1988).

As we have seen, this medium is time-bridging and distance-spanning. It allows groups of people to work together without having to meet face-to-face. They communicate via personal computers across dedicated data networks, or use modems attached to public telephone networks. A host computer stores the computer conferencing software. Communication is in written form only. Group participants send and receive the texts of their conversations at various different times. The medium eliminates all non-verbal channels, and indeed all sensory modes of communication (McGrath, 1990; Hodgson and McConnell, 1992). As we have also seen in the previous chapter, these electronic meetings differ from 'conventional' face-to-face meetings in several respects.

Methodology

The context of this study differs from most other research into interaction patterns in mixed-sex groups in two important ways. Firstly, it is naturalistic rather than experimental. In terms of the frameworks and methods often used in researching gender issues (Thorne and Henley, 1975), those employed here included observation, ethnography and textual analysis. Additionally, empirical data concerning interaction patterns was gathered. Secondly, the study involves analysis of groups that met for extended periods of time.

Most reported research into interaction patterns of mixed-sex groups has been with experimental groups (Aries, 1976) and with groups that met once only, for a short period of time (Wheelan and Verdi, 1992). Little if any research has been conducted into mixed-sex group interactions in naturally occurring groups. Indeed, although Wheelan and Verdi looked at naturally occurring groups over longer periods of time than was usual in these kind of studies, their conception of longer periods of time was still relatively limited in terms of group development since their groups met from a minimum of 4½ hours to 7½ hours in total. The time span during which the electronic groups researched in this study 'met' was considerably longer, from three months to seven months.

It might be predicted, therefore, that the findings of this research may not accord with those of previous studies because of the differing methodologies used, and because of the larger time spans employed, apart from the more obvious difference of medium.

The Group Conferences

Four mixed-sex asynchronous computer conferences were examined. The conferences were part of a two-year, part-time, computer mediated MA in Management Learning. Over the two years, participants and tutors met periodically for face-to-face workshops, followed by long periods of 'online' (computer conference) meetings, lasting between three and seven months. The concept of a learning community defines many of the educational values of the programme: participants and staff work towards open participation; sharing; collective decision making concerning responsibility for the design and evaluation of the programme; the management by participants of their own learning, and cooperation with others in theirs; a critical reflective perspective on learning; and self/peer/tutor collaborative assessment of each individual's self-chosen assignments. These computer conferences are integral to the programme and are a major focus for participants' learning; they cannot complete the course without participating in them.

Conference one was made up of two females and two males (one of whom was a staff member); conference two had two females and three males (one a staff member); conference three had six females (two staff members) and seven males (two staff members); conference four had one female, who was the staff member, and four males. Each group met electronically for between three and six months. The groups worked intensively on various self-selected issues to do with management learning and development. Participants were all professional management trainers and developers. They worked in public and private sector organisations, higher education institutions or were self-employed. Their ages ranged from late twenties to early fifties. The conferences were run on a self-managed basis (Cunningham, 1981), with much of the activity being around self-development, experiential learning and action learning rather than purely cognitive learning (Pedler *et al.*, 1986). The self-managed philosophy of the groups provided an environment where staff and participants could strive to assume equal status and similarity of roles (see McConnell, 1992, for more details).[2]

The study looked at turn taking, length of textual entries (equivalent to duration of speech in other studies), and initiation of conversational topics. Since it is not possible to interrupt a speaker online in the way that can occur in face-to-face settings, interruptions did not form part of this study.

Each group conference was extracted from the host mainframe computer and converted into a word processed document for analysis. Each conference was analysed for the number of items in it and the number of responses (or turns) within the items. For the purposes of this study, I have considered an item to be a separate topic of conversation; responses are participants' textual interactions within that conversation. In conference one there were 21 items and 338 responses; conference two had 22 items and 804 responses; conference three had 33 items with 479 responses, and conference four was made up of 17 items and 681 responses. To put this into some kind of context, other researchers looking at patterns of interactions base their research on samples of conversations with total turns of between 82 and 119 (Swann and Graddol, 1988); 188 (French and French, 1984); 543 (Brooks, 1982); and between 14 and 111 (Kelly, 1991).

Turn Taking

Turn taking in groups refers to the phenomenon of one person talking and then giving way to another person. This may appear rather too simply put, since those involved actively construct the production of the conversation at the same time. In turn taking analysis, however, we are concerned with determining who is speaking at any one time, and not with how the speakers have co-constructed the conversation.

Turn taking is often used as a measure for looking at the participation of male and female members of groups in formal educational settings. Turn taking is thought to be a universal phenomenon in conversations of all kinds:

> Sacks *et al.* (1974) suggest that speech exchange systems in general are organized to ensure that (1) one party speaks at a time and (2) speaker change occurs. These features are said to hold for casual conversation as well as for formal debate and even high ceremony. Thus it appears that the range of speech exchange systems found in our society (and possibly all societies) is constrained by some form of turn-taking mechanism' (Zimmerman and West, 1975, p. 107).

It is difficult to translate this to an environment like computer conferencing, where turn taking as described above does not need to take place. People do 'take turns', but they do not have to wait for the current speaker to stop talking, or to interrupt them in order to take the floor. There can be various simultaneous conversations. In a CSCL environment, whatever piece of textual communication an individual enters is counted as a turn, eg it may be one word, a sentence or a longer piece of text. The system informs participants each time someone takes a turn, and the text of that turn is presented to all participants.

This distinction between turn taking in face-to-face environments and turn taking in electronic forums is important. Turns in a CSCL environment may differ from those in face-to-face environments in several ways. For example, they may be much longer than would be possible in a face-to-face meeting. This may be due to the way in which participants sometimes prepare their responses offline, when they have time to think and plan the content of the response. Such responses sometimes take the form of a well thought through piece of prose. It is unlikely for someone in a small group to talk for such periods of time, or to present what they wish to say in such a well thought out way.

Even when responses are not prepared offline, there is the possibility to take time to respond as fully as you wish in online environments because there is no fear of being interrupted. This exchange system seems to differ from that proposed by Sacks *et al.* (as reported in Zimmerman and West, 1975), whose model of turn taking is based on the assumption that there will be interruptions, and that those involved in the conversation will administer turn order and turn size.

However, not all turns in online groups are long or well prepared. It is possible to have a conversation which approximates to a face-to-face one in which people use short 'unit types' (Zimmerman and West, 1975) of several words or short phrases.

The general phenomenon of turn taking is described by David Graddol:

> The dynamics of face-to-face talk allow for many inequalities, however. The turn taking mechanism is such that successful participation in conversation is often a competitive business requiring speed and confidence: a maxim of 'first in gets the floor' seems to operate; one person can interrupt another and prevent them from taking or completing a turn. The need for contributions to be topically tied to the current topic means that those who cannot or do not wish to participate in that topic have limited powers to change the topic to another. There is instead, a continuous thread in which current participants have more control than those listening and a current speaker has first rights to select the next speaker' (Graddol, 1989).

It is often suggested that computer conferences allow for a more participative dynamic than face-to-face meetings (Harasim, 1987; McConnell, 1988). There is no need to wait for your turn to talk since the architecture of a computer conference permits multiple, simultaneous conversations. There is little sense of interrupting others, and topics need not be tied to any current topic since new items can be set up for new topics. The power relations of the members of the group, in theory, can be shared more evenly.

Given all of this, do computer conferences additionally support equality of participation among males and females? Or are the gender differences in participation and talk that are often cited for mixed-sex face-to-face groups still in operation?

Computer conferences lend themselves to this kind of simple turn taking analysis since it is easy to establish how often anyone 'talks', or takes a turn. Table 4.1 shows the results of turn taking by gender groups in the four conferences.

In three out of four cases, females took more turns than males.

When we look at the 'expected' ratio of turn taking to the actual ratio for males and females, a similar trend can be seen. In conference one,

Table 4.1   *Turn taking analysed by conference*

	Conference 1	Conference 2	Conference 3	Conference 4
Number of participants	4 (2M, 2F)	5 (3M, 2F)	13 (7M, 6F)	5 (4M, 1F)
Male turns	144 (T=23%)	414 (T=25%)	272 (T=13%)	536
Female turns	194	390	207 (T=9%)	145 (T=21%)
Average turns per male	72	138	39	134
Average turns per female	97	195	35	145
'Expected' ratio of turns	50M:50F	60M:40F	54M:46F	80M:20F
Actual ratio of turns	43M:57F	51M:49F	57M:43F	78M:21F

Notation: F denotes female: M denotes male: T denotes tutor.

while females comprised 50 per cent of the group they accounted for 57 per cent of the turns. In conference two, females comprised 40 per cent of the group but they accounted for 49 per cent of the turns. In conferences three and four, females and males accounted for similar proportions to those expected.

The average turns and the ratio of turn taking between males and females indicates a trend for female members of the conferences to take a greater ratio of turn taking compared with male participants.

When we look at turn taking per item in each conference we see a similar trend.

Table 4.2 indicates that in three out of the four conferences, female members took more turns than males in each item when measured across all items in each conference. The trend is therefore towards females taking more turns per item. However, in the remaining conference (conference three) males took the highest number of turns in nearly four times as many items as females. This may be due to the larger size of this

Table 4.2   *Highest/Most turns taken in each item*

	Conference 1	Conference 2	Conference 3	Conference 4
Total number of items	11	22	33	17
Highest/most turns per item				
Males	2	9	15	6
Females	9	10	4	9
	0 equal	3 equal	14 equal	2 equal

Interpretation: In conference 2, females took highest number of turns in 10 out of the 22 items.

group, and may suggest that it is necessary to examine interaction patterns in larger groups to see if similar trends exist.

An analysis of interactions by individuals in each conference suggests a slightly different perspective (see Figure 4.1).

F1 has more turns in conference one, but generally there is an even distribution of turns. In conference two, M2 and M3 took lower turns than the ratio of turns per individuals might expect. In conference three there is wide variation in turn taking, both between and within sexes. The males have the larger percentage of turns. Two males, M4 and M5, have more turns, taking 37 per cent of the turns between them. But also some males took very few turns (eg M2, M3 and M6). There is a similar trend amongst the female participants, but it is not as marked as for the males, with a greater 'sharing' of turns between females. There therefore appear to be no simple trends when looked at by individual turn taking.

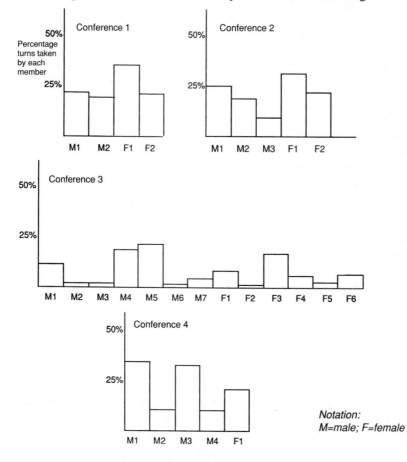

Figure 4.1 *Turn taking by individuals*

Length of Exchanges

Another measure of the dynamics of male and female participation in groups is the length of exchanges, or the duration of speech. One way of measuring duration of speech in a computer conference is to count the words entered by each individual. This gives a measure of the length of each entry.[3]

As can be seen from Table 4.3, males entered more total words in three of the four conferences. This is perhaps to be expected given that there were more males in each of these conferences than females. In conference one where there was an equal number of males and females, females entered more total words.

Table 4.3 *Number of words entered by conference*

	Conference 1 (21 items)	Conference 2 (22 items)	Conference 3 (33 items)	Conference 4 (17 items)
Number of participants	4 (2M, 2F)	5 (3M, 2F)	13 (7M, 6F)	5 (4M, 1F)
Total words	47,754 (T=18%)	114,319 (T=26%)	40,302 (T=19%)	98,704 (T=16%)
Total entered by males	19,078	64,786	23,898	82,926
Total entered by females	28,679	49,533	16,404	15,778
Average number of words entered by males	9,539	21,595	3,414	20,732
Average number of words entered by females	14,340	24,766	2,734	15,778
Difference	4,801	3,171	680	4,957
'Expected' ratio of words	50M:50F	60M:40F	54M:46F	80M:20F
Actual ratio of words	40M:60F	57M:43F	59M:41F	84M:16F

Notation: F denotes female: M denotes male: T denotes tutor.

Looking at the average number of words entered by gender, we can see that there is a fifty-fifty split between the sexes. In two conferences females dominate the conversation, by 5,000 and 3,000 extra words more than males on average. In the other two conferences, males dominate by 1,000 and 5,000 extra words on average.

Looking at words entered relative to the proportions of males and females in each conference, we can see that females had a greater proportion in conference one than might be expected, and a slightly higher proportion in conference two. Males had a slightly higher proportion in conferences three and four than might have been expected.

These results indicate a degree of equality between gender groups in the length of talk in these conferences.

Table 4.4 shows the average words entered by individuals per turn. In each conference the individual person who enters the highest number of

Table 4.4   *Average words entered by individuals per turn*

Conference	Participant	Words Entered
One	M1*	110
	M2	160
	F1	151
	F2	144
Two	M1*	151
	M2	150
	M3	189
	F1	136
	F2	115
Three	M1*	72
	M2*	259
	M3	10
	M4	120
	M5	69
	M6	59
	M7	78
	F1*	60
	F2	87
	F3*	87
	F4	58
	F5	93
	F6	83
Four	M1	135
	M2	132
	M3	168
	M4	205
	F1*	109

*Notation: F denotes female: M denotes male: *denotes tutor.*

words per turn is always male; but it is also always the case that these individuals have the fewest number of turns in each conference.

In conferences two and four, individual females consistently added fewer words per turn than individual males. In conference three, two males dominated overall, followed by a cluster of females, which in turn was followed by a cluster of males. The contributions of females in conference one, although less than the dominant male, are on a par with the males.

These figures indicate that there is not a simple dominance by gender when looked at on an individual participant level. There is much variation between genders and between those of each gender. Nevertheless, there does seem to be a trend for males to enter more words than females per turn.

When we look at each conference and make a rank order of speaking by gender, males consistently come out top. In each of the four conferences, males ranked as first; females were never first. In three out of the four conferences, males ranked as second; females ranked second in one conference. In two out of the four conferences males ranked as third; females also ranked as third in two conferences.

Table 4.5 *Rank order of speaking by gender*

Rank	Males	Females
1	4 out of 4 conferences	0 out of 4 conferences
2	3 out of 4 conferences	1 out of 4 conferences
3	2 out of 4 conferences	2 out of 4 conferences

These results suggest that again male members of the conferences talk longest.

Which gender group entered the highest number of words per item?

Table 4.6 shows that in three out of four conferences analysed, the trend was towards males consistently entering more words when measured across all items, than females. Once again, put simply, males tend to say more, or talk longest most often.

Who Directs the Conversation?

The third measure of conversational patterns concerns control over the direction of conversations. One way of measuring this in computer conferences is to determine who starts new conversations by setting up new items in each conference (what actually happens in the items, eg

Table 4.6 *Numbers of words entered by item*

	Conference 1 (11 items)	Conference 2 (22 items)	Conference 3 (33 items)	Conference 4 (17 items)
Number of items with highest number of words by gender				
Males	2	12	19	12
Females	9	10	14	5

Interpretation: in Conference 2, males entered most words/said most in 12 out of the 22 items.

which ones get followed or picked up by participants, is the focus of another study).

The figures in Table 4.7 indicate that, on the whole, there are no major differences in who directs conversation when measured by who sets up new items in the conferences. In conference one, however, females did set up more items in total suggesting that they tended to dominate the direction of conversation in this group.

Figure 4.2 shows the degree to which each individual initiated conversations. In conference one, the two females dominated the direction of conversation, adding 36 per cent each (72 per cent total) of the items. In

Table 4.7 *Initiation of conversations by gender*

	Conference 1 (11 items)	Conference 2 (22 items)	Conference 3 (33 items)	Conference 4 (17 items)
Number of participants	4 (2M, 2F)	5 (3M, 2F)	13 (7M, 6F)	5 (4M, 1F)
Number of items set up by males	3 (T=1)	14 (T=5)	17 (T=3)	14
Number of items set up by females	8	8	16 (T=2)	3 (T=3)
Average number of items set up by males	1.5	4.6	2.4	3.5
Average number of items set up by females	4	4.5	2.6	3
'Expected' ratio of items set up	50M:50F	60M:40F	54M:46F	80M:20F
Actual ratio of items set up	27M:73F	61M:39F	52M:48F	82M:18F

Notation: F denotes female; M denotes male; T denotes tutor.

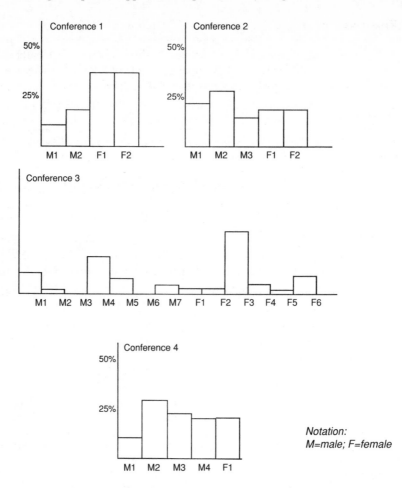

Figure 4.2 *Initiation of conversations by individuals*

conference two there is a fairly even distribution of items added by gender, as is the case also in conference four. A female participant dominated in conference three, setting up 30 per cent of all items, followed by a male member who set up 18 per cent. Then there is a cluster of people (male and female) who started 6–9 per cent of the items each, followed by another cluster (males and females) of people who set up 3 per cent of the items each. Two males set up no items at all.

Overall, in some conferences (eg conference four) there is a fairly even spread of the direction of conversation by gender. In others (eg conference three) there is wide variation within and between genders (from this simple empirical comparison it is not possible to say why this happens; this is the focus of an other study to be reported in a follow-up paper).

Discussion

The findings of this study appear to differ from those of other researchers in some ways, and seem to support them in other ways.

In terms of turn taking or frequency of speech, we can say that females as a group take more turns in these computer conferences generally, and within individual items in conferences. They also take a greater ratio of turns than might be expected. These findings differ from those of other researchers who consistently report that males take more turns than females in mixed-sex face-to-face groups (eg Eakins and Eakins, 1978; Brooks, 1982; French and French, 1984; Swann and Graddol, 1988; Kelly, 1991 who all found that the male group was dominant in speech frequency or turn taking).

We might, therefore, tentatively say that in the context of this MA programme, this medium appears to support turn taking by females as a group.

But when looked at on an individual participant basis, there are no major differences in turn taking irrespective of gender. This concurs with findings elsewhere (French and French, 1984; Kelly, 1991).

When we look at words entered, or the length of speech, we can say that individual males tend to enter more words per turn than females in these computer conferences, ie males talk longest. Males also enter more words per item than females. This is similar to the findings of Eakins and Eakins, 1978; Brooks, 1982; Swann and Graddol, 1988 and Kelly, 1991.

Therefore, patterns of interaction when measured by word length appear to be no different in this medium than in face-to-face meetings.

There is no difference in the average words entered by males and females in these conferences. This differs from other research findings (eg Brooks, 1982) which suggest that individual males dominate in mixed-sex conversations.

The issue of who directs conversational topics by setting up items is a little more complex. In some conferences there are no major differences by gender groups in who initiates discussion by setting up items in conferences. In other conferences, females dominate. This differs from other research findings. For example, Michard and Viollet (1991) say that males choose the themes in conversations. Aries (1976) reports that males initiated more interactions.

In some of these computer conferences there are no differences between individuals (irrespective of gender) in who initiates conversations. But in other conferences, female members initiate more topics of conversation. As was said above, it is not possible from these simple empirical comparisons to say why this occurs, although a follow-up study may throw some light on this.

It can therefore be said that, in the context of this MA programme, this medium appears to support equality in initiating discussion topics more than is usually reported for face-to-face meetings. It is also the case that, in certain instances, females are able to dominate the direction of conversation in this medium.

Other Verifying Data

The perceptions of members of these online meetings about gender issues add to these findings.[4] For example, a female member reported that she didn't always know HOW to respond in her group. For her, the dialogue of the male members was 'too much in the head' and she felt she could not be herself. Her preferred style was 'just to babble on and chat', rather than having to intellectualise about everything, which was what she experienced male members doing. A male member said that he was conscious of what he was putting into some conferences: issues that were 'wholly about thinking and not about feeling'. He was aware of feelings not being expressed by himself online.

The female participant's perception of herself as 'just chatting' seems to beg the question about her perception of the educational function of 'chat'. She seems to have felt that chatting was intellectually less acceptable or appropriate than the more formal, structured conversations that some male members indulged in.

Many educationalists believe that much learning takes place when people 'just chat'. They believe that there is probably some underlying logic or structure to such informal talk. Researchers in Britain have looked at the educational functions of chat and informal talk in classrooms. It is argued that learning takes place when students are allowed to chat freely. David Graddol explains the rationale behind this thinking:

> The rationale was twofold: first, the act of planning and uttering was regarded as psychologically beneficial to thinking and problem solving. Second, it allowed the joint negotiation of knowledge, and cooperative learning. Even talk which appears off the topic may provide a vital forum for adventitious learning (Graddol, 1989).

Freeflowing, informal 'off the topic' talk has a learning value in itself, and one which is just as important and educationally acceptable as structured, 'logical', formal talk.

The experiences of these female and male participants indicate some wider issues about the ways in which males and females work in groups, what they might be looking for in terms of how to work and what kind of language might be appropriate in carrying out that work. It seems that there are differences in the ways males and females perceive the use of language:

> I can remember so clearly the first stuff that one of the men put on. I don't understand what this guy is talking about. I went over it again and I thought I don't even understand the words that he's using... I thought, what the hell is this man saying... he's using language that I can't identify with (quotation from an interview with a female participant).

Another female member commented:

> Stephen online and Paul online certainly, I mean as individuals regardless of sex, they have quite different ways of saying things to Helen and Jenny.

and she continues:

> It's perfectly OK in our set conference to talk about how one churns up inside about something, or just life in general... If I put that on to Stephen, Paul, Jed and Alan – I'd tend to think they'd drag it into the intellectual and bring it straight back into their head; and I'm not in my head, I'm in my heart and guts (quotation from interviews with participants).

What might this mean?

The perceptions of participants in these electronic groups appear to confirm other findings into the dynamics of mixed-sex groups in face-to-face situations (eg see Jones, 1980; Haas, 1979). Women are often cited as being more 'chatty' than males. Deborah Jones (1980) suggests that such talk has the social purpose of maintaining the unity, morals and values of a group. She also suggests that 'chat' and gossip is a female proclivity, a point which I personally would dispute but one which would seem to have some common currency in the literature. Males are cited as talking more in mixed-sex groups, and for longer. Whether these interpretations stand for the situation of male-female talk in online (ie typed contributions) environments requires more research. Certainly, the above findings suggest that females are more chatty online in the sense that they take more turns at talking; but whether what they talk about could be termed 'chat', and whether male members do not chat in the same way is not clear.

There does seem to be some evidence though that some female members of these online groups see themselves as wishing to be expressive in ways that to them appear to be different to male members. There is a clear wish to engage in dialogue that is not 'heady' and overly intellectual (a wish to talk from the heart and guts as one of them put it). And they view themselves as more willing to participate in disclosure issues online, and talk more about themselves as people rather than just talk about intellectual issues. All of this also accords with existing research into gender in groups: females are more likely to disclose; and they talk more about people than things. Males talk more about 'things' and business issues and are factual/knowledge based in their dialogue. They tend to debate and argue rather than discuss (Haas, 1979; Brooks, 1982).

However, although we have to acknowledge some major differences between sexes in terms of the dynamics of group work and talk, it is also too simplistic to imagine that these rather stereotypical views of males and females apply to everyone. For example, in one mixed-sex online group, we found that people would often read an entry and if they had no immediate response they would enter nothing. This had the effect of disconfirming previous speakers' entries, and the participants found this a problem in their communications. The suggestion was made that all participants should enter something, anything, to confirm a speaker's entry (eg an entry such as 'I've read this but have no comment at the moment'). The point is, this strategy – which was suggested as a way of involving all participants and encouraging everyone to feel wanted and heard in the conference – came from a male member. Yet in stereotypical terms, we might have expected a female member to be concerned about such issues and to take the initiative to do something about them.

How do we begin to understand what is going on in CSCL environments from a gendered perspective? (Another question might be: how do we begin to understand the construction of new kinds of gendered identity? See eg Yates, 1997.) Perhaps we need to find a way of allowing males and females to use language in ways that suit them and yet still maintains their gendered positions:

> Another precondition for satisfactory dialogue is an appropriate language of exchange. Traditional women's talk centres on experience and feelings, men's on analysis and logic. The challenge is to find means of bridging these differences, without compromising either register or forcing either party to speak wholly in a foreign tongue (Judy Marshall, as quoted in Hardy and Hodgson, 1991).

The notion of finding ways of allowing people to speak in their own register seems highly appropriate. But to suggest that all males talk in a certain way, which is different to the generalised ways in which all females talk, is surely rather too simplistic. Experience suggests that we can talk in different ways at different times in online meetings, depending on the context and people involved in the conversations. We can control our talk, and when necessary match it to the circumstances we find ourselves in. We can cross the sex barrier (Thorne and Henley, 1975).

In general, though, I agree with Judy Marshall's precondition of an appropriate language of exchange for satisfactory dialogue. This must be particularly true for our use of language in a medium such as computer conferencing where words and language are the only means of communicating. Everything else is stripped away, and all we have is language.

Conclusions

In this chapter I have drawn on analysis of online group dynamics, field research interviews, group reviews with tutors and participants on a computer mediated MA programme, and my own personal reflections and experiences of working with groups in online environments, to say something about the nature of mixed-sex group work in educational computer conferences. In it, I set out to explore rather than define. In some ways the chapter raises more questions than it answers. This is no bad thing, given that the focus has been on examining a new medium of learning, one which we still know little about in terms of its educational potential.

Nevertheless, the findings discussed here suggest that, within the context of the particular setting of this research, this group learning medium may offer new opportunities for female members of mixed-sex groups. As a group, females appear to be able to take more turns at speaking than in face-to-face settings. As individuals, they have equal chance of speaking for similar lengths of time to males. They have equal opportunity for directing conversational topics, and on occasion appear to direct the conversations more than the male participants. Females therefore appear to be at less of a disadvantage in online discussions, at least in the contexts which have been discussed here. However, males still tend to talk longest even in this environment, even though there is no difference in the average words entered by individuals generally, irrespective of gender. This suggests that the medium does allow for a more democratic form of participation in some respects.

In general terms, we can also interpret these findings to indicate that there is in some respects a flattening out of participation patterns in this environment. The dominance of males consistently reported in most other research seems to be decreased, and the dominance of females seems to be increased.

Indeed, the findings of this study appear to challenge the conclusion of Zimmerman and West:

> We are led to the conclusion that, at least in our transcripts, men deny equal status to women as conversational partners with respect to rights to the full utilization of their turns and support for the development of topics. Thus we speculate that just as male dominance is exhibited through male control of macro-institutions in society, it is also exhibited through control of at least a part of one micro-institution (Zimmerman and West, 1975, p. 125).

But perhaps this suggests that the differing methodologies, contexts and time spans of research in this area are unlikely to lead to generalisable outcomes. Each study paints a picture of a case in time. The wider generalisability can be provided by the reader who is able to relate their own experiences to those offered by the researchers.

I am not trying to suggest that computer conferences themselves overcome the problems of social interaction inequality in mixed-sex groups. It is the culture of any programme of learning, the goals of those involved (learners and tutors) and the local circumstances which largely determine this (Mantovani, 1994). This research may only show that it is possible, using this technology, to support the values embodied in this particular MA course, and not that the technology intrinsically supports equality of participation. The social contract of the MA acts towards resolving the social questions about the ways in which participants cooperate in the computer conferences. Questions about group norms and values, equitable role structuring and so on are central to the programme and are the focus of discussions between participants and tutors. The technology is only a vehicle through which these values and beliefs are mediated and worked out.

What I have tried to indicate is that computer conferences CAN make a contribution to soothing these inequalities. For those who fear the use of such technologies in learning situations, thinking they will only exacerbate these inequalities, this research suggests that in suitable supporting contexts, the medium can offer some opportunities for redressing some of the inequalities of participation.

The starting point of this chapter was a wish to try and establish, from empirical data, differences in the interaction patterns between males and females in CSCL. More research into the patterns of conversation in mixed-sex groups using this medium is needed. It would be useful to look at patterns of interaction in larger online groups, and in groups working in different learning contexts such as undergraduates; those learning in mass distribution distant learning settings, such as open universities; those participating in occasional online seminars; and so on.

The next stage will be to go beyond the empirical work of looking at patterns and examine and interpret communications between male and female participants in these electronically mediated groups, always remembering that the particular context, culture, goals and so on of those involved will be the major factors to take into consideration when making any judgements about the nature of the communications. Attention should be given to what actually happens in these online learning groups, from a gendered perspective. What do male and female participants actually talk about, and why? Who attends to who in a computer conference? If females do direct conversations more in this environment, how do they do it? By asking questions? By making suggestions? And are they actually being listened to? What gets followed up in these mixed-sex conversations, and by whom? In general, are conversational forms, topics, content and usage (Haas, 1979) in this environment similar to those stereotypically reported for males and females in more conventional face-to-face settings, or are there differences?[5]

Notes

1. CSCL-type media have been reported to be used in management studies at the Western Behavioural Sciences Institute (Rowan, 1986, pp. 71–74); Henley Management College, UK (Jameson, 1991); the UK Open Business School (Mason, 1993); the Management School, Lancaster University, UK (Hardy *et al.*, 1991; McConnell, 1992) and in various management settings in large organisations such as Digital (Gundry, 1992) and IBM (Rueda, 1992).

2. The self managed learning status of the groups, and an educational philosophy which strived to assume equal status and similarity of roles between 'students' and 'tutors', has led me to present the results of this study largely in a way which does not differentiate between staff and students. This is deliberate since to constantly break down the data into the two groups would make a differentiation between them which, largely, did not exist.

   However, in order to address this possible concern, when it seems appropriate to point out differences I do so in the text. As an example, the following breakdown of turn taking and initiation of conversation gives some indication of any possible outcome differences, and may indicate if there was any bias from staff making more contributions than students (see Table 4.8).

3. There are of course other ways of measuring duration of speech. For example, the measure could be at the level of sentences or paragraphs. A word count was used here mainly because it is a common measure used in other similar studies.

Table 4.8 *Tutor involvement*

Percentage of turns taken by tutors by conference

Conference 1 (4 participants)	Conference 2 5 participants)	Conference 3 (13 participants)	Conference 4 (5 participants)
23	25	22	21

This shows that staff took on average between one quarter and one fifth of the total turns in each conference.

Initiation of conversation by tutors (ie percentage of items set up by tutors)

Conference 1	Conference 2	Conference 3	Conference 4
9	23	15	18

This shows that in terms of directing or initiating conversations, tutors varied considerably as a group but did not appear to direct the conversations any more than students. Qualitative analysis of the conference transcripts is needed in order to determine exactly if this is the case.

4. The findings in this section are taken from a series of in-depth interviews with participants on the computer mediated MA programme at Lancaster University, and from participant and tutor reviews of the MA programme. The interviews were free-flowing, focusing largely on participants' and tutors' experiences of working in online groups. This research is reported in Hardy *et al.* (1991) and in Hodgson and McConnell (1992).
5. At another completely different level, the 'issue' of gender interactions is turned on its head by the assumption of multiple identities in online environments. Many people are choosing to hide their gendered identity, or choose roles that may or may not relate to male or female identities while communicating online. This is perhaps less likely in formal learning settings of the kind discussed here, where everyone knows everyone else. But it is quite possible to hide or change your identity online, and the consequences can be challenging (Van Gelder, 1991).

    Sherry Turkle (Turkle, 1995) has examined the adoption of multiple identities in MOOs, and she says:

The Internet has become a significant social laboratory for experimenting with the constructions and reconstructions of self that characterise postmodern life. In its virtual reality, we self-fashion and self-create. What kinds of personae do we make? What relation do these have to what we have traditionally thought of as the 'whole' person? Are they experienced as an expanded self or as a separate from the self? Do our real-life selves learn lessons from our virtual personae? (Turkle, 1995, p.180).

Acknowledgements

The research on which this chapter is based was funded by the UK Economic and Social Research Council, research grant no R000234531.

5 | Designing for CSCL

Introduction

In Chapter 1 I indicated that in many cases, cooperative learning produces greater benefits to the learner than traditional, individual learning. Which learning designs lead to greater production in cooperative learning groups compared with individual effort? In this chapter, I will discuss this and other questions concerning the design of computer supported cooperative learning.

The Philosophy of CSCL

In his book *Freedom to Learn*, Rogers (1969) indicates some of the factors limiting meaningful learning:

> When we put together in one scheme such elements as a prescribed curriculum, similar assignments for all students, lecturing as almost the only mode of instruction, standard tests by which all students are externally evaluated, and instructor-chosen grades as the measure of learning, then we can almost guarantee that meaningful learning will be at an absolute minimum.

Breaking down the traditional view of learning to one that becomes more meaningful to the learner and more socially acceptable to those offering a course of learning, necessarily involves viewing the learners as individuals capable of playing an important role in the decision-making process concerning the design of the course. Learners usually have a wealth of experience and skills which can be used in their education.

The thinking behind CSCL derives from several questions:

- How can the various backgrounds and experiences of the learners and tutors be acknowledged and used in the development of the course?
- How can the different needs of the learners be met in the course?
- How can the learners be encouraged to be active learners, take control of their own learning, contribute to the learning of the group as a whole and participate in issues of course design, assessment and evaluation?

Additionally, using CSCL will pose some important questions for staff in their initial discussions about any courses of study they are planning, and later between staff and learners during the negotiated, ongoing design of the course:

- What kind of educational/training philosophy are we involved in?
- What kind of learning is being designed for?
- What kind of knowledge are we trying to encourage and explore? What here constitutes knowledge? What kinds of knowledge are there?

It is with such questions and issues in mind that we approach the design of CSCL environments.

But before looking at how we might go about designing for CSCL, it will be useful to reflect on some of the differences between traditional forms of learning and cooperative learning. This will help establish issues to do with the nature of, and theories of, knowledge implied by cooperative learning (its epistemology). This in turn will guide us in designing computer supported environments for cooperative learning.

Cooperative Learning and Traditional Learning Compared

Cooperative learning environments differ from traditional learning environments in a variety of ways. Table 5.1 offers a comparison between traditional forms of learning and cooperative learning. This comparison does not necessarily suggest that cooperative learning and traditional learning are always at opposite ends of a spectrum, but it does help to emphasise the main underlying characteristics of the two forms of learning. This comparison can help in illuminating differences between the two learning environments in terms of:

- the processes of learning: between active, problem-centred learning and passive or book learning
- the nature of knowledge: that there are different forms of knowledge, for example, personal knowledge gained from real experience, compared with 'absolute' knowledge gained from textbooks
- the different ways in which we can gain knowledge: through action learning and research used to construct new knowledge, compared with ways of learning which emphasise that knowledge exists independently of the learner

- the tutor-learner relationship: relationships based on egalitarianism rather than those based on authoritarianism and control
- assessment: assessment based on self, peer and tutor evaluation rather than one based on unilateral tutor judgements.

Table 5.1 *Comparison between traditional forms of learning and cooperative learning*

Traditional	Cooperative
Little opportunity for learners to take initiative, to express themselves, and for direct interaction with their peers; little control over their work	Learners encouraged to take initiative: self-expression is central; dialogue and interaction with others is very important; the degree of control can vary depending on the particular situation – but being able to make decisions about their learning is central
Not social – classes are not seen as a social unit; viewed as individuals with no/little social contact; when social interaction present, usually occurs in formal (controlled) situations (eg, seminars). Learners encouraged to work individually and to compare themselves with others	Classes seen as social units where individuals have a need to interact; interaction is seen as an important source of learning. Learners have freedom to form their own social groupings to further their learning. Learners encouraged to see each other as collaborators. Support and challenge within group work.
Inherently competitive and envious; zero-sum learning – gainers and losers	Competition less likely; reduced envy since everyone working on their own issues; reference point is self, not others; non zero-sum learning: everyone can 'win'
Learners treated as undifferentiated similars	Learners seen as diverse individuals with a variety of different interests/ needs/capabilities
Emphasis the static, passive regurgitating aspects of learning	Emphasises the experiential process in learning–rethinking and rephrasing of ideas and problems

Table 5.1 *Continued*

Traditional	Cooperative
Emphasises absolutist knowledge: – tutor/teacher is the repository of knowledge – institution sets learning criteria and judges achievement – knowledge exists independently of learners	Emphasises personal knowledge: – rigorous testing of ideas against relevant experience – honesty – drawing personal conclusions in context of dialogical learning – considering alternative ideas – testing ideas in action – knowledge is constructed by learners through processes of engaging in discussion with others and attributing meaning to the world
Development of learners viewed largely in terms of academic developmentonly: 'development' not viewed as central	Development of learners is central – personal, social, moral, ethical, etc. development as well as academic development
Level 1 learning, ie learning a body of knowledge	Level 2 learning, ie learning to learn
'Courses' are based on a syllabus which is organised, defined and packaged by the teacher/tutor.	'Courses' based on problems, ideas, interests, needs of learners and tutors; involves negotiation, planning, decision making, experimenting, rethinking.

Cooperative learning can be highly developmental, engaging the learner in making sense of their learning and in reconstructing knowledge. Traditional forms of learning are concerned more with transmitting largely predefined forms of knowledge (Boot and Hodgson, 1987).

Knight and Bohlmeyer (1990) are at pains to point out that different cooperative learning methods will differ among themselves too, and that such things as the social influences on the learners, the ways in which they learn, the ways in which the group work is presented to them and structured, the ways in which they are rewarded for their effort and the roles of each participant may well be important in promoting and sustaining cooperative learning, but they may not in themselves influence academic achievement. The research into cooperative learning illuminates the degree of uncertainty about what does and does not promote cooperative learning. There is, therefore, little certainty about what really promotes academic achievement using cooperative learning methods. We need more information about what exactly happens in cooperative learning groups in order to further clarify these issues:

> Different cooperative learning methods may or may not function in similar ways... the variability in the methods, as well as the variability in the specificity in which the methods are described to teachers, suggests that much more detailed information is needed on exactly what the teachers and students are doing in the various types of cooperative classrooms... (Knight and Bohlmeyer, 1990, p.19).

Knight and Bohlmeyer suggest that greater knowledge of what brings about academic achievement in cooperative learning will enable researchers to be more confident about recommending which methods to use in which situations, will provide greater conviction in making recommendations to sceptical practitioners, and should provide information for improving current practice in cooperative learning methodology.

CSCL Designs

What constitutes a useful design for CSCL, and what issues need to be addressed in designing CSCL environments? Practitioners of CSCL do not have definite answers to these questions. CSCL is too new and untested for anyone to be prescriptive and in any case, different designs will be needed in order to meet requirements of different tutors, learners and institutions.

These questions raise the issue about what exactly CSCL is. It is becoming fashionable in advanced learning technology (ALT) circles to apply the term CSCL to any use of ALT. Perhaps this does not matter, as long as the focus is on learners working together in some way through the use of ALT. The variety of new ALTs will suggest and enable a wide spectrum of ways of designing for CSCL, as we shall see in a later chapter. So anything we say about designing for cooperative learning using advanced learning technologies is not, at this stage, definitive.

From my own experience, and the experience of working closely with colleagues on CSCL programmes, I have found the following to be useful and important aspects of CSCL design:

- openness in the educational process – the learning community
- self-determined learning

- a real purpose in the cooperative process
- a supportive learning environment
- a collaborative assessment of learning
- assessment and evaluation of the ongoing learning process.

These aspects of CSCL design should not be considered to be separate or mutually exclusive. They are part of a whole, and are only presented here as seemingly separate for the convenience of description and discussion. Taken together, they combine to suggest a philosophy of, and set of procedures for CSCL.

Openness in the Educational Process – The Learning Community

Openness in the educational process is an overarching design feature which permeates CSCL generally. Openness does not only relate to aspects of the administration of any learning event or course, where barriers to openness such as when and at what pace a person can study are relevant. Openness, perhaps more importantly in computer supported cooperative learning, relates to freedom around issues to do with the relationship of the learners to such things as course content and method, choice and negotiation within the course, self- and peer assessment, and tutor-learner relationships. It is also to do with their willingness to share ideas and be open with their intellects; to be open to new ideas and to the possibility of change.

CSCL courses should support openness in learning. Learners should be in a position to make decisions about their learning, and feel they have a large degree of freedom in doing so. They also need the power to exercise their choices. In some circumstances, the degree of openness will be greater than others. For example, in some cases, the degree of openness may well be defined by the constraints of institutional requirements rather than the wishes of those involved in a programme of study.

Research into the ways in which learners learn, and their perceptions of what leads to meaningful, thoughtful learning, indicates the benefits of freedom within learning. The context of learning can have considerable impact on how learners learn. Where learning is meaningful they develop high 'meaning orientations':

> Students who exhibited a high meaning orientation were those who reported having a deep approach to learning, relating ideas in one subject to another, examining evidence carefully in what they read, and being interested in learning for its own sake... meaning orientation was related to the perceived presence of

freedom in learning combined with good teaching... . Freedom in learning included opportunities for choice in what they worked upon, and the ability to study in the way that best suited the individual student, that is, the amount of discretion possessed by students in choosing and organising their academic work (Boud, 1988, p. 35, referring to the research of Entwistle and Ramsden, 1983).

There has to be a mechanism for achieving openness and freedom, and for the exercise of the learners' power. One which works particularly well in CSCL is the concept of the learning community. But before we consider this, let us consider what a community is.

Learning communities
It is difficult to define community. We know that a community is like a group: it has members, a sense of who it is and a set of purposes for existing. It symbolises something to us, as well as offering us a place to carry out some common 'tasks', a place to exist. In analysing the meaning of community one author comments:

> Raymond Williams (1983) has, in an attempt to discover the 'essence' of community, observed that community is not just a bounded locale but also 'the quality of holding something in common, as in a community of interests, community of goods... a sense of common identity and characteristics. These senses indicate a 'particular quality of relationship (as in *communitas*) (Fernback, 1999, p 204).

In conceptualising the meaning of community in cyberspace, it is possible to draw on existing definitions of community and contemporary Western thinking about communities. This will help us to try and understand what a virtual community such as a CSCL community may be. Several writers have tackled this issue (eg see Fernback, 1999; Smith & Kollock, 1998). In a review of the current literature as it relates to computer mediated communication (CMC) environments, Fernback (1999) offers three possible conceptions which can be used to help understand the nature of 'community' in CSCL environments:

1. *Community as place.* CSCL groups can be viewed as communities that meet in cyberspace. CSCL is a place where the community of learners can develop; it has a unifying power to hold communities together. The social relationships possible in CSCL environments help participants form a view of themselves as a thriving community.
2. *Community as symbol.* CSCL communities have a symbolic dimension: participants give the community meaning, and create the community through their interactions and through their norms and

values. This gives them a sense of identity, a place where meaning exists.

3. *Community as virtual.* In any context it is argued that communities live in the minds of their members: they are imagined. CSCL communities might be distributed across a continent or the globe, but to their members a *community* exists because they think it exists. Webs of personal meaning and relationships, and authentic discussion over long periods of time are indicators of the existence of community (Rheingoled, 1993).

The socially constructed spaces of virtual learning environments such as CSCL are places where learners can meet to develop their sense of identity, common goals and community. But what makes them 'learning' communities? The learning community is made up of both staff and learners who have equal rights to manage the resources of the community and the learning that takes place in it. The learning community attends to issues of climate, needs, resources, planning, action and evaluation as a whole community (Pedler, 1981). This requires personal investment, intimacy and commitment (Fernback, 1999). This makes it quite different from traditional, staff-led courses and also from independent studies courses and flexible learning courses (Snell, 1989).

In the learning community, there is a mixture of working for oneself and on one's own issues and concerns, and working with others on their concerns and issues. Traditionally, this might be framed in terms of education: helping yourself; and therapy; helping others (Pedler, 1981). The learning community offers a third dimension, that of development, as shown in Figure 5.1.

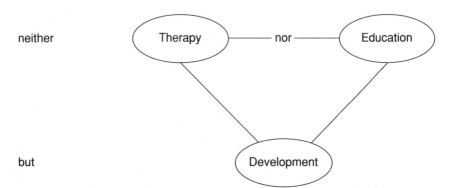

Figure 5.1 *The dimensions of the learning community (from Boydel and Pedler, 1981)*

The use of the word 'development' to describe this third position of simultaneous helping self and helping others via purposeful work in the world is perhaps incongruent with some more individualistic constructings of development. None the less a feature of most age and stage theories of individual development is a movement away from the individualistic and personal towards the altruistic and transpersonal. In this sense development demands a social contribution – a 'giving back' as well as a personal qualitative leap (Pedler, 1981).

In the learning community, 'qualitative leap' means seeing learning, and all that is associated with it in a social context, from new and different angles. Learners begin to address learning from a qualitatively different level. Their experiences in the learning community can help them shift their perspective on the meaning of learning to a meta-level perspective.

Tensions in the community
In the learning community, there is always a healthy tension between the purposes and needs of individuals and those of the community at large. There are two major kinds of tension: one to do with thinking and feeling; and the other to do with acting individually and collectively. These tensions indicate some of the differences between learning in traditional situations and learning in a learning community. In traditional situations, people usually work separately and often competitively, while in a learning community people strive to work constructively in cooperation with each other. However, in a learning community, there can be a tension between oppressive collectivism, so shutting out minority view and differences, and constructive collectivism which strives towards meeting as many needs as possible within the wider framework of a group (Figure 5.2).

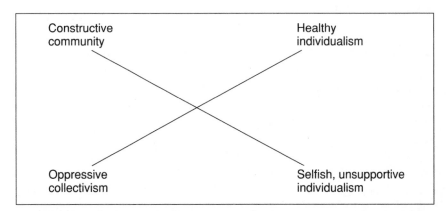

Figure 5.2 *The individual community chiasm*

In a learning community, differences are seen as a cause for celebration, rather than a problem. The learning community allows individuals to address issues of minority interest. This works towards ensuring that minority interests and people are not marginalised and that simple solutions are not applied to complex personal and social issues. Choosing to be different, or to think and act differently does not mean choosing to be marginalised.

In traditional classes learners are usually taught to think the same and feel differently, while in the learning community participants feel together but think differently (Figure 5.3). These tensions are what Cunningham (1987, p.53) calls chiasms, or cross-wise transpositions of words. He suggests that the concept of the chiasm helps learners develop ways of thinking about the group, helps them develop appropriate maps and rules about the group, and helps them see that it is possible to work as a group without violating principles of cooperation and openness.

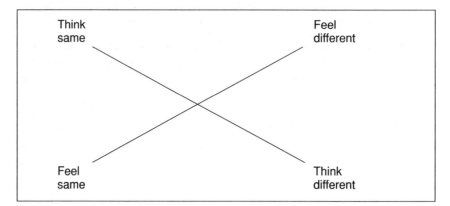

Figure 5.3   *The think-feel chiasm*

The success of cooperative groups depends on each member feeling responsible for the success of the group. Learners working in CSCL environments require an understanding of how to work in cooperative groups: how to relate to others and how to work in groups generally. They cannot usually be expected to understand the nature of group work, and they will probably require training in small-group skills in order to work cooperatively. The interpersonal skills of each member may well determine the eventual level of success of the group.

The role of the tutor in all of this is crucial. The tutor has to address issues of authority and power, and has to be aware of how best to use their special experience in a community where everyone is equal, or at least where everyone has equal rights. The power imbalance between learners and the tutor has to be worked on. The tutor has to become more of a 'tutor-participant' and has to acknowledge that traditional forms of thinking and acting around their role have to be changed to suit the circumstances of a learning community. Notions of there always being a 'right answer' or a 'right way of doing something' have to be put aside. In a learning community there will always be a variety of ways of doing and thinking.

Tutors still have a legitimate role to play in offering their expertise and particular know-how, but always in the context of others being able to do likewise. By doing this, tutors help surface issues about authority and the use and abuse of power in the minds and discussions of the learners. Talking of the 'greater knowledge' of the tutor, Pedler (1981) notes:

> If his (sic) 'knowledge' ie his awareness, intuition, experience, articulation, is 'superior' ie more relevant, lengthier, sharper, more in touch with the collective will, in this situation, then surely he has a duty to make it available. But how can we be freed, made autonomous, through being led by someone with superior knowledge? Knowledge confers power to those that hold it and enslaves those without it. The contradictory stance of many of us seeking to promote 'learner centred designs' through an imposition of what we referred to earlier as 'unstructured' [design], is apparent.

Self-determined Learning

Self-determined learning means that each person takes primary responsibility for identifying their own learning needs. At the same time, each person is responsible for helping others identify and meet their needs and for offering themselves as a flexible resource to the community. Sources and materials for learning include each other; one's own learning practice; books, journals, etc; reflection on, and 'unpicking' of, learning experiences in the here and now, and so on. Current socio-cultural approaches to learning emphasise the importance of self-determination within learning (Salomon and Perkins, 1998) and within cooperative learning environments where knowledge building is the central learning process (Scardamalia, 1999).

In CSCL, one aspect of this self-determination is learning how to learn. Learning to learn is embedded in CSCL processes. It is not of the study skills variety where an expert tells learners how to learn. By playing a major role in determining their own learning and by working cooperatively with other learners and tutors, learners will have to face issues of learning how to learn within the processes of the cooperative learning group itself. Taking this kind of control of your own learning helps in addressing how you learn and why you learn in that way:

> If we have access to and can examine the theories about how we learn, we may be able to undermine them. If we can critically analyse theories about our behaviour, and have the freedom to reinterpret them, we are not necessarily bound by them. This allows us to undertake second order meta-level change (Cunningham, 1987, p.42).

In CSCL, learners become aware of how they learn through interaction with other learners. They are forced to think about how they have learned to date, and how they might go about changing their learning patterns. Working cooperatively with others makes learners aware of alternative ways of learning.

Research into learners' experiences of learning throws some light on this issue. People approach learning in different ways, often depending on the context in which they find themselves. Three approaches to learning from texts have been suggested:

- Surface approach – learners focus on the words and phrases used in text books and try to remember these
- Deep approach – learners focus on the meaning of the text and try to understand what the author is saying. They also attempt to re-interpret the meaning in relation to their own understanding
- Achieving approach – learners work out whether a surface or deep approach is being called for, or which one is likely to produce best results, depending on what they think they are being asked to produce at any time (Boud, 1988).

Learners do not necessarily always adopt, or show, only one or other of these approaches in their style of learning; rather, they tend to weave between them.

In being self-determining, learners are more likely to adopt deep approaches to learning. The responsibility of managing your own learning within the learning community quickly makes it clear to you that how you learn and why are largely up to you. Other learners and tutors in the community work with you around your concerns and interests, but you have to make the choices about how and why you are learning. This requires, and leads to, deep approaches to learning where you engage with the material, situation, issue, etc in a meaningful way, and attempt to bring your own understandings to bear on it in doing so.

This does not mean that a self-determined learner will never use surface approaches. But it is more likely that if they do, they will be making a choice to do so at a given period of time within a wider context of appropriate learning strategies for a given purpose. But the relationship of the learner to the process of learning will be of a deep approach in self-determined contexts, because that is what is called for. And if the community is working as a learning community (sharing, supporting, challenging, critiquing, questioning, etc), learners will constantly be faced with working at deep levels.

A Real Purpose in the Cooperative Process

Cooperative learning requires a real purpose in the cooperative process. This is often best achieved through a problem-centred, or issue-centred, approach to learning. This can take many forms. For example, each learner may define his/her own problem and the other group members may help that person think through the problem, design ways of examining it and carry out the work around the problem. This is typical of action learning or action research groups, which will be described below. Alternatively, the problem or issue may be defined by the group as a whole (or it may be defined for them by a teacher) and they work together on the problem as a team. No matter how the problem is defined, or how the group works towards it, when working cooperatively learners need to be sure that each individual is offering something useful to the group.

When the problem or issue is defined by (or for) the group, each individual works towards a common goal to be achieved by the group as a whole. In such cases a high degree of positive interdependence is required (Johnson and Johnson, 1990). Positive interdependence is the knowledge that you are linked closely with others in the learning task and that success (personal and for the group) depends on each person working together to complete the tasks (the 'sink or swim together' metaphor). There are two types of positive interdependence:

- Outcome interdependence – this is the desired goals or outcomes of the groups' work. Learners' perceptions of these will determine the way they relate to the group and the tasks of the group.
- Means interdependence – this is the actions required by each group member. They are the means for achieving the mutual goals, eg roles in the group, resources available.

Group members need to understand their role in the mutual group work, and they must believe that each person is important and vital for the general success of the group. They have to actually see for themselves in real action and individual behaviour that this is the case. If someone is treated as being dispensable then they are likely to opt out of the group's work. Similarly, if someone is seen as indispensable they are likely to be put into a 'guru' position which might well change group members' attitudes to working cooperatively.

This poses a question: is it more important to have each individual working to help others achieve their own goals (positive goal interdependence) or is it more profitable to have a group reward, such as a group final grade, to which the group is aiming (positive reward interdependence)? Researchers interested in this issue are in some disagreement about the relationship between goal versus reward interdependence and its effects on promoting cooperation and achievement. Johnson and Johnson (1990, p.29) report a study which suggests that the combination of goal and reward interdependence is the most effective, since the impact of the two seems to be additive.

When the problem or issue is defined by and for each individual, the support of the others is geared towards helping that individual meet their own, specific learning goals.

Action learning

Whether the problem or issue is defined by (or for) the group, or by each individual, the process of working together can be similar in many respects and has much in common with the cyclical nature of action learning and research. A problem or issue is posed and is diagnosed; this leads to a series of action steps being imagined which need to be taken in order to investigate the problem or issue; the action steps are carried out in whatever form has been imagined; the outcomes of this action are evaluated, and this in turn leads to a re-examination of the problem or issue in the light of the experience and knowledge gained, and a new cycle is engaged (Figure 5.4).

The cycle of action learning or research is one to which each member of the group contributes. If the group is working on a collective problem or issue, then they will each have an active participatory role to play in the four steps of the action cycle. It is likely that they will make decisions about who should do what and when in order to complete the cycles.

If the members of the group are working on individually chosen problems, then the focus will be on helping each member address his/her chosen problem. Here the group functions in a supportive way, helping

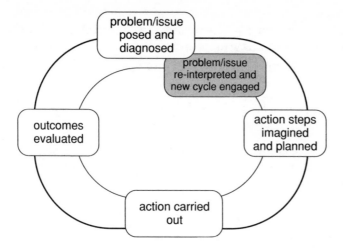

Figure 5.4 *The action learning/research cycle*

the individual work through each step of the cycle while offering thoughts, ideas and comments of their own.

Action learning and research are ways of dealing with real-life problems and issues. They are ways of both generating new knowledge about something while at the same time trying to change it. The 'it' might be as large as a social system, or it might be a narrower concern such as one's way of learning or working. Whatever it is, action learning and research can generate new ways of knowing about the issue. Action learning and research differ in their focus from traditional forms of learning and research:

> Conventional social science aims at producing new knowledge by solving scientific problems. Action research adds solving practical problems to create new general knowledge. In other words, action research aims at producing new knowledge that contributes both to practical solutions to immediate problems and to general knowledge (Elden and Chisholm, 1993).

At a meta-level, action learning and research inform the learners about how they are learning. The constant process of reflecting while learning, which is inherent in the action cycle if carried out thoughtfully, raises issues to do with how the learning is taking place and why, and how it could be made different: 'contemporary forms of action research also aim at making change and learning a self-generating and self-maintaining process in the systems in which the action researchers work' (Elden and Chisholm, 1993).

It is also a way of producing theory grounded in the reality of everyday experience. This relationship between the learner and the development of grounded theory is a powerful one which in itself can contribute to helping the learner understand how knowledge is generated and theory produced:

> The important product here... is participants learning how to learn to develop their own, more effective practical theories. Becoming a better 'practical theorist' is a key to empowerment... the new ideas about action research... can be related to a re-thinking of the relationship between science, knowledge, learning and action. Can ordinary people not formally trained as social scientists engage in the kind of learning that leads to valid, reliable (ie 'scientific') knowledge propositions which enhance their ability to achieve shared goals in a given context? (Elden and Chisholm, 1993).

The process of action learning is another aspect of self-determined learning, mentioned above.

A Supportive Learning Environment

One important aspect of the supportive learning environment is the need to have considerable interaction between members of the groups. Learners must encourage and facilitate each other's efforts. This might involve them helping each other, providing feedback, challenging each other, suggesting ways forward, acting in trusting ways, and so on. Each member has to feel that they will be supported by the others. This can then produce the conditions for learners to take risks in the learning process, to try out ways of working, thinking or acting which they consider to be different to 'the norm', but which might produce novel results or ideas.

A major constraint in interactions is group size. If a group of cooperative learners is too large then the possibility for frequent interaction between all members will be low. What constitutes a large group in CSCL? A difficult question to answer. In my experience, anything greater than six or seven is large; four or five is perhaps best.

The work of the political scientist Robert Axelrod in cooperation theory supports the view that small groups are needed to foster interaction (Axelrod, 1990); frequent interaction also helps promote stable cooperation. Interaction leads to cooperation; cooperation begets cooperation; absence decreases the possibility of cooperation. This is also confirmed by two of the leading practitioners of computer mediated communications systems (CMCS) who, in talking about ways of dealing with social interaction and information overload in these systems, state that, 'we believe that one of the basic principles of CMCS design should be to encourage relatively small task-oriented groups and communities of interest' (Hiltz and Turoff, 1985). In programmes of study with large numbers, it is fairly easy to sub-divide into several small groups, each of which is managed along the lines being discussed here.

A supportive learning environment does not, however, suggest a lack of challenges. But a challenge in a supportive environment can be received, accepted and dealt with in a different way to a challenge in a non-supportive environment. If learners have a large degree of trust in each other, then challenges will become part of the culture of the group and will be seen as productive.

Linked to this is the need to work without fear. Where learners do not know each other and where there is little concern for being supportive and cooperative, they will be fearful of taking risks, of sharing and being open. Where there is a cloud of uncertainty in learning relationships, learners will act with caution for fear of 'making fools' of themselves or 'showing themselves up'. Seemingly unrelated things can be tied up by fear and avoidance. Making CSCL environments safe places to work in can create stimulating, challenging and exciting learning opportunities. Learners and tutors engage in dialogue more freely and openly, as we shall see in the example of a CSCL programme discussed in the next chapter.

Collaborative Assessment

In CSCL, learners have a major role in choosing what they work on for their course assignments. They also have an important part to play in assessing their own and other learners' work. Collaborative assessment is a natural corrolary of cooperative learning; it supports the cooperative learning process. One leading British practitioner in the field of self- and peer assessment writes:

> I have long argued that an educated person is an aware, self-determining person, in the sense of being able to set objectives, to formulate standards of excellence for the work that realises these objectives, to assess work done in the light of those standards, and to be able to modify the objectives, the standards or the work programme in the light of experience and action; and all this in discussion and consultation with other relevant persons. If this is indeed a valid notion of what an educated person is, then it is clear that the educational process in all our main institutions of higher education does not prepare students to acquire such self-determining competence. For staff unilaterally determine student learning objectives, student work programmes, student assessment criteria, and unilaterally do the assessment of the students' work (Heron, 1981).

At one time, self- and peer assessment may have been considered peripheral to the educational process; now they are seen as an important, integral part of the preparation for life and work generally (for example, see Boyd and Cowan, 1985; Stephenson and Weil, 1992; Bostick, 1999; Stefani, 1998; McConnell, 1999; McDowell and Sambell, 1999; Shafriri, 1999). Although by no means universal, there is now a wider belief in the educational and social benefits of such a process. A survey looking at quantitative self-assessment studies showed that there was considerable consistency between marks assigned by teachers and students in peer and self-assessment situations (Falchikov and Boud, 1989), so dispelling some of the criticism that students are not able to effectively assess themselves and each other.

Boud (1986) reports that graduates rate the ability to evaluate their own work very highly, yet many of them feel that their university career does not prepare them to do so. They think self-assessment is an important life skill, and think universities and colleges should play a greater role in helping them develop those skills.

Research into the relationship between assessment and learning has shown that learners will often choose how to learn, and what to learn, on the basis of their understanding of what is to be assessed, and how it will be assessed. Learners seek cues from staff about what to learn and what is actively to be examined in the course, and work instrumentally to achieve this (Miller and Parlett, 1974). What students focus on in their studies, and indeed their whole view of university life, is largely governed by what they think they will be assessed on (Becker *et al.*, 1968).

Students are sometimes resistant to undertaking any unassessed activities: 'Activities which are unrelated to the assessment, class contact or even peer pressure are less likely to be taken seriously. Students have a habit of bypassing author's intentions' (Cox and Gibbs, 1994, p.23).

Research into students' perceptions of self-assessment (McDowell and Sambell, 1999) indicates several dimensions of self-assessment: a qualitative–quantitative dimension and a dependent–autonomous dimension. At the qualitative end, attention is focused on the processes of assessment, with an emphasis on students showing understanding – 'internal assessment'. At the quantitative end, attention focuses on the quantification of learning: scores and numerical judgements – 'external' assessment. At the dependent end of the other continuum, self-assessment is seen to be controlled by the lecturer, and students experience this as them having to fit into the lecturer's view of the world. At the autonomous end, self-assessment is experienced as promoting autonomy – the student makes the rules and negotiates these with the lecturer.

The importance of this to cooperative learning and collaborative assessment seems clear. If learners are actively involved in decisions about how to learn, what to learn and why they are learning, and are also actively involved in decisions about criteria for assessment and the process of judging their own and others' work, then their relationship to their studies will be qualitatively different to those learners who are treated as recipients of teaching and who are the object of others', unilateral, assessment. Because learners in cooperative learning situations make decisions about their learning and assessment, there will be no need for them to seek cues from staff about assessment or seek to find ways of 'playing' the system. They determine the system themselves, in negotiation with other learners and staff.

Collaborative assessment within cooperative learning situations is likely to be a method which is difficult for staff and learners to make the shift towards. It is perhaps one of the most controversial aspects of CSCL, and as such warrants some detailed discussion here.

Assumptions about collaborative assessment
The concept of collaborative assessment in cooperative learning environments is based on several assumptions:

- The learner should be actively involved in assessing their course assignment since they are the person who has decided the focus for the assignment.
- The learning that has taken place as a consequence of producing the assignment, and as evidenced in the assignment itself, is personal to the writer. The validity of the learning that has taken place can be based on the writer's intentions – these might be personal and not obviously visible to others, in which case we have to be informed about them to some extent during the collaborative assessment process. The validity may be more public in the sense that we can discern from the assignment the level of rigorous testing of ideas, degree of relating to the writer's own experience, critical perspective on the topic, and so on. Collaborative assessment based on discussion seems appropriate.
- The peer assessor is appropriate because they have also gone through a similar learning experience. They will be in a position to relate their own experiences to that of the assignment writer, ask relevant questions and take part in the assessment from a closer 'learner's' perspective than the tutor.

127

- The tutor is appropriate because they have a special place in the overall conduct of the course. They are the link between the learners and the specific institution offering the course or training event; they have special responsibilities around representing the institution's requirements, rules and methods of working. Tutors also have professional experience in working with learners in this way, and can bring their skills in facilitating collaborative assessment methods into the group's processes. This is not, however, to suggest that the tutor will always 'know best', but they will work in the interests of all those involved and not just their own or their institution's interests.

Learners assess their own and others' learning through the negotiation of criteria and methods of assessment, and by participating in judgements about such things as pass/fail and grades or marks. Collaborative assessment is designed to have a positive effect on the learner's ability to learn, and on their ability to make judgements about their learning, and in setting and achieving criteria of excellence. It is highly developmental in that it can produce shifts in understandings about the nature of assessment and how to carry it out.

This aspect of cooperative learning often poses the greatest problem for learners and can initially produce strong feelings of antipathy. There is often a general feeling of uncertainty about participants assessing themselves, and more strongly about assessing each other. It is important to spend time discussing the meaning of such assessments in an effort to understand what is involved and what the learning benefits might be. Some of the points made by students at this time are:

- It is somehow inappropriate for them to assess themselves and each other. They have no experience of doing this.
  One of the points of collaborative assessment is to help learners develop skills in assessing themselves and others.
- There is concern that they might be too subjective in their assessments. Could they therefore be sure that they would be fairly assessed by their peers?
  An assumption here is that if tutors were to assess unilaterally they would be entirely 'objective'. With an appropriate methodology for the collaborative assessment process, and an openness in carrying it out within the view of others in the group, the degree of purely subjective assessment will be diminished and can be guarded against.
- How can they begin to assess work in areas in which they are 'only learners' themselves?

Many of us do that all the time as teachers and trainers. Collaborative assessment processes help the learner develop understandings about how to develop appropriate criteria for assessing, and how to make judgements about the application of these criteria to their own and others' work.

- It is the lecturer's job to assess, not the students'.
  Collaborative assessment is, in this sense, subversive. In carrying it out, we are implicitly questioning the status quo of education and training, and the roles of tutors. Collaborative assessment opens up issues to do with tutor control, democracy in the learning process and the position of the learner within all of this.

In working with collaborative assessment I have become aware of the concern of some learners in being involved in this process:

> The concept of triangulated assessment [where there is self-, peer and tutor assessment] was definitely new to me. Initially I was not sure what to think but I took the line that I am here to learn and this might be a very valid experience. However, it was obvious that a number of the others were very concerned. Some of the suggestions made me feel very uneasy and the insecurity seemed to spread through the group... (learner comment).

However, the irony of this concern with assessment is not lost on some learners:

> I hope this week's apparent obsession with assessment doesn't become too unhealthy. It's odd how we can accept without a murmur of protest the 'normal' means of being assessed from other lecturers, yet find Dave's proposal a problem. And this from teachers who in their schools would surely object to the iniquities of the current exam system (comment by a school teacher on a MEd programme).

By taking part in their own assessments, they can begin to understand what it could be like for others to be involved in such a process. They are also in a position to begin to address some of the unquestioned assumptions about the assessments that have been carried out on them to date. Discussions with learners about collaborative assessment certainly address these points.

The collaborative assessment process
In carrying out collaborative assessments, it can be helpful to draw up guidelines about the purpose of the task. These can be used for discussion as much as guidance, and might include:

- Collaborative assessment should be seen as a learning experience in itself (for students and tutors alike).
- Collaborative assessment is not only a way of giving a grade to an individual's assignment. The feedback from others and ensuing discussions can be separated from the assessment element.
- The focus should be on discussion of the learning that has taken place, and its meaning to the individual concerned.
- During collaborative assessment, students and tutors often focus on the following concerning the background, approach and outcomes of the assignment:

  What led you to choose the assignment topic?
  What were you trying to do in the assignment?
  How do you feel it went – both the process and the product?
  Would you approach the topic in a different way if you were to start it afresh?
  How satisfied are you with what you have done?
  How useful will the assignment be in your work/life situation?

- The minimum group for collaborative assessment is the triangulated group, ie the learner whose work is being assessed, a tutor and one other learner. I call this 'triangulated assessment' because it aims to view a learner's piece of work from three different perspectives, or viewpoints, in order to provide the broadest possible view of their work. If is often the case that more learners will be involved; often the group size can be four to six. As much freedom as possible is given to who works with whom in the process.

The collaborative assessment process involves deciding on what is to be assessed, setting criteria, giving and receiving feedback, and assessing.

What to assess?
A simple answer to this is that it is the work of the group, or the work of each individual, which is the focus for assessment. But does this involve the processes of the work, or just the product at the end? In some cases it may be that both process and product are assessed; in other cases it may, more likely, be the product alone that is assessed.

There may be scope in a programme for choice in these matters – a group or an individual may be 'allowed' to decide on what is to be assessed, or there may be statutes or rules governing the kind of things which can be the focus for assessments. For example, it is often cited that there has to be some concrete product which others outside the programme (eg, external examiners) can have access to in order to make judgements abut the validity of assessments and the quality of the work in a programme. This may have consequences for what the group or individuals can ask to be assessed.

In my experience though, there need be few limitations on what can be assessed, as long as evidence of some kind can be supplied to show that it took place. A *process* can be the focus of assessment, as long as it is possible to provide evidence of that process.

Setting the criteria for making judgements

Criteria for making judgements about each learner's piece of work have to be devised. Who determines what the criteria are? The tutor unilaterally? The learners unilaterally?

In traditional learning situations, the tutor will unilaterally decide on the criteria. In cooperative settings, decisions about criteria are in the domain of the learners and tutor alike. The setting of criteria is therefore not controlled by any one person, but is negotiated along the continuum.

There are various ways in which this can be approached. The group as a whole can work on determining which criteria they want to be applied to each piece of work, or each individual can devise their own criteria in consultation with the members of the group. It is sometimes the case that there is a mixture of group-determined criteria and individually-chosen criteria. The tutor may help the group in thinking through what they mean by 'criteria', and he or she may offer some examples from past experience that could be used. It is important though that the degree of self-determination and negotiation about criteria is high, otherwise by default the burden will be assumed by, or placed in the hands of, the tutor.

The criteria are usually chosen at the very beginning of the overall process, before the learners begin their work. The benefits of this can be that the learners know in advance what they are working towards in terms of assessment. But it is sometimes the case that in carrying out their work, the learners become aware that what they had planned for at the beginning changes in the light of experience. In such cases the criteria are often renegotiated.

Unilaterally determined by tutor	Unilaterally determined by learner(s)

Figure 5.5 *Setting criteria for assessment*

Giving and receiving feedback

Having set the criteria, each learner works through the various stages of the action learning cycle described above, and completes their piece of work, which is then submitted to the group for comment and feedback. How the group starts this process is often determined by the learner.

The learner may choose to start the process. He or she may talk about his or her reasons for choosing a piece of work, what he or she was trying to achieve and why (this may relate to their own personal criteria for assessment). He or she may talk about how in practice it worked out, what issues arose in carrying out the work and how they were or were not resolved. He or she may discuss how they might go about doing the assignment again in the light of experience. The learners may ask the members of the group to provide specific kinds of feedback about the assignment, or to focus on particular issues that he or she would like to have some discussion about.

Others in the group may be requested by the learner to start the process. They may begin by asking questions of clarification about the completed piece of work, by offering comments about it, or offering critiques of it. They will also show their appreciation of the learner's work and point out what they felt to be interesting or stimulating from their perspective.

Whether it is the learner or the other members of the group that start the process, there will be considerable dialogue between the particular learner and the others, and between the group as a whole. The feedback process is a learning event. Each person engages in discussion which informs him or her about the content of any piece of work, and the processes and learning methods around it. This process is demanding intellectually and emotionally and has to be conducted with commitment, sensitivity and respect, and should be free of malice. It should also be liberating, rather than oppressive (Boud, 1994).

After the group has exhausted issues to do with feedback on each piece of work, or after an allotted time, they will move onto assessment. The tutor's role in all of this will depend on the experience of the group members in carrying out the process. It is likely that in the early stages of the process the tutor will play a major role in facilitating the group, and in helping the group process its work. With experience, the need for the tutor to facilitate to this extent will be reduced as learners become skilled in the procedures themselves.

Assessment

As with the feedback process, each learner may choose to start the assessment process him- or herself, or invite the others to start it. In either case, the criteria previously negotiated guide the group in the assessment. Each person in turns says whether each criterion was achieved or not, in their view. Usually some justification is also given for what they say. The person whose work is being assessed also takes part in this process, as of course does the tutor.

It may be sufficient in some circumstances to conclude the assessment process at this stage. But if a grade or mark is needed, then the group will have to decide on the degree to which the criterion has been achieved, for example by using a rating scale. In carrying this out, issues which may arise include:

● Some criteria may be so personal to a learner that the other learners and tutor cannot fully rate that learner's work according to them, eg a criterion of 'helping me develop my ideas' about some particular issue might be difficult to fully assess. The group might want to ask the learner to describe how the piece of work helped them develop their ideas, and ask them to point to the learning in the assignment paper or elsewhere that shows that this did in fact occur.
● Each criterion may have a different 'weighting' or importance to the others. Some criteria may be thought to be more important and therefore worthy of a greater weighting in the overall assessment. If this is the case, a percentage of the overall mark can be assigned to each criterion, and achievement level on each criterion decided. These are then summated to give the final grade.

This process of assessment is not trouble-free. There is always scope for the inclusion of personal judgement of a kind that cannot easily be 'defined' or transferred into a grade. The group has to work at trying to understand and live with some of the difficulties of assessment. It can be as much an art as a science. Dialogue around difficult issues is necessary in order that people can explain their viewpoints and justify their positions. Disagreements do occur, as might be expected, and should not discourage the use of this form of assessment. After all, many experienced tutors are not reliable assessors in every situation and it is not entirely uncommon for different tutors to disagree on their assessment of the same piece of work. It is important to keep in mind some of the wider purposes of triangulated assessment, and to respect and live with disagreements:

> Self assessment can be a valuable learning activity, even in the absence of agreement between student and teacher, and can provide potent feedback to the student about both learning and educational and professional standards (Falchikov and Boud, 1989).

The assessment process is often concluded with the group examining the whole process of feedback and assessment, once again to see what they did and why, and to imagine how they might go about it next time round. This degree of reflection is important in helping group members learn from the process, and in helping them be better prepared and skilled for the next assessments.

Outcomes of collaborative assessment

The initial fears and concerns about collaborative assessment usually give way to very positive feelings once participants take part in the task. With few exceptions, learners find this a most worthwhile use of time and one that offers an opportunity to go beyond the confines of the assignment topic itself, as the following comments suggest:

> Initially the idea of someone else involved seeing my assignment was quite daunting but in fact it was very helpful. I am sure this third dimension made the assignment more valuable. Talking about the assignment, explaining, giving reasons and so on was a learning experience – valuable to think about and reflect upon the task as usually 'handing in' is completion, when in fact once the deadline is past you have the chance to surface, reflect and evaluate what you have been doing.

> On the subject of assessment, I must say the triangulated form it took for the main assignment was very useful. Having had Open University essays marked and read the comments on them, I have felt that more of a two way process was desirable for more learning to take place. However, sometimes when I have finished a piece of work I have sent it off with a sigh of relief, thinking 'That's the end of that. If it is not good enough too bad.' With the triangulated assessment one has to re-read one's own work and can find out how it has been received by two others. That fellow students are going to read it may well influence the way you write it, and publishing the titles so that we could choose whose work to assess meant that I have asked a couple of other people if I might read their assignment. This I would have been reluctant to do if the assessment had been done by the tutor alone.

> The triangulation was good in that it removed the abstract element which exists in most formal assessment. I felt that I was writing for an audience and I think this sharpened my approach. I was also pleased to construct my title as a 'problem' and as I mention earlier in this diary I am a firm believer in assessing through setting problems.

I experienced what were two stimulating tutorials on subjects that interested me. Both when my own work was being examined and when I was looking at a colleague's I felt my knowledge and experience was being extended. Both my colleague and myself would probably be able to make considerable improvements to the written work as a result of the close discussion it underwent. And yet, the discussion led interestingly into further areas. The atmosphere of both sessions was informal and constructive... and trusting.

Other similar comments are often made: 'I was amazed at how useful the triangulated assessment was'. For a very few there may still be some concern over the validity of the exercise, their lack of training in carrying it out and their position vis-à-vis the tutor in taking on such responsibility ('You're the lecturer, you should assess!'). With experience, these attitudes change and collaborative assessment is often the most positively thought of aspect of cooperative learning.

Assessment and Evaluation of the Ongoing Learning Process

Any ongoing evaluation of the cooperative learning process must be carried out with the learners' knowledge that there is a real opportunity to change the design of the learning process. Within CSCL, this is carried out by the learners and the tutors or teachers working together.

Periodic and regular group processing

Group processing occurs within the learning community and within each cooperative learning group. By reflecting on the way in which the group is working, the group will be in a position to change its patterns and relationships in order to better achieve what it is aiming for. Regular group processing is needed for this.

Sharan (1990) also emphasises the importance of group management techniques and skills for the success of small cooperative learning groups:

Cultivation of social management skills among the students was shown to contribute to a range of important consequences for the students. These include the students' own satisfaction from participating in the groups, and the chance for lower-class and low-status pupils to participate in, and derive both social and academic benefits from, their membership in small mixed-ethnic groups (p.292).

He goes on:

Students need management techniques and skills to be able to reach their goals. The authors of cooperative learning textbooks have consistently taken that position from the start. Yet probably because such management and team building techniques, largely taken from the group dynamics literature, are not ordinarily part of a teacher's professional repertoire, students are often placed in groups and expected to function reasonably well without any preparation for assuming such a role. When the approach fails, teachers can become disenchanted with cooperative learning as too difficult for the students to cope with, or too complex to implement.' (p.293).

Group processing and review are mechanisms for surfacing issues in the effective running of the learning community or cooperative group. They are also ways of promoting learning about working in groups from an experiential viewpoint. Successful group strategies have to be able to survive, and new varieties have to be able to emerge (Axelrod, 1990). The tutor or teacher has to be aware of some of the techniques, models and ways of thinking about working with small groups in order to help the groups review their own processes.

The norms and roles associated with cooperative groups help eliminate the competitive nature of traditional educational environments. As I have indicated, mutual acceptance is the norm, rather than interpersonal antagonism. But training in the skills of group work is needed before this is likely to take place.

A real willingness to change

It is not sufficient just to have management skills, important as they are. What is vital is a real understanding of the purposes of evaluation in the learning community, and a real willingness, especially on the part of the tutor, to be open to change on the basis of reflection on the experiences of everyone involved. This has to be a cooperative effort. If it is seen to be addressing only the tutor's concerns and experiences then it is unlikely to succeed. And if there appears to be significant blockage on making changes then learners will feel disempowered.

In the next chapter, I will discuss some of the mechanisms used in one particular CSCL environment for working with change.

The Place of the Tutor

The Tutor in Cooperative Learning Generally

Within CSCL environments, the role of the tutor is in most respects no different to their role in face-to-face cooperative learning situations. In the broadest possible terms, tutors are there to facilitate the groups' work as and when necessary, and to offer themselves as resources for learning within the learning community as a whole.

In cooperative learning, the tutor is faced with a set of 'dilemmas' concerning the maintenance of boundaries. Some of these are organisational, some are learning boundaries. For example, the tutor manages boundaries around:

- the tutor as leader
- the tutor as designer and establisher of learning settings
- the tutor as the repository of knowledge
- the tutor as the representative of the university or college or organisation
- the tutor as evaluator and assessor (punishing and rewarding).

I suggest these are 'dilemmas' because, in formal learning situations such as colleges and universities, the cooperative learning tutor is caught between trying to establish an open learning community of the kind discussed earlier in this chapter, and working within the confines and rules and restrictions imposed by the college or university. Tutors have to work at maintaining the boundaries between the organisational requirements concerning learning, and the requirements of a cooperative learning philosophy.

Some of these issues as they are experienced in CSCL environments are discussed in the next chapter where we look at a CSCL programme in action.

The Tutor in CSCL

There are, however, some particular functions in CSCL contexts that tutors have to actively work at.[1] The tutor will be the person most knowledgeable about cooperative learning in CSCL contexts, and they will have the job, initially at least, of helping the learners understand how to work in this new environment. They will have to facilitate the learners' development in the use of CSCL. As time proceeds, the groups themselves will take control of much of this as their understanding of the system and experience of using it develops.

Below I describe some of the more important aspects of the tutor role, at least in the initial stages of CSCL work (see Collins and Berge, 1998; Green, 1998; Rohfeld and Hiemstra, 1995; Paulsen, 1995a, 1995b; Mason, 1991; Feenberg, 1989, for additional ideas and views on facilitating in CSCL).

General
The tutor:

- invites the participants to join the CSCL environment. This may be done through the usual procedures for starting a course or training session on campus or within an organisation, or it may be as part of a distance learning set-up with learners working from their home or place of work. In any case, this will involve helping them to access the host computer and learn how to use the CSCL system, as described in Chapter 2
- opens the CSCL working environment. With computer conferencing, this involves setting up the conferences to be used for the groups' work
- customises user lists – the user list determines who can join which CSCL groups, and what kind of 'rights' they have, eg the right to read only what is happening in the group. Decisions about this may also be taken by the learning community, once it is established
- writes the conference greeting – this usually defines the focus of the group's work, and is usually written in consultation with the groups involved
- starts off the conference – although this can often be carried out by someone else in the group. Item one in a conference is often used to discuss the purpose of the group's work.

Fostering group self-management
The tutor helps motivate learners, fosters social interaction and encourages the group to take responsibility for their own and others' work and the management of the CSCL environment, for example by:

- developing and maintaining a supportive emotional climate
- encouraging the groups to examine (by reflection) their own social processes
- encouraging members to talk and share with each other
- encouraging setting-up of protocols for using the medium, eg how often people will come online and other expectations
- sharing responsibility for running and managing the conference
- creating a sense of ownership amongst participants
- helping groups set targets for work.

Implicit message of the CSCL environment
The tutor works with the learners in helping them understand what message is implicit in the computer conferences. The use of computers

138

generally in education implies a technocratic and positivist view of learning (Chandler, 1990). Within CSCL, the implicit message is largely about emphasising social interactions.

Meeting of minds
The tutor has to ensure that there is a real meeting of minds, and not just unassociated pieces of text. As the groups begin to work together, this in itself will ensure a real meeting of minds since the nature of their cooperative work will necessitate collaboration.

Making the unfamiliar familiar
Working in CSCL environments will be new to most learners. They will require some initial guidance on how to transfer their existing, familiar metaphors for learning into this new medium. The tutor has to help in that process by suggesting what communication models to use. For example, common learning metaphors can be applied to computer conferences, so that they are viewed as a:

- seminar
- tutorial
- question and answer forum
- debate
- discussion
- notice-board.

These help the groups understand the purpose of any conference and the expectations they may have of each other in them.

What 'genre' to follow
Similarly, with the styles of communication:

- narratives – telling stories
- expositions
- dialogues
- essays.

Ways of using the medium
- Logical discussions/dialogues – here the focus is on a progression from one person's comment to another's.
- Holographic – this might involve free-floating 'essays' around a common theme.

- Group text production – a single text with several authors (not a collection of single-authored texts).

Conference weaver

The tutor can act as someone who sees patterns and makes connections – between ideas and comments, and between people – and reflects these back to the group. In time, members of each group will adopt this role themselves as and when necessary.

Personal presence in CSCL

Marshall McLuhan said that 'The medium is the message'. *How* we communicate is as important as *what* we communicate. The tutor helps learners understand how to communicate in CSCL. The tutor, often through personal example, points out how to personalise conference text. We can personalise text in CSCL environments just as we personalise the spoken word (Figure 5.6).

CSCL text comes somewhere between face-to-face talk, which is highly personalised, and written texts such as letters. The conversational nature of CSCL supports informal, personalised forms of communication quite naturally (see Brochet, 1985; Feenberg, 1986; Kerr, 1986, for elaborations on the above points).

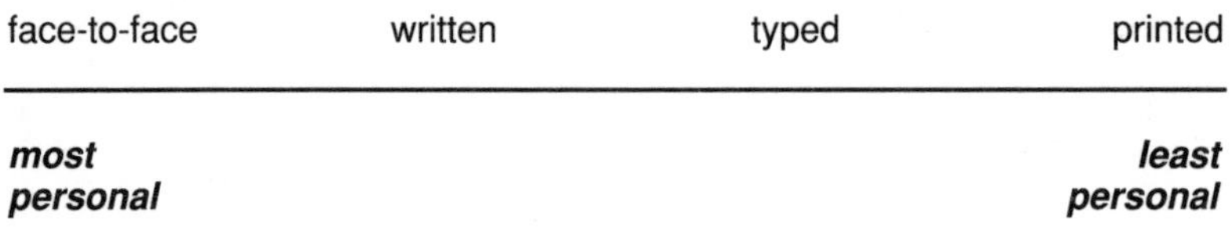

face-to-face	written	typed	printed
most personal			***least personal***

Figure 5.6   *Communication media*

Staff Development for CSCL

It is inevitable in a book with as wide a scope as this one, that some topics are not discussed in as much detail as I would like. This is particularly the case with the development of staff in running and supporting CSCL groups and programmes.

The complexities of working with groups, and working with them in CSCL environments in particular, are perhaps best experienced rather than read about. Staff development programmes in institutions of further and higher education, and within training departments of many organisations, offer opportunities to learn about and experience group work (see eg Fisser and de Boer, 1998; Hilkaa *et al.*, 1998; Levy, 1998; McConnell, 1998; Sharpe and Bailey, 1998). There are in addition many courses available outside these institutions, such as group training methods courses, T group workshops and the like; similarly with learning about the use of CSCL technologies and the potential for learning that they offer (see eg details of the MEd in Networked Collaborative Learning offered online at www.shef.ac.uk/uni/projects/csnl).

Working with colleagues who are already familiar with group work methods and the use of CSCL can be particularly worthwhile. The emergence of networked learning support staff (Levy, 1998) is also an important trend in supporting staff and students in their development. Taking time to reflect on your professional practice while actively involved in CSCL work is perhaps the most beneficial form of professional development (Boud and Walker, 1998).

Finally, there is a wide range of literature on working with groups in education and training that can be referred to, some of which is mentioned in the reference list at the end of this book (see also Laurillard, 1993 for a framework for using educational technology in teaching generally).

Design into Practice

Making the bridge from traditional forms of learning to cooperative learning requires tutors and learners to reorientate themselves. Many tutors will have to reconsider much of their existing professional practice. Learners will have to change many of their expectations about learning. This is difficult in itself. Making the link between cooperative learning and *computer supported* cooperative learning is perhaps more difficult because few tutors and learners will have the experience of working with technology in this way.

One mechanism for facilitating this reorientation will be for tutors and learners to learn about successful experiences of CSCL. In the Centre for the Study of Management Learning at Lancaster University, we have been running a CSCL programme for several years, and some discussion of this may be useful in seeing how one design has been implemented. In the remaining sections of this chapter I will discuss the design of the Lancaster programme. The next chapter will be devoted to an analysis of the programme itself.

The Computer Mediated MA in Management Learning

The computer mediated MA in management learning (CM MAML) is a two-year part-time programme for professionals in Management Education and Development. Participants range in age from mid-20s to early 60s. We try to get a balance of genders on each cohort, and a spread of public, private and voluntary sector organisations as well as those who are self-employed.

The design of the MA is based on educational principles broadly shared by staff, who nevertheless bring influences from different academic backgrounds (including organisational behaviour, educational research, educational technology and linguistics). These principles are:

● Participants should have as much choice as possible over the direction and content of their learning.
● They are responsible for 'managing' their own learning and for helping others in theirs (Salomon and Perkins, 1998). The notion of a 'learning community' is generally used to denote this: a community of course participants and tutors that manages its learning needs through negotiation and discussion (Pedler, 1981; Snell, 1989a).
● The work of the programme integrates the idea of critical perspective in the academic tradition, with participants' day-to-day professional experience.
● The opportunity presented to the students by the MA should be as much for learning about and developing themselves in their professional roles, as for engaging with relevant ideas and concepts in the public domain.
● That the marked degree of participation inherent in the design assumes a commitment to taking collective responsibility (by participants and tutors alike) for attending to the 'process' of the community, ie reviewing and modifying the design, procedures and ways of working.

In practice, this means for instance that the staff often, but not always, design in some detail only the first day or so of each workshop. Thereafter, activities are planned collectively. Reviewing progress and subsequent planning is also a collective activity. Topics which arise emerge from the interests of staff and participants, as does the choice of methods and the online (CSCL) tutorial groups. The topics for course assignments are the choice of each learner and assessment is 'collaborative', ie peer, self- and tutor (Hardy, *et al.*, 1991).

Open Learning Philosophy

The concept of liberation education (Freire, 1972) is at the root of much of our professional practice: 'liberation is a praxis: the action and reflection of men (sic) upon their world in order to transform it'. This educational philosophy is underpinned by the challenge of uniting action and reflection (Freire, 1985). This leads to informed action (Carr and Kemmis, 1986). In our case, with students and staff who are management trainers and developers, action is based on reflection on one's professional practice, as well as on one's role as a learner.

We espouse a theory of knowledge which has much in common with Habermas' knowledge constitutive interests (Habermas, 1972). Knowledge is not a commodity made up of a series of 'truths' (scientism); it is not propositional, but rather a process of knowing in which we engage with our reality, and through dialogue with others and with ourselves we give meaning to the world. This process acknowledges that there are different forms of knowledge, including tacit or personal knowledge (Polanyi, 1958) and experiential knowledge (Kolb, 1984).

One of our principles is the integration of reflective practice (Boud and Walker, 1998) and a critical perspective to participants' academic and professional work. Talking of a critical social science, Carr and Kemmis (1986) state that:

> its epistemology is constructivist, seeing knowledge as developing by a process of active construction and reconstruction of theory and practice by those involved; that it involves a theory of symmetrical communication (a process of rational discussion which actively seeks to overcome coercion on the one hand and self-deception on the other), and that it involves a democratic theory of political action based on free commitment to social action and consensus about what needs to be and should be done. In short, it is not only a theory about knowledge, but also about how knowledge relates to practice.

The dialectical nature of the educational enterprise is supported by the medium of CSCL. Here we can engage in praxis in a way that may not always be possible face-to-face. If we see this medium as an empty space to be moulded or designed in whatever way supports our purpose, then it is not difficult to imagine it supporting a form of education which is based on a resolution of the contradiction of the teacher-student relationship; without this resolution 'dialogical relations... are otherwise impossible' (Freire, 1972). This is a fundamental aspect of our approach to academic professionalism on the MA.

The programme is a form of open learning, not of the 'conventional' packaged learning or distance learning variety, but one which is based on a philosophy of openness (Harris, 1987) rather than of expediency (Boot and Hodgson, 1988). It emphasises considerable social interaction and cooperation between the learners (who we prefer to call 'participants'), and between the participants and the staff running the programme. The programme has much in common with current ideas about 'communities of practice' and situated learning (Lave and Wenger, 1991; Wenger, 1998).

Why CSCL?

We chose to work in this CSCL environment for several reasons. A group of us at Lancaster had just completed a funded project on Information Technology-based Open Learning (ITOL). This was a theoretical project looking at the possibilities of extending conventional university teaching and learning through advanced learning technologies to learners outside the University. We developed an ITOL model (see Hodgson *et al.*, 1989) which helped us design our MA programme. In addition, we wanted to try and overcome some of the problems (as we saw them) in running the department's existing part-time MA programme. This is a well-established programme which has a series of workshops over a two-year period, with day-long face-to-face tutorial meetings in between. The underlying educational philosophy is similar to that described here for the computer mediated MA.

It was felt that a computer supported cooperative learning environment might allow the whole learning community to continue discussions started at workshops (there is little, if any, opportunity for this on the conventional programme); that there might be discussions between different learning sets in the CSCL environment (impossible when they meet in different locations face-to-face); that the opportunity to develop online resources such as databases, bibliographies and the like might enhance learning; and that there might actually be qualitatively better discussions in the electronic learning sets than in the face-to-face ones. These aims have largely been achieved, we think.

The Programme Design

The programme is structured round two learning environments – a residential one and a CSCL one. The residential learning environment is made up of six intensive residential workshops spread fairly evenly throughout the two years, at which participants examine relevant research and theory, and experiment with and plan alternative strategies for their continuing learning in their normal working contexts.

In the CSCL environment, there is continuation of some of the issues raised in the workshops, and a 'meeting' of tutorial sets. The sets usually consist of between three to five participants and a tutor. Their main purpose is to provide support for each individual in choosing, planning and writing course assignments. Participants also discuss matters arising out of the programme and out of their work experience. These activities are supported by a CSCL environment made up primarily of computer conferencing and e-mail (we use the Caucus system), with access to online databases and library catalogues. The whole year group also has the opportunity to 'meet' via the medium. Participants on the programme link into the system from various parts of the UK (and from overseas from time to time), using a PC (or Mac), modem and communications software. Tutors (usually three per programme) use the local area network on campus, or link in from their homes).

We use the CSCL environment for many different purposes and activities:

Communication between participants:
- to keep in touch
- to share ideas

- as noticeboards
- as resources.

Formal learning processes:
- electronic tutorials, seminars and meetings
- decision making about the programme as a whole
- discussions and other participatory learning events
- development of ideas about design issues.

Additionally, we are all concerned at one time or another with looking at the role of CSCL in management learning and development.

The course concludes with a two-day residential period which is used to review participants' dissertation work and their plans for future development. Figure 5.7 indicates the way the various activities are distributed throughout the two years.

Design of the CSCL Environment

As with most of the programme, the design of the CSCL environment is managed by participants and tutors alike. At each workshop participants and staff take part in 'set formation' in which learners and tutors make decisions about who to work with over the forthcoming online period. Each learning set then has a specific computer conference set up for it.

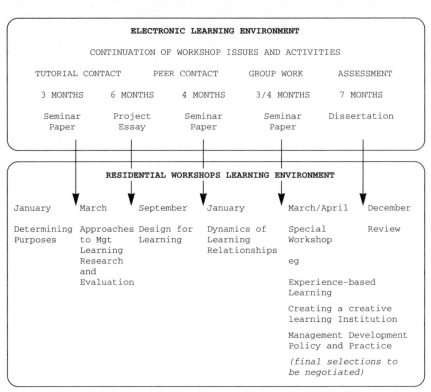

Figure 5.7   *The computer mediated MA design*

The set members discuss how they proposed to work as a set online, and what protocols they imagine they will need in order to communicate effectively. Each set usually has different strategies for working online. For example, people in a set might decide that each person should set up an item for themselves to discuss their next piece of assessed work – this is their own item and is clearly visible as such in the list of items in the set conference. Other items might include one called 'dates' (to keep track of when people are away); 'postcards' for participants to talk about what they have been up to recently; 'assessment' to discuss the process of assessment and for people to provide ideas about their preferred method of being assessed, or the criteria that might be used to assess pieces of work (see Figure 5.8).

Items are set up by both participants and staff. Table 5.2 shows a list of items in one set conference (the conference was called 'Energy'). While at

146

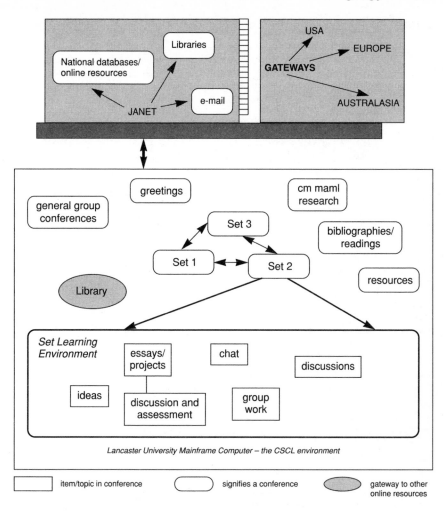

Figure 5.8 *The electronic learning environment*

the residential workshop, the whole group decides on the name for a conference where they can all 'meet'. Typically, this is a conference where discussion about issues arising in the workshop might be continued; where general discussions about management learning can take place; where people can keep each other informed of their work situation, and so on. Once again, items are set up by both participants and staff. Table 5.3 shows the items in a 'general' conference.

Table 5.2 *Example of items in a set conference*

Item	Title
Item 1	exhausted, but 'raring' to go
Item 2	ENERGY CONTRACT
Item 3	Postcards
Item 4	Elaine's Project Essay
Item 5	Mag's Project Essay
Item 6	postcard from Stroud
Item 7	//
Item 8	Helen's assignment
Item 9	this should go with item 8 –sorry everyone – upload probs
Item 10	//
Item 11	Helen's assignment assess. still upload probs
Item 12	//
Item 13	RESPONSE TO ELAINE'S BIOGRAPHY
Item 14	at Borwick all week
Item 15	STUART'S – TO KEEP IN TOUCH WITH ASSESSED WORK, ETC.
Item 16	Thoughts on Computer Conferencing
Item 17	CRITERIA FOR ASSESSMENT – GENERAL/NOT INDIVIDUAL SPECIFIC
Item 18	HOW ARE WE GETTING ON AS A SET?
Item 19	ENERGY STIMULATED RECALL
Item 20	FEEDBACK ON HELEN'S PROJECT ESSAY
Item 21	MAG'S SEMINAR PAPER 2

Table 5.3 *Example of items from a 'general' conference*

Item	Title
Item 1	rules – see 1st response
Item 2	DYNAMIC WORKSHOP – MARCH DATES
Item 3	UPDATE ON ALL CM MAML CONFERENCES
Item 4	CSML Conference
Item 5	ACCESSING LANCS COMPUTER
Item 6	ISSUES AROUND THE COMPUTER MEDIUM
Item 7	Sharing biographies?
Item 8	WORKSHOP 3 – MUSICAL(?) REVIEW
Item 9	Have we been hacked?
Item 10	NEWS
Item 11	BIOGRAPHIES
Item 12	A FREEBIE THAT MAY INTEREST YOU!!
Item 13	//
Item 14	Values research conference
Item 15	Conference news
Item 16	EXTERNAL EXAMINER (PT MAML) MEETING

Table 5.3 *Continued*

Item	Title
Item 17	CHRISTINE DYTHAM NOW ONLINE
Item 18	Conference Reports for general 3
Item 19	SOMEWHERE TO STAY THE NIGHT BEFORE NEXT WKSHP
Item 20	DYNAMICS – ITEMS 20 ONWARDS
Item 21	SEASONS GREETINGS
Item 22	MEETING CM2ers ONLINE
Item 23	resources for workshop 4
Item 24	Stephen diary disaster
Item 25	Guy Claxton seminar
Item 26	Management Competence Issues
Item 27	CAL91 conference
Item 28	Guided tour of Caucus

In addition, other conferences may be convened as and when there is a need. For example, some of the other conferences are: 'readings', where people enter précis, summaries of other information about books and journal articles they have been reading; 'research', a conference set up for us all to participate in researching and evaluating CM MAML; 'resources', a place to put any useful learning resources; 'tutors', a conference where tutors discuss their professional practice as it relates to the CM MAML programme (other participants have 'read only' status in this conference). Sometimes a special conference is set up to deal with the design of the next residential workshop.

Some of these conferences are 'live' throughout the whole programme (eg, readings, research, tutors). The set conferences are intended to run between each workshop, after which new set conferences are convened. As it turns out, several of the set conferences run for longer periods, so that people often belong to several different set conferences at the same time. There is also a conference for people on the different cohorts of CM MAML to communicate. In addition to the conferences, participants have access to each other and to the members of the department via e-mail.

In the next chapter, I will discuss some of the outcomes of working with this CSCL design.

Conclusion

In this chapter I have attempted to compare cooperative learning and traditional forms of learning, and have discussed six aspects of CSCL design which, in my professional practice, have been found to be very effective. These are:

- openness in the educational process – the learning community
- self-determination in learning
- a real purpose in the cooperative process
- a supportive learning environment
- collaborative assessment of learning
- assessment and evaluation of the ongoing learning process.

The place of the tutor in CSCL is also discussed. The chapter concludes with an example of a particular CSCL design, which is offered as a way of seeing how to make the link between cooperative learning and *computer supported* cooperative learning.

Notes

1. I refer here to formal learning events in which the tutor is actively involved. Not all CSCL actively involves the tutor (see eg McAteer *et al.*, 1997 for an analysis of some CMC seminars where the students worked completely on their own).

6 | CSCL in Action – A Case Study

Introduction

In Chapter 5 I discussed in some detail a particular view of CSCL, and a series of aspects associated with this view which I have found to be useful in designing CSCL learning events or programmes.

In this chapter I want to address some issues to do with using computer supported cooperative learning in higher education and in training and development settings, using the design features of Chapter 5. The focus is on the design and management of CSCL in open learning contexts, in particular a cooperatively designed, open learning MA in Management Learning which uses a mixture of computer conferencing, e-mail and periodic face-to-face workshops. I want to focus specifically on the nature of professional practice in such online environments.

Although the particular focus here is on the use of CSCL within a postgraduate programme, the underlying principles, ideas and methodologies are likely to be applicable in other post-compulsory educational settings (such as undergraduate teaching) and within organisational training and development settings also.

Some Characteristics of the Programme

In order to indicate some of the issues concerning the use of CSCL in higher education and in training and development contexts, I have chosen to focus on three aspects of the open, cooperative learning process as practised on the programme: the process of feedback and assessment of participants' course work; decision making on the programme; and the role of the tutor in the programme. I will also say something about the dynamics of these online groups and of people's experience of working in CSCL. In doing this, I hope to show how the medium offers a unique environment for putting into practice those principles of computer supported cooperative learning outlined in the previous chapter.

The Process of Feedback and Assessment of Participants' Work

Our aim of providing an environment where participant choice about what to work on for the course assignments (there are five assignments over the two years) requires a context and process whereby each person can talk about their interests, knowing they are supported by other participants and tutors. We manage this by forming computer supported cooperative learning sets – small groups of three, four or five participants and a tutor. We usually do this face to face, prior to working online, and it is achieved through collective, mutually agreeable action.

The exact methodology for forming sets is devised uniquely on each occasion. Put simply, participants and staff spend a considerable amount of time discussing their interests in working with each other in the CSCL sets. We might try forming sets, then review the procedure and the outcome, ie how do the sets 'look' and 'feel' to us. This sometimes leads to a re-run of the set formation exercise; sometimes it is sufficient to carry out the exercise once. Set formation is one of the most complex and at times difficult aspects of this programme. It brings out many 'hidden' agendas, and surfaces emotions and feelings that may have been lingering in the community. However, we see this as an important aspect of the learning of the community.

Once sets are formed, each group opens its own computer conference and sets up procedures and practices for supporting the group members in their assignments, amongst other things. In the preparation, feedback about and assessment of the assignments, each participant and tutor is involved in the following process:

- Each participant offers suggestions on what they would like to do for their assignment. This is done in an item in the computer conference opened by them for that purpose. Other participants and the tutor offer comment, and a dialogue evolves. Participants' approaches to their assignments often change as we discuss their proposals and offer references and other resources for them to consider.
- Each person plans their assignment and writes it; at the same time:
- Criteria for assessment are mutually agreed, and we think through what's involved in assessing each others' work (prior to this in the workshops we have collectively discussed the nature of a learning community, part of which involves each participant being willing to assess other participants' assignments. This is an important role for participants to play on the programme, and they do it willingly and

with much enthusiasm once they have experienced it. Of course, tutors are also involved in the assessment exercise).

- Copies of papers are sent from one member to another so that we all have copies to work from.
- We start the process of giving and receiving feedback. The exact way in which this occurs depends largely on the members of the group. Sometimes the writer of the paper begins a review of their work, mentioning those aspects which they see as being in need of clarification or modification, or talking about some of the learning issues that emerged for them in writing the paper. Sometimes the writer asks for others to start the conversation about feedback. What exactly we focus on depends to some extent on the wishes of the writer and the interests of the other participants, including the tutor.
- We assess/mark each assignment (self/peer/tutor assessment).

This may appear rather idealised, but in reality it is not far from the truth. Other events sometimes get in the way of the process, so prolonging the exercise; but eventually all six stages are covered in one way or another.

In order to illuminate some of the processes and issues that arise during feedback and assessment, I will discuss two items from one of the early CSCL set conferences on the programme. The first item was set up for the exploration of issues around people's criteria for being assessed, and for discussion about the assessment process itself (item 11). The other item was set up by one of the participants to plan and discuss her current assignment, here referred to as her Project Essay (PE) (item 17). Each conference is of course also concerned with other issues which are 'happening' at the same time (in this particular set-conference there were about 24 items in all).

Dialogues about assessment

Item 11 was set up by the tutor involved after a general discussion at the first residential workshop about assessment (the programme started in January). At the workshop staff had introduced three criteria that they use when assessing participants' work. This was the starting point for the item.[1]

Item 11   *30-JAN-91   23:05 Daniel*

CRITERIA AND ASSESSMENT – THOUGHTS ON

Thought it might be useful at this point to start an item to look at criteria that you all want to think about using for assessing your assignment, and also maybe give our thoughts on the nature of peer/self/tutor assessment?

124 Discussion responses

11:1) Daniel   *30-JAN-91   23:18*

Some of my criteria that I implicitly use when 'assessing' someone's essay:

- does the essay look at issues critically ie is there critical thinking or are things merely seen as 'unproblematic' or taken for granted
- is there a combination of personal thoughts and ideas as well as some use made of theory, concepts and ideas from what you have been reading
- is the essay about some aspect of Management Learning/Development (you can make your own case for saying it is!!)

Needless to say I also use the criteria that you want to apply to your essay too. What are your thoughts.........?
Daniel

What followed (124 entries, 20,084 words) was an exploration of the nature of learning and assessment. Participation in the item, in terms of the number of entries made and the total number of words entered, is fairly evenly spread, apart from Greg's contributions which were relatively low (see Table 6.1).

Table 6.1   *Entries made to items 11 and 17*

	Daniel	Malcolm	Mary	Greg	Sandra
Item 11 (criteria and assessment)					
entries (N=124)	27 (22%)	21 (17%)	36 (29%)	10 (8%)	30 (24%)
words (N=20084)	5388 (27%)	2872 (14%)	4984 (25%)	1908 (9%)	4932 (25%)
Item 17 (Mary's project essay)					
entries (N=49)	12 (25%)	9 (18%)	20 (41%)	3 (6%)	5 (10%)
words (N=10660)	3492 (33%)	1236 (12%)	5040 (47%)	636 (6%)	256 (2%)

A content analysis of the item shows the main activities engaged in. The diversity of activities gives some indication of the issues discussed in the item and the quality of the experience, including:

- participants explaining the criteria they would like applied to their paper
- people voicing concern about their 'ability' to meet some of the Lancaster criteria
- people organising the set's 'work' against timescales
- self-disclosure
- statements about the focus of participants' assignments
- some direction (from tutor and participants)
- discussion about theory
- checking out understandings
- posing questions about each others' work
- planning
- making (collective) decisions about contracts for working as a set; timescales; how we would assess each others' work
- summarising discussions so far
- asking for support and help
- giving support and help
- dealing with technical problems/issues
- giving feedback on people's papers
- some self-analysis/critical reflection
- reviewing.

Are participants engaging in a self-managed, cooperative learning enterprise? I think they are. On analysing the transcripts of this and other items, two sorts of activity which are particularly important indicators of this can be seen to be happening: participants taking control of the learning process, and participants reflecting on the nature of what they are doing in the assessment process.

The following extract from the item shows something of the way in which the participants were beginning to assume responsibility for managing the learning process and making decisions about how to proceed with assessment (the group had already given feedback in other items on each others' assignments).

11:88) Sandra   14-APR-91   20:26

Daniel, Mary, Thanks for all that, how do you think we should go about this, any ideas? If we are going to assess each other's work and our own with the Lanc givens, and our own criteria to give a % has anybody got any 'plan' as to how we should do it? I feel that this is dragging on a bit as we are now in April and we have not started to 'talk' about our next piece of work.

Can we have a timescale when we agree to have it done by. I know we all agreed to have the feedback and assessment completed by a certain date but that does not seem to have worked, I might be wrong, what do you all think? Sandra... (edit)

11:93) Malcolm   16-APR-91   15:56

I agree with Sandra about this issue dragging on and feel we need to take the plunge, getting into the marking. I thought Greg's suggestion of grades at 13.8 (why there Greg?) rather duplicated the suggestion Daniel made at 11.33. Like Mary (11.80) I think we should use Daniel's marking scheme. If I haven't said so clearly elsewhere I would prefer to use the %age mark and Daniel's 'b)' suggestion.

We appear to have personal criteria for everyone except Greg, unless Greg you have tucked it away somewhere, could you say what yours is? My 'plan' for getting over this impasse, is that we all need to record our % marks for all the papers including our own. If there are any significant differences (and by significant I mean the mark being outside the bands Daniel's item 11.33 suggests) we discuss that difference and agree a mark collectively. Otherwise for the sake of convenience agree an average mark which will be within the bands anyway. Does this make sence (sense)?... (edit)

I am ready to put in my marks if everyone else agree the format for doing so. I will check each day to see if we have agreement. Malcolm.

11:94) Mary   16-APR-91   20:27

Malcolm – Your suggestions above all look fine to me and I'm happy to go with what you suggest. Like you, I'll therefore check daily. I'm very conscious of being a beginner at this and so I like your idea of agreeing a mark collectively if poss. Thanks.

Although the tutor had offered some suggestions about the assessment process (mentioned by Malcolm), he held back from initiating the process itself, waiting for the participants to address the issue. Within the dynamics of the programme, this is not as contrived as it may appear. There is no expectation that the tutor should necessarily 'lead' discussion, nor initiate the assessment process. By holding back, the tutor was 'allowing' the participants to take control themselves. This action is part of the trust-building that is needed for participants to know that they are indeed being allowed to manage their own learning.

The next extract shows a participant reflecting on the nature of what she is doing in the assessment process. She is struggling to understand the educational process she is engaged in, and reflects on similar experiences in other settings and acknowledges that our relationships online are an important aspect of the process.

11:102) Mary   *21-APR-91   21:41*

This is my 1st attempt at uploading solo, so here goes…
Here's my assessment of our seminar papers.
I'm finding this quite difficult and was trying to work out why. I've had a couple of goes at assessing work our managers at (organisation) have done on the management development progs. we run and so it's still quite a new thing for me to do. However, I haven't found it too difficult. I think the difference between assessing them and assessing you all and me, is that we're needing to work fairly closely together and we've been through (and no doubt are continuing to go through), some pretty fraught times together. I'm feeling very aware I suppose of potential 'halo' effects on how I do this and the differences in our relationships with each other. I'm struggling therefore, to put all this aside, (I shan't succeed of course!), and look with clear eyes on what we've tried to do and how well we've done it.
     Having now experienced this process, I really have felt that the feedback has been the most valuable part of it all – apart from writing the actual thing of course!! I've also found seeing what we've all chosen to do and how we've approached it a useful experience (edit – she proceeds to give her assessments).

The next extract (from another set-conference) again shows the participant struggling to make sense of the whole assessment process. She points out some of the difficulties and contradictions we are often faced with in the programme (and on reading it I am reminded of something Freire (1985) says; 'Existence is not despair, but risk. If I don't exist dangerously, I cannot be').

21:2) Anna   *25-APR-91   17:11*
(edit)
Some reflections on assessments – and subsequent discomforts.
For me the first seminar paper was undertaken in three broad phases:

THE PRODUCTION OF THE PAPER

this involved reading; writing and rewriting; dialogue; struggling; testing out ideas; being confused and becoming clear and then confused again; excitement; application of learning to improve my professional practice; challenging myself; making things explicit, or trying to; gaining confidence; identifying learning needs; discovering; using my work to know both myself and others better.

FEEDBACK

this involved… struggling with defensiveness; proactivity; risking being first; self disclosure;… touching; enjoyment of what had been created.

ASSESSMENT

this involved receiving; being judged; wanting to move on; being involved in a game I didn't understand; being focused on what hadn't been achieved; feeling afraid and little.

When I reflect on the phases described above it occurs to me that in phases 1 and 2, I felt as if I was managing the process and was engaged, whereas in the third phase I was submitting myself to an introject. Painful. And running away. Painful... (edit)

My current position regarding academic assessment is that I don't know the rules of the game. It would be relatively easy to pretend. I have done much pretending in my life and have some well developed skills which I could use. However, I don't want to waste my time or abuse the work of others. Nor do I want to create processes which are introjects.

I have still to learn how to engage in academic assessment, in a way which is congruent with my concept of self managed learning. I am also struggling with the notion of numeric assessment as an integral part of the MAML programme. Perhaps colleagues have perceptions of the process which might facilitate my understanding. I would be grateful for dialogue to enable me to move on (edit).

As time passed, the group proceeded with giving feedback and finally assessing each others' work; the dialogue became reflexive as they began to use their experience of the process to talk about the nature of the enterprise. This example of experiential learning (Kolb, 1984) was not unique to the assessment process (much of the programme is experience based, using our experiences of work and learning as a basis for future learning), but it brought here an urgency to what the group was doing and made a bridge between theory and practice (Boot and Reynolds, 1984).

The process is not problem-free. It not only involves intellectual engagement, but just as importantly it involves legitimate emotional engagement (Snell, 1989b). Although heavily edited so as to make them easier to read and follow, the following extracts give some indication of the emotional impact of feedback and assessment. They also show how the impact of learning in the face-to-face workshops can be carried over into the online group work:

11:107) Sandra   22-APR-91   20:03

Mary, Greg, Malcolm... Like Mary, I am finding this very difficult. The assessment that Daniel has given us all has not sat well with me. If my paper is the weakest of them all I have no idea how to move forward, and because of this I have had problems just making myself go online. As for the assessment of your papers, I will now try to complete this task... (edit) *(she proceeds to give feedback on others' papers).*

The tutor comments on this the same evening.

11:109) Daniel   22-APR-91   22:27

Sandra... I'm trying to understand what the issues are for you around this feedback and assessment process... I'm sorry if this experience hasn't helped you to move forward – if you could tell me what sort of feedback WOULD help you at this point then I would try to respond to that, as I guess everyone else would too? (edit)

Why do you look at your mark as suggesting you are weakest in the set? I wouldn't take that view – at this point in the programme I've tried to be as honest about the grades as I think I can so as not to produce any 'falseties' at this point… I'd be grateful for any comments on my feedback so that I can try and change/progress and give you all something meaningful and useful in the future if you feel that hasn't been the case so far (edit).

The next day, other participants enter comments.

11:110) Greg   23-APR-91   15:05

I will need to read the last three responses before being able to comment in any detail. I am a little concerned that Daniel seems to be the focus of Sandra's attention but I need to consider what has been said in the past to see if I can help in this. I agree with Daniel that this is something we all need to deal with and not leave Daniel to cope with it himself. I will be back soon.
Greg

11:111) Mary   23-APR-91   18:15

Can I echo Greg's comment too. I'll try to get back to this later this evening. I hope we can deal with some these feelings online.

11:112) Sandra   23-APR-91   21:14

Daniel, Greg, Mary, I am aware that yet again I appear to have raised my thoughts and feelings and that has caused some grief, and for that I'm sorry… (edit) to sum up it is not the feedback that I have had difficulty coming to terms with, the feedback I felt went OK. My strongest feeling is about the summing up and the grades… (edit).

At the moment I feel that my relationships with some set members is a relationship that I do not feel comfortable about… (edit). I do however feel unhappy about being the one that has raised yet again 'problems' as I see them. They might not be problems for anyone else, and therefore I do not want to 'waste the set's time'.
Sandra

11:113) Mary   23-APR-91   21:24

Daniel – I'm responding here to your questions to all of us in your 11:109 to Sandra.

How I felt about your feedback…

For me, it was helpful both in content and style. I liked the way you queried some things I'd said, as that made me think about them more clearly. I also like the way you picked up on and endorsed some things and commented about what they meant for you.

That all gave me a sense of how far I'd met my own personal criteria as far as you were concerned.

The 'general' comments bit was useful too and I found that altogether your comments helped me think as objectively as I could about my own paper. In transactional terms, my response felt like 'adult to adult'.

What I should have liked more opportunity for, from everyone, was to continue with the dialogue about our papers (which I think Sandra was referring to). Time is really the problem here I know, but I enjoyed responding to people's feedback to me and feel some regret that cos of time constraints that has really had to get cut off in a rather peremptory way. It felt for me, that I was still learning a lot more, both in terms of my paper, but also about other's perceptions, which I feel is very useful for us in learning to work together as a set (edit).

She goes on to discuss the process of feedback, and online discussions in general.

The next day, the tutor returns to the discussion.

11:117) Daniel   24-APR-91   10:38

Thanks Mary for your thoughts on feedback... I do get concerned about the focus and level of feedback that I should give on essays etc and what you've said has helped me considerably... (edit). I agree about the discussions around essays not being long enough... (edit).

It seems it takes something of a 'crisis' to make us address some of these important issues; that's a pity I think cos when we're under pressure and feeling hurt and all of that then we don't always see these issues in a clear light? But maybe that's the only way that some really important issues CAN emerge here? Daniel

Sandra comments:

11:121) Sandra   24-APR-91   20:20

Mary, Daniel, Greg. I think there is a great deal in what you say here. Sandra

11:122) Sandra   25-APR-91   19:59

Daniel, I have given what you put above some thought... (edit).

Some of the information that you need, I am sorry but I do not feel that I am able to put it online because I know it can be read by a number of people... (edit).

As I said, others from the large group *(the previous workshop)* did and said things that have had an effect on me and relate to other members of this set. I think that I have been carrying this around with me since the last workshop and it has resulted in a number of things... *(she elaborates on these)* (edit).

Also I have talked about support, I do feel that there is support from the set when there is a problem...

I know that you will not know half of what I am on about, and I should be able to put it online. If I felt that it would be constructive I would. But I feel that if I did it would not be at all constructive (edit)... so I will finish there. Sandra

Later that evening the tutor replies:

11:123) Daniel   25-APR-91   21:44

Thanks Sandra for your thoughts – I can understand that if you don't feel able to discuss some of the issues affecting you at the moment because they might have an effect on others that you don't want, then you shouldn't talk about them. It does make it a little difficult to understand some of what you are saying though.

It's good tho' to hear from you and I hope we might find the opportunity to get into some of these issues that affect you and us all at some time in the future. Daniel

Sandra later mentions that she has asked someone outside the programme to act as a mentor to her, to help her think though some of these issues. She asks the set how they feel about this, and Greg replies:

11:131) Greg   06-MAY-91   14:55

Sandra – you asked about our views on your mentor. Only you will know if this is the best way of tackling the issues you are facing. My initial reaction was to feel that in some way I have not been able to help in the way that you needed it – I feel I have let you down. Having said that I know that there are some things you are not ready to discuss online and I recognise that a face-to-face helper might be able to help where I and the rest of the set cannot. I, like Daniel, would be a bit worried if I could not help you with the process of coming to grips with your learning (edit).

He goes on to offer some thoughts on the issues raised by Sandra.

These extracts show that for some participants it is not always easy to articulate their feelings in this medium, and that, in any case, there are times when they feel it is inappropriate for them to talk about some issues with the set members. The extracts also show that the process of working in sets is not problem-free. Working cooperatively in this way is complex and requires judgement from everyone about their level of involvement, and their relationship to the emerging issues.

Working with emotions in an online environment is a new experience to us all. We don't shrink from it, but we tread softly because we are unfamiliar with some of the consequences of doing so in this new medium.

Support in doing assignments
Item 17 was a place for Mary to make explicit issues relating to her assignment. Its dynamic was different to that of item 11 (see Table 6.1), as might be expected from the purpose of the item. She started off by talking at some length about what she wanted to do for the project essay (PE) ie, how to get managers in her organisation more involved in the

development of their staff, carefully outlining her own position in relation to the managers (she is a management developer), defining her
terms, offering justifications for tackling this issue and presenting her
initial thoughts on the way she might go about doing the research. This
opening statement was a very detailed and well-constructed statement of
some 684 words. She concluded this opening entry by inviting us to join
her in working through this.

17:1) Mary   04-MAY-91   12:01

(Edit). To progress on this, I'd really like comments on my ideas from you. I am
wondering whether it's too big an area to tackle for the PE, but I'd really like to
do something towards it if poss. To help me along the way, I've been dipping into
'Management Development – Strategies for Action', Alan Mumford and 'A
Manager's Guide to Self Development', Mike Pedler, John Burgoyne and Tom
Boydell. I've also come across a very helpful article in 'Personnel Manager' on
the manager's role in staff dev, but I don't have it at home with me, so forget who
wrote it!
    What do you think?

Here is a place for Mary to be 'heard' by the others; for her to use for her
own purposes. The level of dialogue and engagement between Mary and
the others in the set was high. There is evidence that participants are
listening to what she is saying and engaging in a meaningful exploration
with her about her work.

17:2) Malcolm   06-MAY-91   15:15

Mary – getting the involvement of the line manager in the development of their
staff is a big issue with the (her organisation), and my dept. One of the problems
I can see is that there are many people all too keen to come up with instant
solutions without looking at the issues first. I think your Project will/would help
address this problem for (his organisation).
    I am tempted to start to discuss the problems with you but I will hold back for
now and concentrate on the methods you are proposing to use. In establishing
what development means to the policy makers I wonder if you should go a step
further and establish what it means to them in terms of practical outcomes.
There seems to be a gap between what is 'policy' and practical 'application'.
Would it be useful for you to discover what methods policy-makers use to evaluate their policies... (edit). The communication process between policy makers
and managers might also be an area for work... (edit).
Malcolm

And later:

17:33) Malcolm   24-JUL-91   10:40

Mary – I find it really exciting to see how you are progressing with your PE and
to read your thoughts on conducting research... (edit).

I was interested to see you had taped an interview. Do you think it affected the quality or depth of the information you obtained? I have not attempted this as I believe that using it with the senior managers I have interviewed will inhibit them from being fully open. One or two have noticeably altered the body posture when they have seen I was taking notes! This is an assumption I plan to explore in my PE... (edit).
Malcolm

Also, Mary's thoughts on her PE are having an influence on other participants' ideas for their own work:

17:10) Greg   16-MAY-91   0:50

Hi Mary
I have just downloaded your item 17 to view tomorrow and will join in the discussion. I would like to contribute now only its 12:45 and I'm getting a little tired. There are questions in my mind from reading your initial proposals from the PE in looking at managers and their staff which may also help me to focus my thoughts from the FE (further education) point of view but I will come back when my head is clearer.
Cheers
Greg

He came back the following night:

17:11) Greg   16-MAY-91   23:45

Hi Mary
I have been reading the issues in your item and two thoughts came immediately to mind and I'm sure a few more will follow. The first question is around comments of Daniel and Malcolm that of involving both parties in identifying and understanding 'development'. For example is this just a manager developing staff or do you see this as a team development process. I have two models in my mind from my own experience which may have no bearing on your thoughts what so ever but here goes... (edit).

He then proceeds to explain the two models and how they apply to developing managers.

What I think we can see happening here, and in similar items set up by participants in this and other set-conferences, is a supportive group dynamic; one which has indicators of self-management, openness, cooperation and a willingness to share and take some risks.

Making Decisions about the Online Environment

Decision making and the ongoing design of the programme are cooperative activities. Much of this occurs in the residential workshops as well as online. The collective involvement of us all in these processes means that ownership of decisions and programme design lies with us all, and not just the tutors.

The negotiation of decisions about the nature of our online work and the design of the conferences is a major aspect of this. Each time we do this it is inevitably different because we are always building on past experience and reviewing past plans and decisions in the light of experience. Even for those tutors who are now 'experienced' in the use of the medium, the procedure of reviewing is appropriate and necessary in order to engage them in thinking about *recent* experience with the *present* group of participants. We do not believe that the experience of one group cannot inform that of another, but we do believe in the uniqueness of each group and that each has its own dynamic, purpose and 'life'.

How do we go about doing this in practice? The following extract from notes taken at a workshop give some indication:

> Tuesday evening – met in the large group (all participants and all tutors) to discuss the assumptions and 'taken for granteds' around the programme and around the concept of learning sets. Question and answer session with tutors being put on the spot about their 'taken for granteds'. Decided that we needed to meet in our present sets to establish how we are working together and to review business that requires completion, before deciding on the design of the online environment for the next period.

> Wednesday afternoon – met in our present sets to review past experience and think ahead to what we need to do online in order to finish the business of the set. Had some frank discussion about online relationships...

> Wednesday pm – reviewed in large group such things as 'purposes' of online environment; possibility for forming new sets online rather than face-to-face at the workshop. Discussed how to have fun online. Reviewed how we make decisions, how they work-out in practice and people's subsequent engagement with them. Posed the question: how we accommodate everyone's needs within different designs of the online environment?

> Thursday am – met in the large group to deal with where we are individually in relation to the programme, and where we are in relation to sets and the next period online. Discussed various ideas for new ways of working online. Eventually decided to try working as one 'large' online set, rather than three smaller ones. Thought through the implications of this (eg possibility of over thirty items in the conference and consequently considerable information to deal with). Decided it was worth trying. Thought through the design of the conference and how to manage it.

These reviews and decision-making sessions have allowed us to collectively design our online environment and put a social as well as educational focus on the use of technology in the programme. By doing this we are taking into account 'the boundaries around the computer' (Kling, 1991). This I see as being similar to what Kling describes as the ('infrastructure of the computer support'): dealing with the computer system, the people who use it, their own computer equipment at home, and the ways in which we all take part in this online experience, in order to make sense of what is happening. Some innovations that we have tried as a consequence include the following.

'Snapshot' conferences

These are conferences where each of us has our own item to use for personal review of the programme. We call the conferences 'snapshots' since essentially each item becomes a series of snapshots about our experiences of the programme. The conference runs for the duration of the course (two years), and affords us all a series of personal evaluations of being on it. Procedurally, we can read each others' item but not contribute to them. The intention is for each of us to have a 'space' of our own in which to talk in any way we want about issues to do with the programme. The conference is grounded in personal ownership (the idea came from one participant and was discussed by us all before being agreed). No one has to 'hear' other people's thoughts at any particular time. It allows us to decide when we want to listen to each other by going into others' snapshots when we are ready to. The experience is similar to talking to yourself in a personal journal or log – but you are also being heard by others and getting some full attention. In practice, people comment on others' contributions in their own item. The items are also being used to 'talk' about personal professional practice in the workplace.

Large learning set-conferences

In these we work as one large learning set, instead of the usual three smaller set-conferences. This design emerged from discussion about people's experience of set-conferences to date. Some felt that the idea of being able to 'look into' but not contribute to other set-conferences wasn't working for them. It took too much time to keep up with the other set-conferences as well as actively contribute to your own, and there was sometimes a sense of frustration at not being able to take part in the dialogue of other sets – a feeling of being 'barred' from them. We discussed the possibility of each of us having our *own* open conference which people could join if they were interested as an alternative, but thought that this would be too cumbersome and could lead to some people being forgotten all together. The preference for one large set-conference with items for each individual completely open to us all seemed worth trying, although there was some reservation about how we might deal with the mass of information that would inevitably accumulate (the number of words at the 'end' of most set-conferences is considerable, often in the region of 40–50,000).

We (participants and tutors alike) spend some time reading each item and responding to those we choose to. Once we have established who we want to work with, we make any other items invisible to us (this is done easily by telling the system to 'forget' those items), so progressively limiting the number of items we visit and the amount of information we have to deal with. We then have a tailored environment to suit our present interests and concerns. Tutors are part of this process, and some negotiation takes place between them and participants about tutors' interests in participants' proposed work, so that each participant has a tutor to work with in addition to working with other participants. The items we work in (and therefore the people we work with) are the focus for discussion about the current assignment, amongst other things. Triads (self/tutor/ peer) for assessment are formed, with people inviting a tutor and another participant into their item for that purpose.

Readings and resources conferences

The purpose of these is for us to share what we are currently reading – papers, books, etc. The conferences had an initial flurry of activity with some very detailed summaries and reviews, and draft papers people were working on, placed in them. However, activity soon waned. The act of preparing a review or summary solely for the purpose of putting it into this conference is perhaps inappropriate given that people talk about their readings in their set-conferences as a natural part of dialogue with their colleagues. The potential benefit of sharing those readings formally with everyone else perhaps wasn't enough to justify the time and effort required to do so.

Tutor conference

This conference was the outcome of a face-to-face staff meeting at which we were aware that we were not involving the participants in our staff reviews of the programme. This seemed somehow inappropriate given the open philosophy of the course. We do still continue to have our 'closed' offline staff meetings (there are issues, often relating to our role as a representative of the University, which we feel cannot always be discussed with everyone, although this has been a point for debate amongst staff), but try to report back to the course members in this conference. In addition, the conference is a place for tutors to discuss general issues to do with the course, and is a bridge for staff between each new programme. Participants have 'read only' rights in the conference (the conference is called 'fishbowl'), but those who join it regularly often raise their views on some of the issues discussed by staff in one of the other conferences.

The external examiner for the programme is also a member of this conference. He was invited to join after participants queried his role within the programme. He joins us for discussions about the quality of the programme, and offers feedback on his perceptions of participants' work and the way the programme is running generally.

Joint programme conference

This conference was set up shortly after the start of the second intake of the programme. It is a place for participants on both intakes to come together, share thoughts on their experiences of the course, discuss their professional work lives, plan meetings, and so on. One particularly interesting development in this conference is the formation of a small group to discuss the possibility of running an online PhD learning set once they have completed their MA. This might include some of our part-time overseas research students.

Postcards conference

The experience of working cooperatively online is not one that comes easy to many participants (or indeed many staff). It is usually the case that participants have never used a CSCL medium before, and some struggle to find a voice and a way of communicating solely in text. Some participants feel constrained by the medium, and feel unable at times to contribute at the level they would often do in face-to-face groups. One way of being freed-up to talk as naturally as they would wish is for them to think of their communications online as postcards, sent to friends.

Each member sets up an item for their personal postcards. In this item they can talk about anything they want – their day-to-day life at work and at home, anything that helps them talk naturally. We have found that the metaphor of postcards (an example of online narrative) does help to free-up members to communicate without any formal structures or strictures being imposed. This in turn usually leads to them feeling more able to contribute to the other conferences where there are expectations about content and format.

Comment

These reviews of our online work have freed us up in our thinking about the programme generally. The comment was made that the programme is not made up of residential workshops separated by online activity; rather it is complete and organic. I call this 'seamless activity'. 'We are finding ways of doing the things we *want* to do', was the comment of one participant. Someone else said that usually at the end of other programmes or workshops there is a 'nothingness'; it has ended until the next time people meet. But not on CM MAML. The CSCL environment continues immediately from the face-to-face one and it is often the case that, on arriving home from the workshop, people immediately go online that night, or the next day.

Dynamics of CSCL Groups

It is beyond the scope of this chapter to look in detail at the dynamics of group work in CSCL. However, a glance at some indicators of the dynamics of online communications is possible. This may help to give some idea of how groups work online.

Needless to say, each group-conference has its own dynamics and no particular one can be considered 'typical' of the programme. I have therefore chosen some statistics of activity in a conference set up to design one of the residential workshops (the conference was called 'Dynamics' since the workshop was about the dynamics of learning). I chose this conference because it was set up some nine months into the programme, at a time when most people were beginning to feel 'comfortable' with electronic communications. It involved all participants, but in varying degrees of participation, and so it may offer a reasonable view of activity of a general kind.

The conference ran from late September 1990 to mid-January 1991, at which point the residential workshop took place (there was a follow-on after the workshop to mid-March 1991, when the conference 'closed'). The conference was moderated by a non-staff participant. The final number of items added to the conference was 40. The number of entries in each item varied enormously depending on the purpose of the item (see Figure 6.1). The 'life' of each item also varied, again depending on the purpose of the item.

Activity in the conference, as 'measured' by the number of entries per week, varied considerably (see Figure 6.2 for figures up to mid-January), with the middle weeks (early December) being the time when participants were most active; there was a lull over the holiday period, followed by

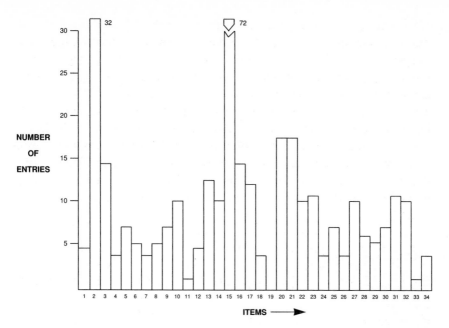

Figure 6.1 *Number of entries per item*

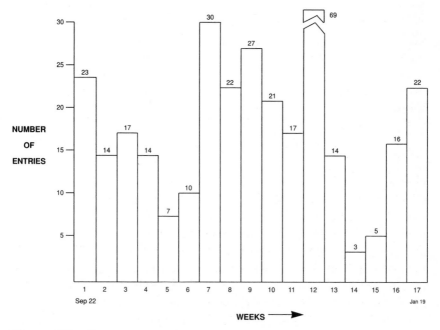

Figure 6.2 *Entries per week*

high activity in the two weeks prior to the residential workshop in mid-January. Overall, staff made fewer entries than participants (68 compared with 268).

Table 6.2 shows the number of visits made to the conference by each member between 22 September 1990 and late February 1991 (when the conference was coming to an end), the number of items each person added to the conference, and the number of responses each made (Mags, who made most visits and entered a large number of responses, was managing the conference). As an example of monthly visits made, during January 173 visits were made; during February 165 visits were made.

Table 6.2   *Visits made to the 'Dynamics' conference*

Name	Number of Visits	Items Added	Responses Made
Stuart (staff)	89	3	54
Kate (staff)	34	1	35
George (staff)	46	1	4
Sally (staff)	35	1	2
Paul	145	3	93
Stephen	124	5	77
Helen	2	0	1
Alan	17	4	15
Mags	206	12	71
Jed	15	0	5
Elaine	58	3	39
Simone	33	4	25
Jenny	18	2	12
Peter	12	0	12
Total	834	39	445

Activity of each member in terms of the number of words entered into the conference overall is shown in Figure 6.3. Using words entered is of course a very poor indicator of activity – it gives no indication of the quality of any entry, nor its purpose and meaning. Also, 'activity' can be a personal judgement: some participants visited the conference often, but did not always enter any new material, yet they might talk of being active in the conference. So, the use of words entered is only one (perhaps crude) measure of 'activity' and is used here for convenience only. (It perhaps should be noted that participants were also active in other conferences at this time too.) Nevertheless, this data may be helpful in interpreting some of the statements made by the participants in the case study. Figure 6.3 shows the wide variation in the number of words entered.

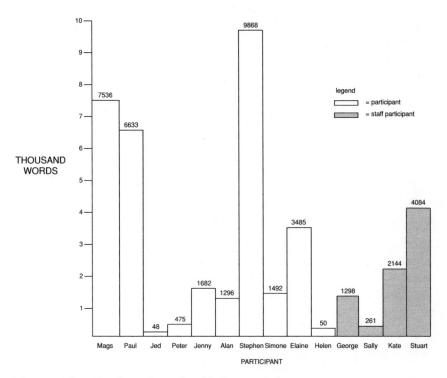

Figure 6.3   *Number of words added per participant*

To complete this overview, Table 6.3 shows a listing of item titles at the close of the conference in late March 1991.

Table 6.3   *A listing of items in the 'Dynamics' conference*

Item and Responses	Title
Item 1 (3)	OUR EXPRESSED WISHES
Item 2 (39)	DESIGN TEAM
Item 3 (14)	Deadlines
Item 4 (2)	WORKSHOP CONTENT
Item 5 (5)	WORKSHOP PROCESS
Item 6 (4)	Power
Item 7 (2)	Conflict
Item 8 (4)	Decision Making
Item 9 (6)	research and evaluation
Item 10 (9)	Appropriate challenging for learning relationships

Item 11 (0)   developing groups for learning
Item 12 (3)   THOUGHTS AND REFERENCES FROM JOHN B
Item 13 (10)   online dynamics
Item 14 (8)   reading
Item 15 (71)   CMMAML group development – on line exercise.
Item 16 (19)   ON LINE 'LECTURE' FOR BEST USE OF TIME
Item 17 (10)   start times at Borwick
Item 18 (3)   Oops sorry don't read this
Item 19 (0)   'dead' item
Item 20 (17)   DESIGN – DECEMBER ON
Item 21 (30)   TRAINER INTERVENTIONS
Item 22 (9)   RESPONSIBILITIES FOR/IN LEARNING
Item 23 (10)   CULTURE AND ORGANISATIONS
Item 24 (2)   PERSONAL POWER
Item 25 (7)   ETHICS AND MANAGEMENT LEARNING
Item 26 (2)   ACTION LEARNING SET
Item 27 (8)   Simone's
Item 28 (5)   CONFERENCE REPORT
Item 29 (4)   CHYFARCHION Y NADOLIG A'R FLWYDDYN
                     NEWYDD
Item 30 (25)   ANALYSING DYNAMICS OF ONLINE
                     LEARNING EVENTS
Item 31 (11)   SCHEDULING THE 'RUNNING' OF SESSIONS
Item 32 (10)   SCHEDULING OUR WANTS/NEEDS FOR THE
                     WORKSHOP
Item 33 (0)   SESSIONS: BORWICK
Item 34 (28)   Celebrating difference
Item 35 (10)   EXPLORING ASSUMPTIONS – CONTINUE
                     WHERE WE LEFT OFF?
Item 36 (29)   FROM CM1 TO CO-LEARNING/SUPPORT
                     GROUP
Item 37 (1)   cancelled
Item 38 (36)   REVIEW OF LAST WORKSHOP
Item 39 (20)   SET FORMATION AT END OF DYNAMICS
                     WORKSHOP 1
Item 40 (21)   March workshop

The Role of the Tutor Online

Conventional CMC wisdom suggests that the tutor should 'moderate' any computer conference (Brochet, 1985b; Feenberg, 1986, 1989; Kerr, 1986; Collins and Berge, 1998; Green, 1998; Rohfeld and Hiemstra, 1995; Paulsen, 1995a,b; Mason, 1991); if not the tutor, then at least it is assumed that someone has to take on the job of moderating. This orientation to the place of the tutor in a CSCL environment is however problematic in a cooperative, open learning context.

The moderator role of the tutor is built on the premise that the tutor should take control of the learning situation. From this premise follows a series of 'leadership' strategies designed to ensure that the conference achieves its stated purposes.

> In most conferences, the moderator's main function is to facilitate discussion by deciding *unilaterally* a great many procedural questions that would otherwise require prolonged and *wasteful* discussion. These questions may include such things as *when to begin discussing a topic*, when to pass to a decision and new topic... what are the *boundaries of relevance*, of emotional tone, of length or complexity of comments, and so on. The authority delegated to the facilitative moderator...' (Feenberg, 1986, emphasis added).

In open, cooperative learning contexts it would be antithetical for tutors to unilaterally decide on any procedures for the use of the medium or the way groups should conduct themselves. Although this orientation may give rise to prolonged discussions about group process, we see them as integral to the purpose of working in a CSCL environment. The process is indistinguishable from the product, and discussions about such things are not only important, they are vital to the proper conduct of the CSCL programmes and for the relationships between all members, tutors and participants alike.

Tutors and participants share responsibility for ensuring that the CSCL environment is operating to their mutual satisfaction. This is consistent with the philosophy of self-management mentioned in the previous chapter. It is usually a tutor who sets up a conference (mainly because it is technically too complex for all participants to learn to do, although several have done so), but only after discussion with participants about its purpose, and after a suitable title has been agreed (we choose conference titles that have some association with our work together, eg when one of the participants was leaving for Hong Kong to take up a new job, we called one of the new conferences 'Orient'). Once a conference is established everyone plays a part in its design – setting up items, discussing protocol, setting contracts, and so on.

In our context too, the need for 'strong leadership' (Kerr, 1986) online would be to view our role as tutor from a particular educational perspective, one which presumably is based on hierarchies and divisions between learner and teacher:

> STRONG LEADERSHIP has been shown to be required in this medium if groups are to be successful... The nature of the medium, including the different kinds of group structures that emerge and the absence of pressure to sign online and participate, create the need for strong and active leadership. The lack of

> adequate leadership is one of the factors sometimes responsible for conference failure; unless a moderator sets an agenda and keeps the group working to its goal, nothing much will occur (Kerr, 1986).

Our experience to date tells us that leadership of this kind is perhaps not necessary in CSCL contexts. If the group has a real purpose for being online and has established a sense of collective ownership of the conference, and if issues of power and control within the group are part of the group's focus and agenda, then the concept of leadership will not only be unnecessary, but it will be unhelpful. Setting agendas, and keeping work to its goals, are activities which we try to achieve democratically. This sometimes becomes difficult at the point in our online work where the group has to work towards completing its current activities. Tutors sometimes have to point out to members that there are certain deadlines that, traditionally, have to be met. But this kind of intervention sometimes leads to discussion about the design of the programme and whether deadlines are needed or in fact important.

Since we are all regular visitors to the conference, issues of information overload (Hiltz and Turoff, 1985) are less likely to be a major problem – although sometimes even an absence of a week can leave someone with a considerable amount to 'catch up' on if activity in the conference has been high. But the need for one person formally to netweave – 'summarizing the state of the discussion and finding threads of unity in the comments of other participants' (Feenberg, 1986) – on behalf of everyone else, on the grounds that participants need to be kept informed of what is happening, is not always necessary. Active participation (most people come online at least twice a week, if not more often) means we are all keeping up with what's happening in a conference. When it appears that a summary is needed, netweaving is often done 'spontaneously' by us all (see, for example, Malcolm's summary of where the group was in the assessment process mentioned above).

Some problematic areas

There are a certain number of areas where our role as tutor in a CSCL context could be said to be problematic. They are some of the dilemmas which cooperative learning tutors face, as mentioned in Chapter 4.

First, there is the question of the impact of our interventions. This is not unique to the tutors, but it does have serious implications for our formal role of supportive facilitator. Our position as tutor can carry with it a power and authority which could be abused (Freire, 1985; Giroux, 1983; Young, 1971). We are constantly confronted with the contradiction of playing the dual role of 'tutor-participant'. This is especially so in the assessment process. Any intervention we make has the likelihood of being received differently to interventions made by other participants. Our wish to remove the iniquity of unequal power relationships[2] takes some considerable time and active work – as tutors, we have to establish a sense of trust and partnership online with participants. But in this medium it is not always possible to be as aware of your interventions as you might be in a face-to-face situation. Participants may construe your intervention in an unanticipated way, perhaps reading more into what you say than you intended. There is no way of checking this out (other than constantly asking how an intervention was received, which would get in the way of discussion if done frequently, although it has to be done from time to time).

You can be aware of the ongoing 'climate' of the conference and glean some information about your position in it and how you are being 'received' and perceived. But from time to time it emerges that a tutor intervention has had some unanticipated effect. Sometimes participants confront us about the issue immediately and we are then able to discuss it (for example, issues to do with giving and receiving grades). Sometimes its effects are dormant and it is only in time, in discussion over other issues, that we become aware of its significance. This may not appear any different to what a tutor has to confront in a face-to-face situation, but online it does have a different impact on all concerned and seems in practice to be more difficult to manage. It requires self-critical awareness through dialogue with participants.

A second issue is how best to obtain a sense of being effective online. In face-to-face situations we receive information (verbal, body language, etc.) which helps tell us something about our effectiveness as a tutor. Online we can only be told (indirectly or directly) about our professional practice. If, however, we are constantly trying to develop honest, trusting and open online learning environments then we can trust our intuition at times to tell us something of our effectiveness (Polanyi, 1958, talks of such commitment saving us from mere subjectivity). Participants will 'say' something about us as tutors in the normal ongoing dialogue, and if the climate is 'correct' we will be able to 'see' ourselves in the process and make judgements about our effectiveness. However, I have found it helpful at times to set up an item about my role as tutor (the contradiction here of forcing a focus on me as tutor in an environment that tries to by-pass roles is not lost on me – although it might be seen as being no different to the individual items each participant sets up to focus on them). This has been reasonably useful and when it works well participants engage in discussion about 'me as tutor' in a meaningful way.

Third, our role as largely non-directive tutors sometimes feels compromised online. This I think has much to do with the asynchronous nature of CSCL, and with attaching meaning to silences online, and to the nature of our 'voices' online. The medium can have the effect of making what we say stand out more than we would wish. Interventions which, when made face-to-face and supported by non-verbal cues which help to present intention and other meaning beyond the verbal words we use, can only be 'said' online. This sometimes strips the intervention of its richness, so that a comment intended to be non-directive is sometimes 'heard' as direction.

Interpreting a silence online is difficult. With the Caucus conferencing system, everyone can check when anyone else was last online. If someone is frequently online but silent, or if they are online but only silent in particular conferences or items, we can assume that they have actively chosen to be silent, so any intervention on our part to draw attention to their silence may well be seen as directing them in an unhelpful way. This is of course a conundrum for a tutor. But if the conference participants are being supportive of each other then it is likely that one of them will offer a way back into the discussion for the silent partner before a tutor has to. Being open and 'able to talk' about one's silences doesn't always come easy in this medium.

The Experience of CSCL

It is beyond the scope of this chapter to discuss in detail the experiences of tutors and learners in CSCL. This is an important issue though, and one which we are currently researching (see eg McConnell *et al.*, 1996; Collaborative Group Work, 1998).

Sifting through many CSCL discussions has produced the following largely unsolicited comments about various aspects of learning using CSCL. A content analysis has produced the following general headings under which the comments can be placed:

- feedback and assessment
- online talk
- intimacy and emotion
- learning through CM MAML
- the medium
- tutor experience.

Feedback and Assessment

'For me, online assessment has been, is, one of the most stimulating aspects of the programme. There seems to be more scope online, compared to the traditional PT MAML (from what I've heard), for exploring the meaning, legitimacy of assessment criteria which can provoke quite deep and protracted self examination.'

'Online assessment can be very full, rich, time-consuming, and when it comes to marking very confusing... In one of our conferences we spent vast amounts of time grappling with the criteria for marks – that was interesting, but on reflection the struggle to agree marks may have been an alternative to much deeper exploration of our papers. My impression is that the depth of discussion about our papers has been much greater through CM than would be likely, maybe even possible through face-to-face.'

'I also find it much easier to cut through the dross and the bull online. It's much easier to focus on the content of what you're assessing and less on the body language of traditional face-to-face meetings. It can also be hard, and frustrating too in making it a more functional approach.'

'I'm conscious of having four dissertations on my table at home and having read them all this weekend (again). I somehow feel more able to deal with the assessment aspect of my/our work, than on previous occasions in the programme. I guess this reinforces some of my perception of 'learning by doing' and I find some of my anxiety eroding.'

'I think that for me, there's something about trying to ensure I give everyone feedback on what I think about their work. I'd like to do it so's I'm also commenting on what others have said. But it's difficult for me to do that online when I've been working, initially anyway, from their work in isolation, and then uploading a file of comment. To refer to others means I either have to refer to printouts of people's responses *and* the piece of work, so that I'm preparing my response from several documents perhaps, or I have to remember what others have said. It's the sheer difficulty of trying to do all that, that for the moment defeats me.'

'In my more brutal moments of introspection I know that often I achieve less than I can, from laziness. I know that I judge – and I need to work hard to judge what I do/don't do, rather than myself. When I enable I illuminate, I explore and celebrate, and when I disable I make judgements using the clumsy model of right and wrong. I value my perception that formative assessment, conducted collaboratively, and for the purposes of celebration and illumination is a more positive enabling process than summative, anthority-led assessment.'

'Greg – Your comments I find similarly helpful. What I found with both your comments on my p.e. (project essay) and on my seminar paper ... is that sometimes you're really looking at something in entirely different ways from me. It's like having light thrown from a different angle so that something new and previously hidden to me is illuminated – it's great!'

'I guess my view is similar to yours Cathy – I love the assessment process and in some cases have achieved (for myself) learning as powerful, maybe more so, than the preparation and writing bits.'

Online Talk

'What I like about this medium is that I can take for ever to answer a question!'

'I'd like to continue cm-ing. I found online talk invaluable as help in thinking through MA work... My MA work was very much about me in my work anyway.'

'I do wonder if it is the continuous discussion that has made writing more difficult. To some extent, debating the issues online is very interesting and has widened the issues considerably... they have affected all our approaches to the hard part of writing!'

'Having to talk through my ideas online with learning set colleagues provided the means for me to clarify my thoughts and set my inner dialogue to rest. Online discussion provided challenge, support and validation for my ideas, thoughts and intuition in an environment in which I have come to feel safe, if not always comfortable.'

'What I've found is that I find it hard to have a dialogue online. I enjoyed the afternoon we had on campus looking at grids... that kind of sparking off each other I find exciting... still waiting for real sparks online, but perhaps the time-lags mean this is not possible????? I do enjoy the support, though, knowing you are all out there somewhere...'

'I have had the opportunity to talk with my learning set at any time convenient to me and with no expensive and tiring travelling around the country. When in networking groups with colleagues from far and wide, I find myself wishing that they too had the technology available. When I have such meetings I also realise the value for me of CM 'chat'. If I don't feel I know the colleagues I'm meeting with particularly well, I tend to find that that feeling of a shared purpose, which I find valuable, is in danger of evaporating too soon when we've gone our separate ways. Whereas I can meet online with CM colleagues more easily.'

'I find it is not easy for me to get excited over the written word, which tends to be... too unspontaneous, trimmed down, reasonable, etc. This (online discussions) is a kind of middle road, ie more spontaneous than an essay (I'm making it up as I go), less so than face-to-face – for me. I find it easier to make synergy face-to-face – to pick up and communicate excitement. Re what Claire says, we don't talk much online about pain, confusion, etc. Is there a gender issue here? The other thing about online communications is it is in short bits. As opposed to a two hour talk! face-to-face.'

'Since joining this programme, ALMOST A YEAR AGO, I have been mindful of how the computer medium is helpful is assisting my communication. I like not having to be spontaneous... Your input helps me focus on the notion that I'm probably learning to respond in real time with the same qualitative essence that reflective responses affords me when I make appropriate use of this medium. Being less spontaneous!!! In order that I can say more about what I really mean. Curious.'

'I am also aware of how this... medium helps me expand the range of my thinking. You make a statement, someone responds, I have time to reflect on both and then respond, and so on. Again, I'm delighted with the potential of the medium, and with myself for taking the risk to choose a programme based on CM conferencing!'

'Hazel – I've been thinking about the question you flagged up about how do I impact on myself, and I must admit I'm finding it difficult to answer. Because everytime I think I have the answer I find myself thinking, 'No that's what someone else thinks.' So I'm finding myself going round and round in circles. Maybe it is also to do with this medium – somehow finding it difficult to say something – because of its permanency. I try now to respond immediately (rather than print it out then respond). Why do I do that? Because I find I am more genuine when I respond immediately – even if that means sitting here contemplating the screen for a while! However, sometimes, when I do respond I find myself reading it and then wondering how others will react to what I have written.'

'The nature of the discussions (which have been extensive at times) have seemed of an authentic dialogical nature – it felt as though we had a mutual interest in what we discussed. So for me it seems like a pretty rounded experience which I'd like to think had something to do with the skills and authenticity of the tutors. I'd like to stress the importance of that authenticity...'

'I have often wondered if it was "worth" accessing Lancaster. Asking myself if anyone else has been online since I last logged-in. However, when analysing this line of thought, I realised what I was doing was expecting someone else to do the "leaving of messages", when I should have taken equal responsibility for leaving messages for others. I was responding to messages, but not necessarily being proactive in starting a line of communication...'

'The actual online communication – it really worked for me. I found myself able to develop relationships, to share intimate information, and to experience empathy. I feel that CMC helped me to improve my relationship skills. I can think of dialogues which seemed possible online, which seemed not so when I encountered those individuals face-to-face. I developed a real liking for communicating online, to the extent that it would without question be my preferred way of working with people in the MAML community. I liked the opportunity to be reflective, I enjoyed the safety of not having to be in 'real time'. I seemed to experience all the richness of face-to-face communication, without some of the risks. My sense of online communication is that of having the opportunity to communicate without a lot of the extraneous 'noise' I associate with face-to-face communication.'

'Working online was not a standard experience, and seems to be influenced by myself and my frame of mind, by my co-workers, and by our interpersonal process.'

Intimacy and Emotion

'Online we put a lot of stuff in there that others might see as very intimate. In fact it almost frees me up to talk about stuff like that on the computer, rather than, maybe I do it more on the computer than I do face-to-face.'

'Reading what you're saying makes this feel extremely personal in a way that I have never experienced before. It felt strange to be hugged via computer – but it was as if I actually felt that... Thank you.'

'I read with horror your experiences with the Board and felt for you. I have been there with senior managers in a couple of Departments and I didn't like that one bit. I wanted to say how I had coped but considered the online as being a poor medium. I saw that you were struck by the intimacy of Caucus but I felt I wanted more, I wanted to be closer – and as a result wrote nothing! If the moment has not passed and if it would help, I am happy to get together if you would like to talk face-to-face.'

'The medium is superb. Really warm and comfortable. My problem in recent weeks has been 'time', ie lack of it. I hope that the next few weeks will see things ease up back at the ranch.'

'I've been offline for a couple of days, largely due to computer link problems... I have found this very annoying – I really DO like to log on each evening to see what's happening, hear from my friends and colleagues, and drop an odd note... I obviously need to feel that you are "there", and call in to establish this contact. I suppose that's why this feels quite a warm medium to me, in that it helps me to feel part of the human race, and that I'm one of a group.'

'The effect of bringing the screenful of participants into the home... I recall Mag talking about some issues re Brian's (*her partner*) reactions to what pops up on the screen. Others have also talked of their partners feelings towards their relationship to the screenful of friends... there is a group of friends on Caucus from whom Geraldine (*his wife*) is excluded, feels jealous and excluded and negative about the whole process in which I'm engaged. If I was on normal pt MAML these feelings may never surface or at least the MAML activity would be compartmentalised and much more invisible rather than visible but obscure. It's like continuously having a private party in the house to which Geraldine is not invited, or at least feels she can't join in.'

'So were my emotions aroused online? Yes, they were. It was not the cold clinical medium of communication I might have perceived prior to the programme. At times, particularly late at night, when the house was quiet, there was a beautiful silence being online, save for the quiet purring of the computer. That gave me a feeling of peace and contentment. I was able to reflect and think.'

Learning through CM MAML

'I am by nature a reflective person... and I do think that MAML has encouraged me to become more so cos it's helped me to understand that through reflection I can still get into practicalities, ie that one enables the other. Pre-MAML, I think I tended to see my reflectiveness as stopping there and going no further, if all that makes sense!'

'The real impact for me has been in the sense of liberation. There have been times when I felt that MAML was designed to order, for me. Like a party in my celebration. Until MAML I didn't know what to do with all this 'rebellious subjectivity' and I guess I was in an anti-authoritarian hole. Finding new ways of working has been a delight – especially workshops and online peer group assessment. I punish myself less now and feel more flexible.'

'Well I have just read this item with great joy – to hear of your experiences of MAML, which echo some of my hopes for it, and also a thrill at hearing Robert describe being in the large group on MAML as "doing philosophy". I had never thought of that, but it makes absolute sense to me and captures the eternal struggles I find myself in there! Reading what has gone before I feel more and more that the programme should not have a pre-determined focus, but that this should emerge (as it does anyway) through collective self-management. I have always been concerned with the term self-management because of its individualistic implications, and so find collective self-management much more appealing.'

'I feel the programme has done something like give me more self-confidence in my thought processes, so that I am more inclined to question and recognise assumptions than I felt I was previously. It's something about working with people (all of you) for whom this is seen as an ok activity and something worth doing. At work, for me, it isn't often seen/experienced by me as ok. Working with all of you feels like a unique experience from that point of view. I am making an assumption that not all other programmes would feel as free as MAML does in this way – it's primarily its self-managed nature I think...'

'It's felt like an amazing experience – being able to switch on the computer and find messages for me, discussions going on, etc. I've loved it. The CM aspect has also helped me clarify my thoughts and their expression. I try to do this in face-to-face communication, but I think the fact that I'm putting something online, usually for several people to see and which will stay there, has made me think twice about what exactly I do want to say... In this way, I feel that I have become more analytical...'

'Since starting the programme I seem to have developed much more of a motivation to learn for its own sake and the sake of my own interest, and that I see as being a massive change/development from my original motivation... I'm also wondering if part of the nature of the conflicts of individuals and organisations in the learning process lies somewhere in the process of determining WHAT is to be learnt and the values that underpin how the WHAT is decided upon?'

'I think we should try hard to see MAML for what it is, a brilliant knowledge-based programme.'

'Yeah, you're right, I do feel constrained by my organisation as I've come to realise what a liberating experience CM MAML has been for me.'

'Jack and Sandra – can I first say thanks for sharing some of your reflections about MAML – I can identify with them very much. I share most particularly the issues of confusion and uncertainty – yet I think I'm pretty clear that I don't regard it all as disabling. For me making some kind of shift from seeing the 'external' world as the arbiter of my worth to being more self-accepting and creating is very potent. It has also enabled a much more accepting view of others' values and differences. I feel bloody good about that and MAML has been worth it for that alone – but I also see MAML as the start of something rather than an abstracted and bounded two-year 'event'. I carry my MAML experience forward with me with a new sense of a world of possibilities. And yes, one of those is some kind of continuation of CM conferencing. Anyone for a CM PhD?'

'One of the things that has struck me about myself since CM MAML formally came to a close is how much it has done for me in terms of my personal development. I think it's fairly safe to say that I haven't person-ally ever felt so intellectually alive. I don't mean that in a capricious or arrogant sense but in a sense of understanding how I see the world and how little I know of it… a response to our coming together and the effect that we had on each other. I feel much more able to understand things and to be in control if you like. This is important for me in as much that I used to defer to others all the time or look for ways in which I could win. Neither do I have an in-built resistance to change even when the change does not appear favourable.'

'For me the smallness of our group has advantages when online as I can really keep track of what people are saying and the various trains of thought, something I lost on 'learnco' *(another, larger online group)* when all sorts of people were dipping in and saying things.'

'It was while working on the computer at Lancaster I suddenly saw the real potential of the CM aspects of the programme. I could 'talk' to the other participants without leaving the house – at any time that suited me. For me, this opened up all sorts of possibilities, which before I had not fully explored. Up until that point I had only seen the CM communica-tion as being of an academic and theoretical nature – that is I saw its primary purpose as to discuss seminar papers, projects or theoretical issues. Some of this line of thinking was, I believe, due to my under-standing of the terms theory and academic… Now I could see it could be a chat line, a help line and a support line. Being a little less fearful of the academic aspects of the programme, the idea of CM communication suddenly seemed friendly and useful.'

'The MA has given me an appetite for learning and exploring which is precious and new to me. I've experienced it engaging the whole me in learning – not just my intellect. This is about my own experience of an MA course, which has quite simply, changed my life (for the better)!'

The Medium

'The constraints are such things as time and telephone bill. For me it has been some of the best communication for quite some time. Oh to have been Caucusing for many years. What it may have led to in the way of thinking, reading and growth!... such stimulating dialogue.'

'It has been so stimulating... Caucus is still appallingly time-consuming. Not just the practicalities of it, but reading and reflecting. Then I think about the time lapse, have things moved on so that what I want to say is no longer relevant. But this has not proved so in practice curiously... E-mail was never mind-blowing like this.'

'I feel wildly enthusiastic about using Caucus in the group learning situation for personal development work – especially as it has evoked such strong and varied feelings in this course... I think the slowness of communication over this medium is a big plus – it really forces one to slow down and become more aware of what one is saying... the record of what has been said is another big plus – changes in one's style of response (and attitude behind it) are made visible by re-reading conference entries.'

'Like you Stephen, if I've met someone face-to-face then I do feel that that affects my online discussion with them in a way that I think it doesn't if I haven't met them. I'm aware that I feel my prejudices less easily get in the way online, if I haven't met the person I'm talking to. I find it a very enabling medium from that point of view.'

'Jack – What I THINK I mean is, what I get from talking with anyone through Caucus whom I've not met, is not any picture at all of them physically, but a sort of jigsaw of their 'mindset' – of the way (or just a miniscule part I guess), of how they might view life... What I feel is that in everyday face-to-face interaction, I'm trying to do similarly... and maybe their sex or physical appearance triggers off some assumptions and/or prejudices in me, which won't come across in Caucus. However, I still think similar reactions can be triggered (in me anyway), by what people choose to say online and how they say it...'

'To return to the CM-ing... I've felt that this has allowed me access to more ideas, people and conversations than I might have found on a "conventional" programme.'

'I feel much happier about using the computer. In fact I want to go straight home and use it. I feel great optimism that it will bring a whole new dimension to my life.'

'The online process... was one of the delights of the programme, both as an aid to reflection, and also as an aid to collaborative, holistic working – the CMC medium helped me sense the MAML experience as an integrated part of my life, rather than as a part-time programme, requiring chunks of my diary, in competition with other activities.'

'This (medium) has given me much needed and welcome support throughout the course. Not only with the academic aspects of my work, but a more personal support through the process of completing the MA. The CM aspect has similarly given me the opportunity to offer the same to others via the curious intimacy I have experienced in using CM communication.'

Tutor Experience

'One of the best things that has happened for me on CM MAML is that we have actually got a sub-task group designing the next workshop using the computer conference to do so...'

'A big plus is the contact with the rest of the community. It enables dialogue about planning and workshops and so on.'

'I'm enjoying being directive, for example facilitating Moira (a participant) in making her choice about her project essay. That felt good and I wouldn't want to deny being able to do that.'

'And that takes us back to the tutor role... I took a firmer line on my first set and forced them effectively to close about two months after the workshop.'

'My model of tutoring as "digging in" is perhaps more suited to CM MAML.'

'I have a sense of what I'm trying to to in face-to-face tutorials... and I feel that, for better or worse, I've got an approach which I feel fairly comfortable with... within CM MAML I'm wondering whether I can do that effectively in this medium.' *(Tutor in early stages of using CSCL.)*

'Wanting not to be discouraging... to get the balance between support and critique... difficult to feel that I was getting that balance right when not face-to-face.'

'I feel more directive now – both feel obliged to be the one to respond, and want to respond.' *(Tutor in early stages of using CSCL.)*

Conclusion

This chapter is an attempt to indicate, by reference to a particular setting and educational context, some of the issues relating to the use of CSCL in higher education, and in training and development settings. CSCL can support open, cooperative learning. It offers learners an environment in which to structure their learning in a way which supports cooperative group work. Of course, without an underlying educational philosophy which emphasises the importance of cooperation, no CSCL system will in itself be effective. CSCL media only offer an environment for such activities. It is the people using them that have to believe in the activities and ensure that they occur.

This leads us into the issue of the purpose and nature of learning in CSCL environments. Cooperative learning is a central value in CSCL. The architecture of CSCL media assumes groupwork. Yet much learning in higher education is done in isolation, with minimal reference to other learners. Teachers and administrators in higher education will have to reconsider much of their educational practice if they wish to use CSCL successfully.

As it is, it is difficult to judge the claims of success being made about CSCL media. Making judgements about the conduct of professional practice and learning in CSCL environments presents us with a new arena for discussions about professional practice generally. The issues are complex – whose reality are we talking about, and what social (and research) standards do we apply to the process of making sense of our claims to 'knowing' and to the development of educational knowledge?[3]

By approaching issues of professional development from a critical perspective, and working out of a theory of professionalism which is based on such questions as 'How do I improve the process of education here?' (Whitehead, 1989), I believe we have a way forward. Otherwise, how will we know if claims often made about the educational benefits of CSCL are not mere rhetoric rather than the outcome of analyses grounded in the realities of those involved?

Notes

1. These extracts are taken from the computer conferences. I have left them largely unedited, but occasionally some minor editing was needed for clarification. Throughout them I have used pseudonyms to maintain the anonymity of persons and organisations.
2. Of course, we have to acknowledge that tutors do have some special roles to play in all of this. They are the representatives of the University, and have a privileged position in relation to knowing about the rules and regulations of the institution. On our programme, the role of the tutor is always a major source of discussion with participants. We work at helping participants (and ourselves) understand the nature of 'the tutor' on a cooperative, open learning programme such as this one.
3. See the following for discussion of such research issues: Lincoln and Guba, 1985; Reason and Rowan, 1981; Whitehead, 1989.

7 | Trends and Developments

Introduction

This chapter is rather more wide-ranging than previous ones. In it, I attempt to make the link between some recent developments in new information and communication technologies (ICT) for learning and their possible use in cooperative learning situations. Advanced learning technologies and electronic networks are becoming established 'tools' and methods of communication in many areas of higher education (see eg Mason and Kaye, 1989; Mason, 1989a; McConnell, 1990; Harasim, 1993; Harasim *et al.*, 1995; Verdejo, 1994; Collis, 1996; Banks, Graebner and McConnell, 1998). Although their use for *computer supported cooperative learning* may not always be very significant, the technological infrastructure needed to support cooperative learning is in place. What might be lacking is an understanding of the educational and training benefits of CSCL, and an awareness of how to implement cooperative learning strategies using these new technologies.

In the following, I will describe some recent developments in the use of information and communication technologies, particularly those systems which are distributed throughout learning organisations by means of local area networks, or which are distributed beyond these institutions by means of wide area networks, such as the Internet. These systems are significant applications of ICT. Some of them are well documented and therefore open to in-depth public scrutiny. Some are being trialled in 'cutting edge' projects, but which are significant for their approach to the use of ICT for cooperative learning.

My purpose here is not to be comprehensive nor to try and cover all new ICT initiatives, but rather to point to some important concepts, projects and applications from which we can learn something about the use of ICT in cooperative learning. The concepts, systems and projects discussed are:

- networked learning
- the ITOL (information technology-based open learning) model

- just in time open learning (JITOL)
- models for European collaboration and pedagogy in open learning (MECPOL) Project
- portable PCs for students
- teleteaching generally.

Networked Lifelong Learning

The emergence of the information society is confronting all education sectors with profound changes. The convergence of information technology with communication technology for the purposes of education and training, known as Networked Learning, creates opportunities for people to learn and communicate with each other in new and flexible ways. At the same time, networked learning is:

- changing the way in which traditional face-to-face, institution-based and distance learning is delivered
- giving rise to new ideas about access to learning and the nature of communities
- beginning to impact on training and development in organisations
- enabling the UK education sectors to reach global markets
- creating online organisations such as virtual universities.

However, the emphasis to date has been on technology rather than on how technology can facilitate learning, particularly through learner-centred and collaborative approaches and the development of skills. The pace of change means that, although the innovative potential of networked learning is still unfolding, the education and training sectors are already having to make complex decisions about implementation and the commitment of resources.

What is Networked Learning?

Many terms are emerging to describe the use of electronic communications and the Internet in education and training. My preference is for 'networked learning', since it places the emphasis on networking people and resources together; and on collaboration as the major form of social relationship within a learning context. The emphasis is emphatically on 'learning', and not on the technology.

We are experiencing a paradigm shift in our thinking about learning. This is occurring at various levels. For example, there is a shift from conventional, second generation distance learning towards virtual distance learning. Face-to-face teaching and learning on campus is now also incorporating some forms of networked learning, freeing staff and learners to work at times which suit them and to use resources, and methods of working together, that were not possible a few years ago. 'Distance' in learning is no longer the issue that it once was: the paradigm of networked learning shifts the emphasis from geographical separation of learners to the ways in which we can 'network' learners together, whether they happen to be on-campus or off-campus, in the same country or situated anywhere in the world.

Learning how to work with the technology and take advantage of networking in learning are the key issues.

In the UK, the Dearing Report of July 1997 (the most important policy document on Higher Education in the UK since 1963) emphasised that communications and information technology (C&IT) will play a very important role in the future of higher education. A National Institute for Learning and Teaching in Higher Education is being set up which will be concerned with professional development, especially in the delivery of online learning.

> For a full and successful integration into learning to take place, staff need to be effective practitioners and skilled in the management of students' learning through C&IT.

> For the majority of students, over the next ten years the delivery of some course materials and much of the organisation and communication of course arrangements will be conducted by computer (Dearing Report, 1997).

This suggests that we are going through a fundamental shift in our thinking about teaching and learning: a paradigm shift from 'conventional' on-campus and off-campus (distance) learning to networked learning.

In 1998, my colleagues Sheena Banks and Celia Graebner and myself, within the Centre for the Study of Networked Learning at Sheffield University, organised the first international conference on 'Networked Lifelong Learning'. The main objective of the conference was to link research and knowledge about networked learning with implementation and current practice, in order to achieve maximum benefit for all parties through collaboration on the dissemination of good professional practice, sound pedagogy and guidelines for quality assurance.

The conference looked at both the theory and practice of networked lifelong learning in relation to:

- the paradigm shift from traditional learning to distributed and distance learning
- internet technologies in learning
- innovation and implementation
- in-house and organisational training and development.

The conference was designed to bring together managers, teachers, lecturers, trainers and researchers from all sectors.

The papers presented at the conference (Banks, Graebner and McConnell, 1998) were highly varied and represented current thinking and practice in the field.[1] They show a cross-section of approaches to networked lifelong learning, from both a research perspective and a professional practice perspective. Several trends are emerging in the practice of networked lifelong learning, and from an analysis of the conference proceedings, some tentative propositions can be made about the educational potential of networked learning.

- Networked learning has a focus on student-to-student collaboration, where students use the technology to learn from and with each other.
- Students sometimes have difficulty adjusting to these new forms of learning. They are required to move away from an expectation of individualism and competition in their learning towards an expectation of sharing, cooperation and collaboration.
- There is a major focus on constructivist forms of learning, ie an approach to learning that suggests that students construct meaning for themselves from engagement, experience and 'making sense' of their struggle to learn.
- Sharing of resources, ideas and experience is central to networked learning.
- There is a greater degree of openness in the learning process, between the teacher and students, and between students themselves.
- Computer-mediated communications can be used to effectively support online discussions.
- Existing learning resources can be integrated into networked learning environments. New learning resources developed and produced by students themselves as part of their learning can also be incorporated.
- In networked learning environments, there is great importance in developing *communities* of learners.
- The Internet and the Web offer rich areas for finding, retaining and using resources useful for learning.

● Collaborative forms of learning reduce the 'authority' of electronic and other forms of publications, by encouraging students to develop and share their own situated knowledge and learning resources.

Information Technology-based Open Learning (ITOL)

ITOL was a research project funded by the UK Training Agency (Department of Employment) which looked into the feasibility of providing electronically mediated open learning provision (Hodgson, Lewis and McConnell, 1989). The ITOL model is still highly relevant today as a significant conceptual framework for considering ICT based distance learning.

The stated aim of the study was:

> to improve the flexibility and responsiveness of vocational education and training provision in Great Britain through producing a plan for the creation of information technology based open learning provision alongside established practices in existing universities.

The project set out to examine how universities could capitalise upon recent thinking about, and advances in, new technology and open learning in order that they could become more flexible and responsive in their vocational education and training provision (ITOL gave rise to JITOL – Just in Time Open Learning – which is a major EC/Delta funded project).

The specific objective of the study was to develop a model of information technology based open learning (which came to be termed ITOL) that was feasible and could be implemented immediately. The model would define how we could employ desk-top computers, modern communications technology and online educational computing in the provision of up-to-date, relevant and supportive forms of open learning for people geographically distant from each other and from the university.

Although the ITOL model was initially developed for supporting distant learners with professional backgrounds, we always had in mind the wider application of ITOL for all levels of post-compulsory education and we believe ITOL is as applicable to these areas as it is to professional training and development.

Benefits to Learners

In working towards the objectives of the project, we kept in mind the needs of client users. From the perspective of the user of the system, there are certain advantages to be gained from taking advantage of this information technology-based ('online') form of open learning.

Time and Space Barriers are Removed
Typical ITOL learners are undergraduate and postgraduate people, and professional people at graduate level employment. With increases in student numbers in the further and higher education sector, access to resources (people resources such as tutors, and other textual and graphical resources) is becoming a major concern. Large classes and lecture-only teaching methods are not always the most appropriate way to learn. With professional people there are perhaps different concerns. Professional people are hard pressed to take time off work to go on residential updating and professional development courses, which can often last between one to five days, and which usually require travel to a distant site.

ITOL would offer an alternative to this. Learners could take part in their studies without the disadvantages of mass lecture teaching. Professional people could take advantage of development activities, without having to leave their workplace. All that is needed is a desktop computer and access to a local area network or a modem linked to the public telephone system. This will link them to ITOL. The flexibility of ITOL would permit them to learn at times and places convenient to themselves – ITOL would be there 24 hours a day, seven days a week all year round, without the need to travel to face-to-face meetings.

Learning Barriers are Removed
A common criticism of current educational and training systems made by participants is that they do not cater for their particular learning needs. The educational philosophy underpinning ITOL is one that works towards allowing the learner to define his or her own learning and personal development needs, with the ITOL system offering ways of reaching these self defined needs. This is achieved through a process of negotiation, collaboration and cooperation between the ITOL learner, the ITOL tutor and the ITOL resources. So ITOL could help overcome the problems of participating in courses which are too general for a learner's specific needs and goals.

This is not to suggest that ITOL can be a panacea for all higher educational and professional development needs. There will always be an important place for face-to-face classes, and for residential courses for professionals. But ITOL can offer an alternative to what are often seen as restrictive methods of education and professional development provision. ITOL will not supplant existing provision, rather, it will supplement and add to it.

Open Learning

From the inception of the project we sought to develop an ITOL model which takes a different and hopefully innovative approach to distant, open education.

As T R Morrison points out in a paper on the potential impact of information technology in the role of higher education in society:

> Some distance educators have become so wedded to particular concepts of distance education, and the belief system that it engenders, that they have become the 'new traditionalists' in an innovative field (Morrison, 1989).

He goes on to say:

> At this point in time distance education needs to be understood for what it is: a technique to overcome primarily, spacial barriers to learning. It is not, in its current stage of development, a process which overcomes cultural, economic and educational barriers to learning.
>
> If it is to fulfil this wider mission, distance education needs to recast conceptually within the broader and more normative concept of an open-learning system (Morrison, *op cit.*).

To claim that we hoped, in developing a model of ITOL, to overcome cultural, economic and educational barriers to learning would not be wholly true. We were not, however, unmindful or unsympathetic to such views as Morrison's, and we did want the model to reflect an open learning educational philosophy. That is, we wanted it to be learner-centred, where learners not only have freedom of choice but also the opportunity and power to exercise that choice and to control and be responsible for their own learning development.

The ITOL Audience

The long-term aim and vision of ITOL is to have an information technology based provision which is widely available and accessible to individuals in further and higher education, and from the whole range of professional and vocational occupational areas. The intention would be for anyone to have access to the necessary guidance, support and resources they require to enable them to pursue their individual learning programme or project.

In the research to develop a model of ITOL we looked particularly at:

a.   the suitability of available (and future) technology and the kind of resources it can give access to
b.   what, in practice, an ITOL type provision might look like.

A model for ITOL developed out of this work that we believe is feasible and educationally viable and beneficial.

The outline of the ITOL model is shown in Figure 7.1. Fundamentally, it allows any individual learner to communicate with a tutor or tutors, or facilitator(s) (most likely university based people, but not exclusively), with other learners and with a series or collection of both university and non-university based resources. In addition, the learner may have available to him or her a counsellor. Finally, as depicted in Figure 7.1, there is a university based resource manager with whom the learner can also communicate.

The ITOL Model in Detail

The ITOL model includes objects and actors within a bounded ITOL system, and similar components outside this bounded system. The bounded system is that large portion of ITOL which is developed and made available by the host ITOL institution. This contains the resources

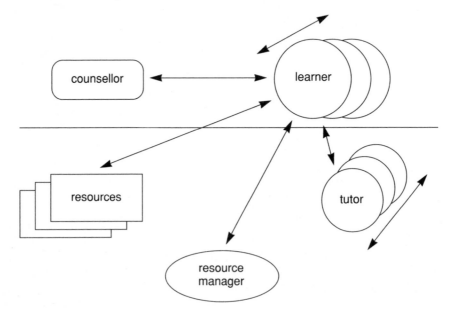

Figure 7.1   *The ITOL model*

available for learner use and the electronic mechanisms for accessing these resources.

Outside this are other resources made available by other institutions and agencies, some of which can be accessed via gateways at the host ITOL system, and others which can only be made available by the institutions or agencies concerned. There may be information on the host ITOL system about resources offered by others, but learners would have to make contact with these institutions or agencies themselves in order to avail themselves of these resources. For example, the ITOL databases may contain information about courses available at other institutions. The learner would have to contact these institutions direct if he or she wished to enrol on one of their courses.

Objects and Actors
The various objects and actors in the ITOL model are as follows.

Learner
The learner is the person who wishes to use ITOL. They may wish to use ITOL for a variety of educational or professional development reasons. For example, students enrolled on self-managed learning courses or other courses where they have considerable freedom in choosing what and how to study could use ITOL. Professional people wishing to tackle some new work-related task, further their own personal development or enhance their career prospects could use ITOL. The learner's needs may be defined by themselves, by the requirements of a formal course offered by the institution or by the needs of their employing company or some other external source.

The learner would need information about the purpose of the system, its scope (the degree to which it covers areas of concern to them in their learning), how to access it via the local area network or public telecommunications system, and how to navigate through it (including details of information resources, communicating with tutors and other learners, requesting further information and delivery of resources, and so on). The learner would also need considerable support from the system itself, eg by way of online help (human) advisers and software.

Each learner would require the use of a workstation to access and use the ITOL system. The basic requirements for a workstation are a stand-alone personal computer with good internal memory and fixed hard disk storage capacity (eg 40 megabytes or higher); good resolution monitor; keyboard and mouse device; suitable text processing and communications software; printer; and modem.

Tutor

Tutors are normally academics or other subject specialists who will help the learners with their learning. Depending on the purpose of the learning event, tutors adopt different roles to accommodate the different requirements of the learners or the course profile. The tutor would not necessarily take on the traditional role of 'leading' the learner in an exploration of the subject matter. They act as a resource to be called upon by the learner when necessary. The relationship between the learner and the tutor is one of professional partnership and cooperation, not teacher and taught. The tutor establishes friendly contact with the learner and helps them think through their issues of concern.

For example, when so requested, tutors may help learners find their way through the various resource materials in order to help them resolve the problems or issues which they wish to address. They may answer queries and questions concerning learners' work and professional development, and generally take part in on-going electronic discussions with learners. They may lead or take part in computer conferences (electronic seminars, tutorials or group discussions) dealing with whatever issues have emerged from the various discussions with individual learners. The purpose of this relationship is to try and meet as many of the needs of the learner as possible, by a variety of methods and resources.

In order to achieve this, tutors require professional development in the use and purposes of ITOL. The role of an online (electronic) tutor has much in common with the more traditional, face-to-face tutoring activities. However, the ITOL medium will be new and strange to most tutors, and it cannot be expected that they will immediately see how to transfer their normal professional activities to the medium without some form of briefing and training in the scope, purposes and uses of the system. Implicit in this will be a need to explore with them the nature of the 'open', cooperative educational philosophy underpinning the ITOL system.

It is likely that after any initial briefing and training, tutors will require on-going support in the educational uses of ITOL. This might best be achieved by perceiving the professional development of the tutors as a form of educational action research which is on-going and developmental, with spirals of learning activities emerging from considered and reflective analysis of their professional ITOL practice.

Each tutor requires the use of an 'ITOL' workstation, as described above for learners.

Counsellor

The ITOL counsellor fulfils the need to have access to someone who can offer assistance in planning a learning programme and counsel learners once they have embarked on their work. In situations where learners are participating in ITOL for company benefits, the needs of the company will have to be taken into account.

Many professional people will be sponsored by their company and will be working towards meeting the needs of their company as much as their own needs. It is likely in situations like this that a company counsellor will liaise with the learner and those running ITOL. The counsellor will be in a supportive role to the learner, helping him or her in their quest for self and professional development.

Resources

The resources available on the ITOL system are largely defined by the domains of application. These include the following forms of resources.

- Resources specially developed and made available by the institution of higher education running ITOL. For example: online addresses and phone numbers of relevant experts (tutors, etc); online addresses and phone numbers of people with similar needs and interests; references to useful textbooks, or sections thereof; references to recent review articles; details of existing and upcoming courses; access to relevant databases; access to electronic tutoring packages; access to electronically browsable texts; and access to pictorial information and video sequences.

  Access to some of these is possible at the moment (eg it is easy to access online databases, electronic tutoring packages and so forth on the Web). Access to others will be possible in the near future (eg video sequences will be accessible when digital telecom lines are widely available). Where learners cannot access the appropriate resource direct, it is possible for them to receive copies on CD ROM.

- Resources offered online by other institutions, and/or agencies which can be accessed via a gateway at the host ITOL institution. Additionally, learners and tutors can access all the human and other resources available on the Internet.

- Human resources in the form of online tutors and other ITOL learners. In addition to the various resource databases and gateways available to ITOL learners, there is a sophisticated interactive electronic mail and computer conferencing system at the core of ITOL. This facilitates communications between ITOL learners and tutors, allowing them to treat each other as a learning resource. The collective intelligence, knowledge and experience of ITOL users is a natural and highly important organic learning resource.

- Other resources not specifically made available by the ITOL host, but available elsewhere, might include video sequences (eg tutored video instruction); tape slide sequences; audio tapes; computer software applications; and so on. These would be made available in resource centres or through the post at the request of the learner.

Resource Manager

The resource manager is the person who mediates between those making decisions about the resources to be made available on the system, and actually putting them onto the system for learner access. This person maintains records of resources and updates and adds to them when necessary.

In addition to the Resource Manager, a systems manager and technical adviser to learners and tutors is needed. The system manager oversees the whole ITOL system and its effective and efficient running. The technical adviser deals with problems and difficulties associated with accessing the system and using its various facilities. Technical advice may be given by a variety of methods, eg by voice telephone or e-mail, depending on the nature of the query.

The Evolution of ITOL: Just in Time Open Learning (JITOL)

This is a European Union DELTA Programme-funded project which has its origins in the ITOL model discussed above. JITOL is a project based on a view of learning which might be described as self-directed open learning at a distance using information technologies for the professional and personal development of individuals (Hodgson, Lewis and McConnell, 1989; NL/192, 1992; Gardiol, Boder and Peraya, 1993).

Central to the JITOL philosophy is the belief that learners have expertise and experiences – a form of knowledge not usually used or formalised in training programmes.

One way to conceptualise this draws on the classic notion of the 'zone of proximal development' attributed to the Russian psychologist Vygotsky. One considers that the knowledge of an individual has a central core which is 'owned' by the individual who is able to use that knowledge in the autonomous performance of tasks. Surrounding the core is a region (the zone of proximal development – zoped) in which the individual has some knowledge, but needs help in performing tasks which depend upon that knowledge. The process of learning takes place as the individual extends their core knowledge to encompass an increasing amount of the peripheral region. This may happen as a result of intentional learning either through experience or using more formal, conventional methods; in either case other humans (tutors or peers) can play an important supportive role.

Of great interest in professional learning is the case in which an occupational group is working together to solve work-based problems. [In] the collective knowledge of the community... the zoped area of one member [overlaps] core areas of others. These are areas where one member may support another and in which learning may take place incidentally. This situation is present in the JITOL analysis in cases where the main goal of knowledge exchange is improved task performance but during which members of the community learn from one another. The most transparent case of learning in which only zopeds overlap, might be what we commonly refer to as the 'research process'. It is here that the exchange of informal knowledge between professionals results in the creation of new knowledge, later perhaps substantiated and made 'scientific' (Lewis, 1995).

From this has emerged the idea of evolving knowledge bases through the process of reification of human-human interaction, so that the knowledge can easily be retrieved 'just in time' (Boder, 1992; Boder and Gardiol, 1995). Part of the JITOL project is concerned with building evolving knowledge bases.

There are three major sub-projects in JITOL:

1. Training of trainers and teachers in the advanced learning technology field, largely using computer conferencing, e-mail and structured course materials. The Norwegian Winix communication system (Haugen, 1993) was trialled through LANs, WANs and dial-up connections. Winix is thought to be particularly suitable for distance learning activities due to its 'simple Windows interface and the special service of including formatted appendixes' (Haugen, 1993).

2. Training of health professionals responsible for patients suffering from chronic diseases such as diabetes and diabetic self-help therapy. The '4 windows' system (described in Chapter 2) is the technological backbone to this trial. This is a multimedia application in which users have access to a database of graphics and real images of diabetic patients' limbs. The database can be interrogated at the same time as users can be making notes of what they view in a personal electronic notebook; they can then participate in asynchronous conferences where they are led by an expert in the discussion of

issues to do with diabetes. Their interactions are captured and reified (Boder, 1992) and made available as 'new' knowledge.

3. Training of people working in banks and computer companies; this is a corporate staff training project. This project also uses the '4 windows' technology. It is concerned largely with training in economics, using traditional course materials supported by e-mail, conferencing, online databases, etc.

Evaluation of JITOL has been fully integrated since the project began. Two evaluation tool sets have been developed (NL/2/92, 1992; NL/6/93, 1993). Of particular interest are three models of JITOL emerging from the evaluation studies:

1. *The virtual classroom.* This model extends the well-known classroom model to a virtual environment, where a group of learners can learn from explanations and questions addressed by the tutor to the group of learners.
2. *Communication.* The focus here is on exchanges and collaborative learning. The objective is to allow knowledge building through social interaction. CSCL puts learners in contact with each other. The constitution of a learning group is central and requires a common project to work on. The focus, however, is still on personal learning.
3. *Knowledge building.* The focus here is on collective knowledge building from exchanges between learners about their practices. It builds on communication but requires some specific conditions:
   - A shift from 'trivial' conversation to an organised debate that has much to do with a structured collective research approach.
   - Others' expertise should be acknowledged without requiring external validation.
   - The debates should not be concerned with taken-for-granted patterns of interpretation but should focus on the transformation of behaviours, habits or routines. This requires time and is rarely compatible with day to day (on-the-job) practice.
   - The debate requires an incentive in terms of intellectual commitment. Participation in a collaborative task helps maintain efforts to keep up the level of exchanges in the debate. This task could be an exercise such as writing a joint paper, setting up a professional knowledge resource base or realising a collective research project (Saunders *et al.*, 1994; Bonamay and Haugluslaine-Charlier, 1995).

In each of these, the role of the tutor varies, the vision of the knowledge building process varies and the management and regulation patterns and requirements vary. All of this depends largely on the underlying philosophy of education of each model.

At a JITOL evaluation workshop (Lyon, June, 1994, personal involvement), a 'brainstorm' of issues emerging from the evaluation posed some interesting questions about the purpose, processes and outcomes of Just In Time Open Learning, and threw into relief the ideology of the 'JITOL approach' and practical experience of it. Some of the issues emerging, in no particular order, included:

- The effects of assessment on participation in JITOL learning environments: does non-participatory learner assessment (as is the practice in these trials) subvert the collaborative processes inherent in the JITOL philosophy?
- What is a 'suitable' practical role for the tutor in JITOL environments? For example, what is the balance between facilitating and leading a computer conference?
- What is the 'real' status of the personal knowledge and experience of professional people in formal learning situations? Is this kind of knowledge 'downgraded' by the learners themselves? How can it be 'formalised' and legitimised in ways that raise its apparent status?
- How can we situate the JITOL philosophy centrally within the learning environment? How can we build on the *processes* of communication?
- What is an evolving knowledge base in practice? What processes are involved in developing it?
- What are the influences of an organisation's culture in the uptake and usage of JITOL-type learning in corporate settings? Our findings are suggesting that the implementation of JITOL within an organisation can, like any innovation, be subverted by the organisational culture, and may not 'match' the expectations of the learners. Opposing and conflicting interests, and the interaction with the ethos of an organisation's training strategies and methods (Reynolds, 1994), all play a part in the eventual outcomes of introducing such an innovation.

These questions and issues point to the complexity of introducing something like a JITOL philosophy into learning and training. Just having the technology does not in itself give rise to collaborative learning. Learners need a context in which to understand the purpose of collaboration, as we have seen in earlier chapters.

JITOL was one of several projects funded as part of the European Union DELTA Programme (details of which can be found in ARTICU-LATE, 1995). Assumptions made about learning in these new DELTA Teleteaching projects are often not borne out by feedback from learners and users. Some teaching staff are dismissive of the collaborative learning model; learners are not always interested in cooperating during the learning process. It is not always appropriate to make generalisations about the effectiveness or ineffectiveness of learning technologies for distance and flexible learning. Statements about learning have to be contextually qualified. The micro-politics of these forms of learning and training have to be understood.

Models for European Collaboration and Pedagogy in Open Learning (MECPOL)

MECPOL was a recent major European Union Socrates Programme-funded project. It focused on the use of information and communication technologies (ICT) as a basis for open and distributed learning in a life-long learning context (specifically in the continuing professional development field).

The project acknowledged that the advent of the Internet and the World Wide Web pose challenges to higher education to rethink traditional, academic ways of organising universities and colleges. New pedagogical approaches and course design models are required in the provision of knowledge in the 'just in time' world of lifelong learning.

The main purposes of MECPOL were to examine:

1. models of collaboration, exchanges and joint efforts between institutions of higher education
2. models for pedagogy, structure, distribution and design of Internet-based courses and learning material for open and distance learning (ODL) at the professional development level.

Details of the outcomes of the first purpose (and of the project generally) can be found at the MECPOL Web site at www.idb.hist.no/mecpol

The second purpose involved carrying out a series of 'user trials' of information and communication technology (ICT) based courses, and evaluating them. These courses were major examples of innovative learning and teaching via the Internet and represent some of the first attempts to develop European-wide continuing professional develop-ment initiatives. As a member of the MECPOL team, I am able to draw on the extensive evaluation work carried out in the project, and report here in some detail on the findings.

The Evaluation Background

The models of ICT-based open learning

Several models of ICT-based Open and Distance Learning (ODL) were described in the project which were in current use by members of the MECPOL team. A selection of courses and modules built around these models were run as part of Internet-based user trials. These courses and modules were the focus of the evaluation.

The Open Learning Models were as follows.

Open Access Model

Here the emphasis is on institutions offering each others' students courses and modules developed for ICT-based ODL. The purpose is around making existing courses more widely available, and therefore increasing access to learning materials.

Composite Model

Here the focus is on institutions joining together to provide larger modules which they could not develop themselves. The purpose is to build on each others' strengths and develop know-how and expertise in unfamiliar areas or subjects.

Joint Development Model

New courses are developed jointly between institutions. There is some possibility for students to be involved in developing these courses. The purpose here is to focus on joint, collaborative designs that will be to the benefit of all the institutions involved.

Open Learning Environment

The focus here is on organisational issues and open educational issues. The purpose is on the development of open learning environments where tutors and students share roles in terms of course design, collaborative work and so on.

Electronic Seminar Model

This model emphasises a tutor-led discussion around a theme which has been introduced by suggested readings. The purpose of this is to 'mirror' conventional university seminars.

Self-help Groups Model

Here the emphasis is on learners working together as a social group, helping each other in whatever ways seem appropriate. A major purpose of this model is to help reduce the sense of isolation that is endemic in distance learning situations.

Directed Collaborative Projects Model

This model has developed from the JITOL approach to professional learning where the emphasis is on communication between a community of practitioners and knowledge building through the process of 'reification'. The purpose here is to focus on the professional learning concerns of participants and help them establish new understandings of their working life – to make their implicit knowledge explicit.

Computer Supported Cooperative Learning Model

This model emphasises the development of a learning community where professional people cooperate in making decisions about the focus, purpose and process of their learning. The model is highly process oriented, where learning is seen as constructing and re-constructing knowledge. A major purpose here is to establish a social space for cooperation in the learning process.

None of these models represents a discrete and exclusive course design. In reality, courses draw on aspects of one or more models. But course designers found them useful in helping to illustrate the most important pedagogical approaches that they were trying to achieve and used them to help describe the differences between their courses.

Case Studies

In order to make sense of these models, and to highlight the specifics of each, a series of case study evaluations of a selection of them was conducted. Two of the courses evaluated are discussed in some detail below. Each case study considered the purposes of each course and the experiences of those tutors and students involved.

Documentary evidence, such as course brochures and handouts, was used to construct a picture of the purposes of each model/course. This included information about:

- what the course/model is trying to achieve
- the learning processes involved
- what is being asked of participants in the course or model
- what roles tutors have
- assessment procedures.

This data was used as a basis for relating course or model purposes with intended outcomes.

The Experiences of Participants and Tutors

The relationship between intended outcomes, as described above, and actual outcomes was worthy of evaluation. This approach signified a problematic relationship between rhetoric and reality. In looking at the experience of the learners and tutors, the focus was on a grounded approach to evaluation where student and tutor 'reality' was examined.

The definition of what constitutes 'learning effectiveness' in each course is a complex issue that requires an understanding of the purposes of those running the course and those participating; the context of each course, and the teaching and learning processes. In some courses, 'learning effectiveness' is perhaps judged by the number of students passing the final examination. In others, it is judged by a set of different criteria. Indeed, in one course there are no traditional examinations: students are judged by the contribution they make to the online learning community as well as their assessment of their own and each others work on the course.

Each case study therefore offers the reader information upon which they can themselves make sense of 'learning effectiveness'.

Evaluation Methodology

Perceptions of students and tutors were collected by questionnaires sent to them via e-mail.

The students were sent three questionnaires, one at the beginning, middle and end of each course. The questionnaires were developed from ones used in the JITOL project, and the associated NITOL (Norwegian Information Technology in Open Learning) project (see eg Saunders and Machel, 1992).

The pre-course questionnaire focused on the students' professional development backgrounds, their purposes for taking an Internet-based course and their familiarity with the technology.

The mid-course questionnaire covered the time they spent studying on the course, their use of resources, their participation in the online collaborative learning processes and their experiences of studying via ICT.

The post-course questionnaire considered their general enjoyment of studying in this mode, the effectiveness of the course and their comparison with other modes of learning.

The methodology of soliciting student views by e-mail questionnaires was not problem free, and the problems and difficulties involved in evaluating the courses in this way are discussed later in this section.

The tutors were sent one e-mail questionnaire asking about: their background; the aims and objectives of the course they were offering; their experience of being an online tutor; their perceptions of the experiences of their students' problems and successes; the time spent working on the course; and their views about online teaching and learning.

Full copies of all the questionnaires can be obtained at the MECPOL Project Web site.

Course One: Pedagogy in Open and Distance Learning (PiODL)

Educational philosophy, open learning principles and model, and organisation of the online course

The course designers described the course as follows: 'In this course we have put together many of our experiences from the NITOL project, a project with four university partners sharing courses by using the Internet.' Some of the main issues covered in the course are:

- Some background information and terms, eg what is open learning?
- A short introduction to the technology used: Web, e-mail and newsgroups and how to administrate Internet-based open learning.
- Pedagogical methods used:
  - Lessons delivered to students, solutions to exercises sent to tutor by e-mail and discussion in newsgroups.
  - What hyper systems are and how to use the technology in ODL.
  - Collaboration between institutions offering ODL.
- Evaluation.
- Design of ICT based learning.
- Cooperative learning.

Aims and objectives
- Dissemination of experiences from ICT based open learning courses.
- Joint development of course material between five or six independent partner institutions, thus testing one of the collaborative models of MECPOL.

Underlying pedagogic model
The course was given through the Internet. Lessons were published on the Web. Some of the lessons had exercises that should be sent in to a tutor for assessment. The students were encouraged to make smaller groups by using e-mail for discussion of problems given in the lessons.

A common discussion forum for all the students was made through a Web-based discussion forum – a sort of newsgroup. This was meant to function as a virtual classroom where all students could raise problems or questions and where they could also comment upon problems raised. The idea was to make some kind of classroom atmosphere on the Internet, to make each student feel 'at home' in their own class.

This way of doing it made it possible for students to collaborate and, if they wanted, they could cooperate in the learning situation as well. Even if the course was not meant to be organised as a cooperative learning course, part of it stressed cooperation so much that the students had to take part in each other's way of presenting and developing lessons. The pedagogical framework was more or less based on participation and learning by doing.

Organisation of the course
The course had 12 lessons distributed weekly on the Web. Each lesson had a course text to introduce the subject of the lesson and some exercises to be answered either as a discussion or in the discussion forum or to be sent to a tutor by e-mail. Students were encouraged to do collaborative work.

They started out by presenting themselves and some of the students took part in the 'social event' the 'Cafe', but there was only a small contribution to this activity. This part seemed to be difficult to extend without hard work from the teachers and, even so, there was an obstacle to overcome. Most of the students were reluctant – and afraid of commenting in writing.

The Experience of Students and Tutors

Table 7.1 *Questionnaire response rates*

	Number returned	Percentage of total enrolled
Pre-course questionnaire	20	29
Mid-course questionnaire	10	14
Post-course questionnaire	16	23 (53 per cent of those completing the course)
Number enrolled	69	
Number completing the course and taking final assessment	30	

Online participation and collaboration
Students
A major objective of the evaluations was to examine the processes of participation and collaboration in each course. Students on this course reported reading messages and comments in the conferences and e-mails. However, the majority said they had not been encouraged to collaborate with other students during the course. Those who indicated they were collaborating with others said that they discussed subject or syllabus problems, talked about issues concerning course organisation or collaborated to get information and advice from other students.

The frequency of reading conference and e-mail comments was evenly distributed between daily readings and monthly readings. A few people read comments weekly. The majority of the students read between one and five conferences, although two said they read none of the conferences. Most people reported that they rarely contributed to the online discussions, though a few did so often or occasionally. Insufficient time was given as the main reason for not contributing.

Everyone said that the conference comments were 'somewhat interesting'. Just over half said that they were rarely useful for understanding or solving course problems, though one person did find them useful and three did so occasionally. Half the students said they were sharing the responsibility for study organisation.

Tutors
All three tutors thought that their students were able to learn effectively from the online activities in the course. Two of them thought the students

achieved most of the course learning objectives; the other tutor thought only some of the students achieved them.

Tutors' views of the extent to which students found it easy to study independently varied somewhat. In terms of whether they thought students met deadlines, one thought they did most of the time; one thought they did some of the time; the other thought they achieved them only a little. Two tutors thought the students completed tasks most of the time; the other thought they completed them some of the time. Communication between students and tutors seems to have been satisfactorily achieved some of the time, although one tutor commented that the students did not ask many questions. Perceptions of communication between students varied: one tutor thought students managed to communicate between each other most of the time, while the other two tutors thought such communication was rare.

The language of the course was English, even though many of the students did not speak English as their first language. However, in the view of the tutors this did not pose any particular difficulties for students or tutors.

Prior to the course starting tutors did not anticipate many problems in teaching the course. One tutor did comment however that he foresaw some possible problems between the tutors involved in developing the course. There were four or five tutors each giving one to three lessons, and this tutor wondered if there might be problems of course coherence. Would the course just appear like a series of separate lessons, rather than one that had some internal structure and coherence. It seems, in the perception of this tutor, that these problems did arise, but they were being addressed in the redesign of the course. In general, the tutors said that any redesign of the course would have to incorporate more student activities, as well as addressing the issue of tutor cooperation.

One other tutor anticipated that the course would be successful if the students completed it and had a positive learning experience; and this, to a large extent, he says was the case.

The tutors were asked to consider a series of possible roles for online teaching, and to indicate which of them they anticipated having to carry out before the course started, and which roles they actually played during the course. They were asked to rate each role, indicating if they thought it was a central one, a major one, a minor one or irrelevant in their particular context.

The roles are shown in Table 7.2.

There was at times considerable divergence in the views of tutors over the anticipated roles they would have to play, and about the roles they

Table 7.2 *The tutor roles*

Lecturer	Presenting and explaining materials and ideas to students
Discussion chair	Mediating, setting timelines, and summing up in online discussions
Facilitator	Posing questions, stimulating discussion, setting goals in response to student needs
Mentor	Giving individual guidance to students on study problems, or methods
Co-learner	Carrying out investigations, looking for resources, and learning alongside students
Assessor	Checking correctness of student answers or exercises and giving feedback on them
Examiner	Checking assessment answers and giving feedback to the institution
Administrator	Keeping course and student records
Technical advisor	Helping students deal with hardware, network connection and operating software problems
Provider of resources	Identifying resources and providing references for study

played in practice during the course. There was also some divergence in their perception of what the role of the tutor on this course was.

One tutor's views of her role did not change at all as a consequence of the actual experience of teaching on the course. What she anticipated her role to be prior to the course starting seemed to match the actual roles she played during the course. She saw herself as having a minor role in lecturing, acting as discussion chair, facilitating, mentoring and providing resources to students. Her major role was in assessing the students' work. She had no view on whether or not she would be, or was, a co-learner, examiner, administrator or technical advisor.

Another tutor's anticipated views of his role also largely matched that played out during the course, though he did indicate that the role he played of examiner changed from a minor anticipated one to a major one in practice. He also did not anticipate having to give any technical advice or to act as a provider of resources, but in practice found these were minor roles for him during the course. He saw himself having minor roles in acting as discussion chair, facilitator, assessor and administrator; this was how it happened in reality. In terms of his major role on the course, he mainly saw himself acting as lecturer and mentor; this was the case in practice.

The third tutor's anticipated roles and actual roles seemed to vary greatest of the three. Prior to the course, this person did not see himself having a relevant role as mentor, assessor or provider of resources, but in practice he indicated that these became major roles for him during the course. He also indicated that the role of discussion chair changed from a major one to a central one for him. His estimation of the other roles before and during the course remained static: he saw himself having a major role in facilitating online activity and discussion and in the administration of the course; this turned out to be the case. He also thought that being a co-learner and acting as examiner were not relevant to him; again this turned out to be the case.

It is not possible to comment on the divergence of views of tutor roles indicated in these findings since there is no additional data to help clarify the various points of view. It might well be that these tutors had been given different roles prior to the start of the course; hence the variance in their views of what their roles were. It might also be that particular roles were not clearly defined and discussed.

Effectiveness of Open and Distance Learning

Just over half of the students felt that the course was very effective, the rest described it as somewhat effective. Similarly, just over half felt it was more effective as a self-study course than other courses they had taken. One person thought it much more effective, six thought it as effective.

The effectiveness of the course lay mainly in the opportunity for participants to study at their own pace and to be able to study when it suited them. A few people thought the course contained all the information they needed. Very few said that they liked sharing information in the discussion conferences or felt that the conferences gave them the information they needed.

When asked which issues made the course a less effective learning experience, the main one that was mentioned by a majority of the students was the difficulty in finding time to participate adequately in the discussion conferences. A few participants said they felt isolated during the course or needed more support and encouragement in order to be able to learn efficiently. Similarly, a few said that the discussion conferences did not give them the information they needed or that the course itself did not include the information needed.

Comparison with other modes of learning

Compared with other methods of obtaining information *there* and *then*, the discussion conferences appear to have been reasonably effective. Nearly three-quarters of the students thought the course was very effective in helping them obtain information there and then, although several thought it less effective in this respect.

Perceptions of an ideal open learning environment
Participants were asked what demands they would set for the technology used to make an open learning system function well. Their comments include:

> It should be more flexible and modern. It shouldn't be like an electronic book.

> Better data transmission ratios, more standardised user interface in the Web-based educational applications.

> More bandwidth for all the students so that multimedia extensions can take place.

> More friendly and modern; the course material reminds me of a book.

> Computers, manuals, educators, libraries.

> Enough capacity and speed on network communications.

> Speed and privacy.

> Powerful servers, higher network (telephone line) capacity.

They were also asked how they would describe their ideal open learning environment.

> Interactive, online, friendly for those who aren't close to technology (like TV: you don't have to know how it works).

> The main problem in an open learning environment is the lack of communication and exchange of ideas within the course via the conferences, mailing lists, etc. The solution to this problem is to motivate the students to participate. The technology itself has great potential in creating a user-friendly environment. However, the teachers should create the learning material in such a way to motivate students to communicate more. Furthermore, the face-to-face contacts are in a way irreplaceable by any means provided by modern technologies.

> Without multimedia extensions, it is really difficult to motivate somebody to be a part of it.

> A teleconferencing environment that led you through the course.

> More active.

> With a lot of collaboration among institutions and students.

Additional support needed to achieve this included:

> The course material should be structured in such a way to motivate and encourage students to discuss topics of the course material.

> Quick network.

> Faster network throughput.

> Making discussion groups a required obligation.

Attitudes to taking another online course
As an overall indicator of 'effectiveness', participants were asked if they would consider taking more courses of this type in the future. The majority said 'yes' and a few said 'maybe'.

Change in expectations about the course
Just over half said that in terms of the course corresponding to their expectations, it turned out to be about as much as they had expected. Three thought it was better than expected, and one less than expected.

All three tutors said they would be happy to work as online teachers again. They thought the advantages of this form of learning were:

- easier access for students
- independent of time and distance
- flexibility.

The disadvantage was:

- more preparation work for the teacher.

They thought there were some advantages of this form of teaching and learning over traditional (print-based) distance learning methods:

- more open, more contact, easier for everyone to get in touch with each other
- material available online
- rapid communication by using e-mail for exercises and course online discussions
- more flexible.

No disadvantages of this form of teaching over traditional distance learning were given.

Enjoyment of studying the course
Half the participants said they enjoyed taking the course very much; the
other half said it was 'OK'.

Course 2: Developing Networked Learning Communities

*Educational philosophy, open learning principles and model, and
organisation of the online course*
The course team described it as follows: 'This module (called a workshop) is the first one on the MEd in Networked Collaborative Learning,
which is a two year part-time 'online' programme for professional people
interested in developing their skills and knowledge in learning and
teaching via information and communication technologies and the
Internet/intranets.'

Aims of Workshop
The workshop is largely concerned with establishing the idea of a
learning community in online learning environments, and with mapping
out understandings of the nature of action research and how it might
apply to this course. We do some reading around these areas and have
some online seminar discussions, via Lotus Notes. There is also a course
Website.

At the same time, participants keep a reflective learning journal and
start working on the course assignment, which is around one or more of
the workshop themes. Both of these activities form two-thirds of the
assessed work on this workshop. The other third relates to participation
in the Lotus Notes discussions.

The workshop starts with a three-day face-to-face meeting, and then
runs online for three months.

Organisation
The Learning Sets
Great educational value is placed on students working together in social
groups. Not only does this act as a way of validating their knowledge as
professional educators, it is also a very beneficial and highly educative
way to learn. Each of the participants therefore work in a learning set
where they manage their own learning and cooperate with others in their
learning, through processes of negotiation and discussion.

The Lotus Notes Seminars
A major purpose of this workshop is to give participants some experi-

ence of participating in electronically mediated seminars using the Lotus Notes computer conferences. This direct experience provides them with an insight into the issues surrounding this form of learning, the delights of learning in a virtual community and the issues that need to be considered when running learning events in this medium.

Workshop Work and Assessment

The aim is largely to help participants think through the issues that they define as being important for their learning, while offering a series of loose but supportive course activities as scaffolding. Getting the balance between the participants' interests and professional concerns, and the tutors' sense of mapping out the territory and helping them weave their way through it, is not an easy or simple task and is not one that is likely to be conflict-free. But it is worth striving for, and the hope is that everyone can collectively work at maintaining a good balance, constantly reviewing as a learning community where they are, what they are doing and why they are doing it.

They recognise the need to involve participants in their assessment processes – partly in recognition of their own ability and need to have a say in determining the 'value' placed on their learning, but also to recognise and emphasise the learning potential of the assessment process, for both participants and course tutors. This is done through processes of collaborative self/peer/tutor assessment.

As course requirements, it is asked that participants:

- Keep a personal, reflective learning journal of their experiences and thoughts about networked learning. This learning journal should offer them the opportunity to reflect on their own learning experiences, and provide a vehicle for exploring their own experiences on the course. From this we ask them to hand in their overview or meta-analysis of the learning journal. This forms one third of the weighting of the Workshop One assessment.
- Choose a topic related to one or more of the themes of the workshop (learning community, action research or self-managed learning) and write a short (about three thousand words) piece on it. Their learning set members help them think this through and offer support and assistance throughout. This forms one-third of the weighting of the Workshop One assessment.
- Participate as fully as they can in the online seminars and discussions. Again, it is not possible to be prescriptive about the exact meaning of 'fully participate' – the different meanings of this are discussed online

– but the online activities and discussions in a sense 'replace' the usual course requirement of attending face-to-face meetings in a 'normal' part-time course. Participants are asked to review their online participation and to engage in some discussion with their learning set members about the 'level' of participation. This forms one-third of the weighting of the Workshop One assessment.

Course work is assessed collaboratively by self/peer/tutor assessment processes.

Seventeen students started the course and all took the assessment and successfully completed the course.

The Experience of Students and Tutors

Table 7.3 *Questionnaire response rates*

	Number returned	Percentage of total enrolled
Pre-course questionnaire	13	76
Mid-course questionnaire	13	76
Post-course questionnaire	9	53
Number enrolled	17	
Number completing the course and taking final assessment	17	

Online participation

All the students said they read the messages and comments in the conferences. All but one said that they had been encouraged to collaborate with others via the net during the course. They said that they were collaborating with others via the Internet to complete the course. The forms of collaboration were varied, including discussion of subject or syllabus problems; discussion of problems concerning course organisation; collaboration to get information and advice from other students; and collaboration to compensate for being alone. Half of them also said they collaborated for other (non-specified) reasons.

The vast majority of the students said that they read the conferences daily. One person read them weekly. Most of them participated in between one and five conferences; four of them participated in between six and ten conferences. A third described their contributions to the conferences as 'often', while the rest described them as being 'occasionally'. No one never participated in the conferences.

Most participants thought the conferences were very interesting, while a few thought them somewhat interesting. In terms of their usefulness for understanding or solving course problems, half said they found them often useful in this respect, and just under half said they were occasionally useful. The majority said they were sharing responsibility for study organisation, commenting:

> We are trying to work to a contract which incorporates this.

> Not to the extent that I should like.

> We collectively agree who does what in our learning set.

> Currently this is not working to schedule due to work pressures.

Tutors
Tutor perceptions of the students' experiences seem to accord with the students' own views.

The tutors felt quite clearly that, in their view, the students were able to learn effectively from the online activities and that they met the learning objectives of the course. The tutors felt that students were able to study independently: they met course deadlines, were able to complete learning tasks most of the time, and they were always able to complete the assessment tasks. Course participants communicated very effectively with the tutors during the course, and it was the tutors' perception that they also communicated easily and effectively with each other.

Tutors anticipated several problems in teaching this course:

- acclimatisation to the hardware and software
- acclimatisation to the asynchronous mode of discussion
- the paradigm shift towards students managing their own learning and contributing to the learning of the community
- the 'heavy' workload associated with discussions and group work online.

In practice, some of these problems did arise. For example, participants did need extra online help and assistance with understanding how to use Lotus Notes. This was dealt with by setting up a database conference where an expert Lotus Notes user answered queries and gave advice on the various functions of Notes. This was extremely successful and widely used by participants and tutors alike. Participants were also encouraged to start reflecting on their experience of working online and present these to the course community. Once again, this proved a powerful source of learning. Issues around working in an asynchronous environment were addressed by the tutor setting times for discussions and completion of some aspects of the online work, and suggesting steps to be taken in order to reach conclusions. In general, tutors commented that they consistently tried to encourage participants to discuss their experiences – indeed this was part of the 'content' of the course: sharing experiences and discussing them in order to throw light on the nature of networked learning generally.

The tutors anticipated that participants would soon become comfortable with the technology and with the collaborative processes of learning. The extent to which this was quickly achieved varied from participant to participant. Quick progress with understanding and using the technology was made by most. Engaging some participants in discussion about the purposes of the course was at times difficult. Some participants needed considerable guidance with their understanding of collaborative group processes – the shift from individual, self-focused learning to a form of learning that is more social and collaborative needs time. Some participants seemed to need confirmation that this was an appropriate and educationally sound method of learning. However, this did seem to be an accepted educational process by most participants.

Tutors commented that knowing how much work to ask of participants in these 'virtual' learning environments is not easy to gauge. One tutor thought they perhaps asked too much of participants: for example, the different levels of reading for self-managed learners. And related to this the time commitment required to participate in the online activities.

The successes included the detailed and high quality help and advice exchanged between participants. Some participants took 'control' of the Lotus Notes learning space and used it very effectively for their own and collective purposes. Participants in learning sets took control of the group processes and engaged group members in some interesting issues and discussion problems.

Those aspects of the course that tutors thought might require change included:

- more discussion with participants about their own purposes for studying the course
- a greater focus generally on what the participants were 'looking' for on the course
- lengthening the introductory workshop
- introducing collaborative tasks (in pairs or groups) as part of the initial assignment
- taking more time at the face-to-face meeting to establish the nature and purposes of collaboration.

Tutor Roles

Both tutors said they had a good idea of their role as tutor prior to the start of the course. As in the previous case study, the tutors were presented with the list of possible teaching roles (see Table 7.1) and were asked to indicate the roles they thought they would have to play before the course started, and the roles they actually played during the course.

For one tutor, the roles she anticipated playing, and those which in practice she played, appear to differ in some respects. The constants were her perception of her role as lecturer and examiner: in both cases she saw these as minor roles prior to the course, and indeed they turned out to be so during the course. She thought her role as mentor would be minor, yet it turned out to be a central role for her. Acting as facilitator changed from being perceived as a major role to turning out to be a central role also. Prior to the course she thought she would have a central role in acting as discussion chair and co-learner; these turned out to be less important and became only major roles during the course. She thought the roles of assessor and technical adviser would not be relevant to her prior to the course, but in practice these turned out to be minor roles during the course. Generally speaking, she commented that a few people experienced technical setting up problems that slowed the process of group meetings, and that considerable differentials emerged between the capacity of group members to organise their learning online.

For the other tutor, five of the roles imagined prior to the course remained the same as those experienced during it: acting as facilitator, mentor, administrator and provider of resources remained central roles before and during the course, while that of discussion chair remained as a major role. Acting as examiner changed from being imagined a central role prior to the course starting to becoming a major role during the course. He anticipated 'acting as lecturer' as a major role, while it turned out to be a minor one. He thought he would have a major role as a co-learner, but in practice this was a minor role, while his perception of being an assessor changed from a minor role to a major one. He commented that working in the way they do on the course means that tutors have many roles to play, and that sometimes these roles are shared with the participants.

Impact of course on motivation to study

The overall impact of the course on participants' motivation to study was very positive: four people said it had affected them very much, while seven said it had affected them quite a lot. One person said it had not had much of an effect on them.

Effectiveness of ODL

Just over half those responding said that they felt the course was very effective, while a third said it was somewhat effective. When asked how they would rank the course compared with other courses they had taken, all but one said it was 'more effective' or 'as effective'. No one thought it less effective than traditional courses.

Those aspects of the course that made it effective were participants' ability to study when it suited them; the ability to study at their own pace; and the fact that they liked sharing information in the discussion conferences. For a few the course was effective because they could get the information they required from the discussions in the conferences.

Those aspects that made it less effective were largely around finding sufficient time to participate adequately in the discussion conferences. A few people said they needed more support and encouragement in order to be able to learn efficiently, and one person said she felt isolated at times.

Comparison with other modes of learning

Compared with other methods of obtaining information *there* and *then*, the discussion conferences were thought to be more effective or as effective by the majority of students.

According to the tutors, the advantages of this form of learning compared with face-to-face teaching of a similar course are:

- flexibility of time and place
- ability of participants to take part who would otherwise not be able to
- access to online references and a wider community of practice
- excitement and challenge of online learning
- possibility of doing some things 'better' online.

The disadvantages are:

- the slow pace of asynchronous exchanges
- attenuated sense of presence in a largely text-based environment.

Compared with a similar course by traditional, print-based, distance learning methods, online learning allows for support for student-student as well as student-tutor interaction. Collaborative learning would be much more difficult in the traditional distance mode. The traditional distance mode would also not be so rich or engaging. One tutor commented:

I need contact with learners and think they also need contact with each other and the tutor. This is not possible with traditional distance learning. Online learning is just so much more flexible, engaging, rich, complex, demanding, rewarding, socially beneficial...

One tutor thought this form of learning was still a privileged and predominantly mono-cultural environment, with serious equity issues. Both tutors felt that more research is needed into the design of online learning environments and the functioning of learning communities.

Perceptions of an ideal open learning environment
Students were asked: 'What demands would you set for the technology used to make an open learning system function well?' They answered:

Time to use it.

Own computer at work and home, local support.

Not sure yet!

Ease of set up. Reliability. Speed of access. Cross platform software which actually is cross platform.

Compatibility.

Computer conferencing is fine, but would prefer more regular f2f.

Primarily, not to crash so often.

Inexpensive and effective video-conferencing.

Fast response time, greater interaction.

For the student to stay with familiar technology.

They were also asked: 'How would you describe your ideal open learning environment?' They answered:

This is ideal for me. I'm comfortable with the technology and appreciate the flexibility of choosing when to study and having the opportunity of working from home and business.

The beach on Little Cayman with a laptop and modem.

Flexible, supportive and responsive.

Probably a wine bar about 200 yards away overlooking the sea or hills with lots of good people there to talk to. I suppose though being provided with a good lap top with everything I need on it with online and local advice.

More time to devote to it.

A comfortable office with reliable equipment/phone lines, but mainly TIME to think!

Support available when needed – knowing where to go for assistance/advice if you wanted/needed it. Availability of others, colleagues and/or tutors, who are able to offer support, act as a resource/facilitator/mentors. Knowledge of available resources.

More direction and guidance, particularly in identifying 'problems' and suggested areas for research. Other than that I am used to studying alone so that poses no problems for me at all.

One that has both electronic and face-to-face interaction.

The tutors thought that an optimal open learning environment should require an integrated and flexible learning environment with a shorter learning curve than is required by the use of Lotus Notes. Cheaper and faster connections would allow occasional synchronous meetings. The offline capability of Lotus Notes (for reflective reading and responding) seemed ideal for this kind of discussion-based course.

Attitudes to taking another online course
As an overall indicator of 'effectiveness', participants were asked if they would consider taking more courses of this type in the future. Over half of them said they would; the rest said 'maybe'.

The tutors said they would be happy to teach in this way again. One tutor commented that he liked the flexibility of online learning and still (after doing it for several years) found it exciting and challenging. He feels online learning can achieve some learning objectives better than traditional face-to-face learning.

Change in expectations about the course
In terms of the course corresponding to their expectations, seven out of eight thought that the course corresponded about as much as they expected, one person thought it was better than expected.

Enjoyment of studying the course
Most of those replying said they enjoyed the course very much, while a few thought it just 'OK'.

What has been Learned from these Case Studies?

The major point to make about these trials is that all the courses were successfully delivered, and received by students, via the Internet. Those students who chose to work towards credit performed very well, and all the courses were rated highly by the students.

The case studies show two successful but highly divergent models for delivering Internet courses. Each course is unique and has its own purposes, processes and institutional context, thus making it difficult, and perhaps unwise, to try and generalise too much from them.

However, it is possible to summarise the main findings from the evaluation and make some suggestions about the collaborative learning processes, a major pedagogical method which featured prominently in each course.

Evaluation Issues

Several issues limited the method of evaluation:

1. Since the trial courses were to be offered throughout the participating EU countries with students taking them via the Internet from their home country, it was not possible to have a form of evaluation that included meeting the students or tutors in order to discuss with them issues around the courses. We were restricted to a method which could be carried out remotely, via the Internet itself. Although not ideal, we decided to use self-completion questionnaires, distributed electronically to each individual student and tutor via the Internet.

    In the PiODL course they were distributed by two means: as a Word 5.rtf file attachment to an e-mail, the formatted questionnaire opening on the participant's PC for them to complete and return; and in the form of ASCII text within the body of an e-mail. The latter type was not of course formatted, but did have the attraction of being simple and easy to complete and return. In the 'Developing the Learning Community' course the questionnaires were distributed via Lotus Notes e-mails within the body of the e-mail itself, so when they were opened they were presented as fully formatted rich text, and returned in this way also.

    We considered providing the questionnaire on the Web itself, for online completion, but were not able to implement this fully within the timespan of the evaluation. It is, however, possible that respondents may not in any case have been inclined to take the trouble to visit the Web site in order to complete the questionnaire. But this method would have been interesting to try out.

In all cases, each e-mail was prefaced with a courteous message explaining the purpose of the survey and offering to discuss with respondents any queries they might have about the evaluation of the courses. Introductory messages are considered an important factor in attaining good response rates to electronic surveys (Witman *et al.*, 1999).

Reminder e-mails were sent to those not returning their questionnaires.

2. Past experience of evaluating these kind of courses suggested that respondents were not very tolerant of having to complete long or complicated questionnaires. The questionnaire had to be easy to complete – especially for those whose first language was not English. This suggested a largely self completion format, with fixed questions and some opportunity for respondents to elaborate on answers where necessary or where they wished. In drawing up the student questionnaire, it soon became apparent that the number of issues we wished to cover was too much for one questionnaire alone. We therefore decided to design three shorter questionnaires, one distributed prior to the course, one during the course and the third after the course. There was only one tutor questionnaire.

Several problems were evident with this method:

- Low returns of some student questionnaires. In the PiODL course there were low response rates, ranging from 14% to 29% (for the different questionnaires) of all those enrolled. The reasons for this are not clear. Some students did not complete one of the courses, and some courses had 'occasional' participants who were not registered, or who did not wish to fully participate, and so perhaps did not feel inclined to complete the questionnaires. It is not clear if the method of distribution of the questionnaires proved too difficult for respondents to relate to. Although we e-mailed those who did not return questionnaires, most of them did not respond to these e-mails. So, our results do not fully take into account the views of all students, and may only reflect the views of those who set out to complete the course (53% of those completing this course did return the post-course questionnaire). Other researchers also report low response rates to online surveys, sometimes as low as 10%, and indicate the potential pitfalls of data collection via e-mails generally (eg

Witman *et al.*, 1999). To what extent conventional snail mail survey techniques (and other research techniques generally) translate to e-mail questionnaire surveys is an interesting research question for those of us involved in conducting course evaluations via the Internet.

- The standardised questionnaires did not always compliment the different purposes and designs of each course. This is perhaps inevitable in this kind of evaluation. Follow up interviews via the Internet might have offered an opportunity for respondents to expand on their answers, but this was not possible to carry out.

- Restricted responses. It is not possible to know the extent to which those responding actually understood the meaning of the questions asked. This is possibly the case with those whose first language is not English. There is some indication in the replies that some respondents did not really understand what some of the questions were asking, or that their understanding of terms and words used had different and unique local and cultural meanings.

- Interpreting written responses. There were occasions when it was difficult to interpret some of the written (typed) responses. We sometimes wanted to ask respondents exactly what they meant, especially some of those replying whose first language was not English. However, this was not possible. So, occasionally some responses presented in the Case Studies may not make complete sense to the reader eg some students said they did not use e-mail in order to get assistance from course tutors: how they did in fact receive assistance therefore remains something of a mystery. Follow up studies would have helped to clarify these anomalies, but were beyond the scope of the evaluation.

Evaluation Achievements
The achievements for the staff involved in this kind of collaboration are:

- learning about ICT-based ODL
- the collaborative design of an international course in Pedagogy of Open and Distance Learning
- diffusion and transfer of knowledge between partners concerning the application of electronic communications and course design
- access to a variety of models of ICT-based open and distance learning

- exchange of courses and groups of students: major significant examples of good practice
- dissemination to others about collaborative processes of ICT-based ODL.

The Students' Experience

Students say that, on the whole, these courses provided a very positive learning experience and they would be willing to take similar courses in the future.

These forms of Internet courses offer flexibility for learners in pacing their studies and in deciding when to study.

Some students did not complete one of the courses. We cannot be sure about why this happened, though we do know that several students took the course for experience only and did not intend to work towards certification of any kind.

Many, but not all, of the students who took the courses were fairly familiar with the technology involved, and had good access to it in order to participate. They were, in many cases, self selected and so in this respect the trials have been somewhat 'skewed'.

Many students found it hard to organise their studies – mainly because time was at a premium as they were all full-time workers.

The perceptions of the effectiveness of this form of open and distance learning varied from course to course. On the whole, most students thought that, as examples of open learning, these courses were 'effective'. Most described them as being just as effective as any other course they had taken by traditional methods.

The Tutors' Experience

All tutors reported that the courses provided a very positive learning experience and that they would be very willing to teach in this way again.

With one exception, all tutors had previous experience of teaching via the Internet. This form of course provision allows for flexibility in the time of day, and day of week for teaching.

Tutor views of their online roles differed from course to course, and at times even within the same course. This might be a function of the differing purposes of each course, and the associated teaching and learning processes. More research is required to understand the relationship between course aims and objectives, and associated tutor roles.

From the tutor perspective, the advantages of this form of learning are:

- easier access for students
- independence of time and distance
- flexibility of time and place
- ability of participants to take part who would otherwise not be able to
- access to online references and resources, and a wider community of practice
- excitement and challenge of online learning
- the possibility to do some things 'better' online (compared with traditional distance learning)
- construction of interactive sessions in lessons
- ability to communicate fast via computer mediated communications eg for asking questions and giving answers; for facilitating discussions and group work
- ability to use hyperlinks to an 'ocean' of relevant information on the Internet
- ability to have group discussions and collaborative work online.

The disadvantages are:

- the slow pace of asynchronous exchanges
- attenuated sense of presence in a largely text-based environment
- more preparation work for the teacher.

The Collaborative Learning Process
A major aim of each course was the involvement of students in some form of collaborative or cooperative learning. This was seen as an important and beneficial educational aim. Web discussion areas (HyperNews) were set up on one of the courses in order to accommodate this. The other course used Lotus Notes for this purpose.

From the evaluation, it became clear that:

- The meaning, purposes and practices of collaborative learning varied enormously from course to course.
- In one course collaboration was mentioned by the course designers as being an important aim, but in practice the course did not actually require students to collaborate: as one student put it, they were expected to 'study alone'.
- One course defined collaboration as being largely discussion of course material.
- Collaborative learning through discussion was a limited success in one of the courses; in the other course it was more successful.

Designing collaboration into the course appears to be the critical factor here.
- Most students seemed to want some form of collaborative learning (or active learning), but sometimes pointed out that they had limited time to participate in the online discussions.

From these trials, a few points might usefully be made concerning collaborative learning:

- If students are required to collaborate then it would seem that collaboration has to be a central part of the course requirement, or course 'content', and not just additional or peripheral to the course. It has to be formally embedded in the course processes.
- Students have to be rewarded for collaborating: course assessment procedures could be used to achieve this.
- Students have to 'see' a real educational purpose for collaborating – there is some indication in one of the courses evaluated that they perceived it as something that the tutors wanted, yet which in practice the tutors did not fully facilitate or support.
- Students have to be organised by tutors in ways that help them collaborate; they have to have a sense of belonging to a collaborative online group. Leaving the collaborative process solely to the students to organise does not seem to work.
- Tutors have to take a central role in facilitating the collaborative learning processes, help students understand how to work together and understand why it is educationally beneficial to collaborate in their learning.
- Tutors have to understand the nature of collaborative learning and believe in it.

Technologies

Different Internet technologies were successfully used in these trials eg Web-based course delivery and discussion areas; delivery and discussion areas within Lotus Notes. All of these appear to have been reasonably successful for their purposes.

There is, however, some indication that Web-based discussion systems are not entirely successful. This may be due to the way in which the course using them was designed, but this requires further investigation.

Portable PCs for Students

The Portable PCs for Students project is at the University of Erlangen-Nurnberg in Germany. The intention is to explore possibilities of decentralised and cooperative learning by the use of teleteaching and computer mediated communications and decision support systems. Behind the project are concerns about the successful management of 'learning enterprises', in which autonomous teams self-organise and self-manage according to whatever problems they are faced with. A major role of universities these days should be to prepare students for working in decentralised teams where cooperation is fundamental.

The project has two major aims:

1. to determine which forms of team-oriented learning and working are appropriate and feasible at universities
2. to determine how these new forms of learning and working can be realised, and to determine which hardware and software systems are required (Bodendorf and Seitz, 1994).

A target group of university students, including students of business science, social science, information science and computer science, was provided with portable PCs, communication equipment and software resources. They were able to access the university's LAN and participate in decentralised courses. The research programme is divided into four steps, as described by the researchers:

1. *Analysis and organisational design.* The first task was to analyse the programmes of study offered by the university. This led to various courses being redesigned to introduce new technologies such as decentralised CBT (computer based training) and CMC (computer-mediated communications). Furthermore, scenarios have been constructed to support teachers and students starting with tele- and teamwork in education.
2. *Applications development.* A suitable infrastructure for computer supported tele- and teamwork has been established allowing students to decentralise parts of their studies and to practice collaborative learning. Teachware used in some practical courses has been complemented with monitoring software agents to observe learners' actions. The student information system contains information about the institution, educational courses, teachers, dates etc. Electronic mail, file transfer and bulletin board functions have been added to the

system. Finally, an integrated electronic meeting system supports asynchronous and synchronous conferences. A communication server provides remote access to all systems mentioned.

3. *Implementation and usage.* Students participating in the project utilise the tools and information systems to complete predefined parts of their workload as teleworkers and/or team organisation.

4. *Evaluation.* A current empirical study examines how students practise flexible task management and how their attitudes change while using the tele- and teamwork technologies provided. To enable comparisons, treatment and control groups undergo the same instructional phases within some specific courses (Bodendorf and Seitz, 1994).

The learning benefits to students are considered to be far reaching. Students can participate in courses without having to attend face-to-face classes; they link in from home. Group teachware allows them to collaborate with other students, and the system allows them to access information more flexibly than is otherwise possible. They have immediate and easy contact with staff and other students. Additionally, they are being prepared for working in organisations that will be using modern communications systems (Seitz and Bodendorf, 1994; Bodendorf and Seitz, 1993).

A variety of communication techniques is being trialled, such as 'one-alone' techniques where the learner interacts with databases and bulletin boards; 'one-to-one' techniques where communication is between two learners via e-mail and file transfer, or where they work collaboratively on the production of a common document; 'one-to-many' techniques, where communication is between individuals in groups; and 'many-to-many' techniques where an integrated text-oriented electronic meeting system has been developed to support synchronous and asynchronous conferences. Figure 7.2 shows the online learning environment.

Evaluation results of the project are very encouraging. Although students had to pay for their telecommunications connections, 83 per cent accepted this. On average, four car journeys to the university were saved each week through the use of the system. Nearly 67 per cent of the students stayed at home more often while participating in the project, and they were able to use their time more flexibly eg by linking into the system late at night. The average number of logins per week was more than five per person. The most widely used parts of the system were the information and communication systems, word processing systems and graphic processing applications (Seitz and Bodendorf, 1994).

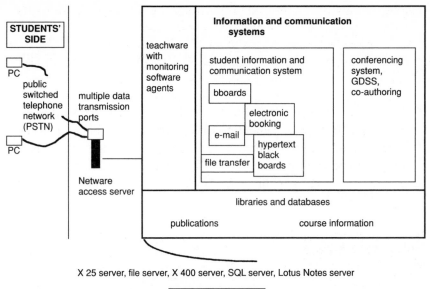

Figure 7.2 *The 'Portable PCs for Students' learning environment*

This collaborative learning and teamwork project uses mainly widely available and reasonably cheap technologies. It is an excellent example of an integrated approach to decentralised teaching and learning in a large city conurbation. Its focus is on both the technology for teamwork and support, and the learning benefits of working collaboratively in distributed 'virtual' environments.

Teleteaching Generally

As with the Internet, it is worth saying something about general developments in the field of teleteaching. Teleteaching is a general term applied to the development and application of telecommunications techniques in teaching and learning. So, broadly speaking, it encompasses those aspects of distance learning and training which use telecommunications. This is an expanding area of learning, training and development, especially in Europe and North America.

Technologies

The most widely used technologies are those which are widely available and relatively cheap to buy. The basic requirements for most teleteaching systems are:

- a workstation for learners and tutors made up of a PC, communications software, modem and a telephone line
- a host computer where group communications software is held (such as e-mail and computer conferencing) and on which other learning resources can be held, and which acts as a gateway to other networks and computers.

New technologies are being trialled and tested to determine their suitability for teleteaching, such as ISDN (Integrated Services Digital Network), a digital telephone service carrying data at high speeds across digital telephone lines (as opposed to the normal analogue lines); fibre optics; DBS (direct broadcast by satellite), and cellular radio. Examples of the use of these technologies in teleteaching include video-teleconferencing and multimedia conferencing.

At the moment, these technologies are being trialled largely in synchronous learning and training situations ie in real time. This has some disadvantages for the kind of cooperative learning which I have discussed in this book, where a value is put on the freedom to work in your cooperative group as and when you wish, and take time to reflect and evaluate your own learning and that of the group. What is additionally needed are trials in the use of ISDN etc in asynchronous learning situations.

No doubt in time these technologies will become mainstream in teleteaching. At the moment, however, there are several drawbacks to their use in the everyday application of CSCL:

- They require access to specially equipped and dedicated studios and buildings where the facilities are kept. In one project experimenting with the use of ISDN-based multimedia distance learning, the facilities required included a specially designed studio with cameras, video-projectors, video-codecs, multiplexers and specialised still image management systems (Coiro *et al.*, 1993). In this example, only two sites were able to participate, linked together through ISDN.
- They require considerable system support. In the above example, technicians, computer experts and trainers would be required.

- They are expensive, involving the cost of the high-speed data connections between the sites; the cost of the special equipment and studios, and the cost of 'people' support.
- They require considerable user training, at least in the first instances. All teleteaching requires some training for users, but the scale of training in the use of dedicated systems such as the one described above is considerably more than would be required for users to learn how to use computer mediated communications systems.
- They are (at the moment) used for same-time (synchronous) meetings. This requires learners and trainees to be present at the same time, so offsetting the advantages of more 'open' learning systems based on asynchronous communications.

Teleteaching Applications

Teleteaching is being used in just about every area of learning and training, including the following.

Medical Practitioner Development

Medical consultants are using telecommunications systems to provide remote diagnosis. Telemedicine is:

> The investigation, monitoring and management of patients and the education of patients and staff using systems which allow ready access to expert advice and patient information, no matter where the patient or relevant information is located (Akselsen and Lilehaug, 1993).

The general scenario is a patient and general practitioner located some way from a hospital who require a specialist opinion or diagnosis. The specialist is contacted via video-conference usually and offers a telediagnosis. Images from microscopes and endoscopes are also used.

There is a built-in professional development aspect of this scenario. Considerable learning occurs for the GP through role modelling – he or she has the experience of practical demonstrations given by specialists; they practise in cooperation with the specialist, and they practise carrying out procedures with expert guidance (Akselsen and Lilehaug, 1993).

School Education

An example of this is the 'Schools in Networks' project in Denmark (Anttila and Eriksen, 1993) where the objective is to explore the use of telematics in collaborative learning between pupils and teachers in schools in over twenty different European and overseas countries. The pupils are involved in a wide range of projects in foreign languages, mathematics, physics, ecology and so on. In addition:

> Students and teachers participating in the above mentioned projects experience not only how much we can learn from each other, and how much we are dependent on each other, but also how important it is to understand who they are and which society they are part of (Anttila and Eriksen, 1993).

Foreign Language Teaching

The field of foreign language teaching via teleteaching methods is set to burgeon. For example, the LINGO service (Beutelspacher and Neubert, 1993) offered 1000 hours of ISDN, flexible language learning provision targeted at the paying market sector. LINGO will cover translation training, grammar training, multimedia language labs and games for language learners at most levels, linking learners with interpreters, language consultants, authors and teachers.

The Berlitz Language Learning Centre is another example of the application of teleteaching to language learning (Davies, Davies and Jennings, 1992). This centre is part of a European-wide network called ELNET, the European Business and Language Learning Network. This project had as its aims to:

- develop strategies for learning in multicultural groups
- develop a low-cost, telecommunications-based European distributed communication infrastructure
- investigate the organisational impact of cross-cultural learning groups
- develop techniques and models for managing distributed learning systems (Mason, 1993).

ELNET used computer conferencing for the exchange of communications between language learners in a student-centred approach. The learners had positive experiences using the system, and the system as a whole was considered highly successful by those involved. But, as with most of the initiatives so far described in this chapter, the experience indicated the enormity of carrying out language teaching via this new technology. The time needed to set up and run the system, learn to tutor by it and manage it successfully were all factors which had not been fully realised prior to the three year project. As with Athena and other projects, the future of ELNET would require the full financial backing of the participating institutions:

The lack of resources at this level of educational provision... led the ELNET team to conclude that on the whole, this was the right technology in the wrong market. The development of computer conferencing at a technical level is ahead of the curriculum and institutional implications of its use (Mason, 1993).

The LINGO project is perhaps more likely to succeed as it is based on a market-led approach which takes into account the full costs of setting up and running a commercial language learning teleteaching system.

EC/DELTA projects
The European Community DELTA Exploratory Action is concerned with the development of learning technologies (Van den Brande, 1993; Rodriguez-Rosello, 1993).

CO-LEARN
CO-LEARN is concerned with experimenting with a range of flexible and distance learning and training environments in collaborative learning contexts. It focuses mainly on access to human resources, such as tutors, experts, working colleagues and peers (Derycke and Kaye, 1993).

CO-LEARN is a multimedia project, using ISDN, audio channels and multiwindowing, where users have their own work-window and where they share other windows with the other participants during real-time learning events. There are four modes of communication:

1. *Real-time teleteaching.* Remote lecturing with remote 'electronic blackboards' and audio follow-ups.
2. *Real-time tele-assistance.* Tutors can monitor learners' screens.
3. *Real-time multimedia conferencing.* Using ISDN, learners participate in a 'virtual classroom' where documents can be shared and spoken communications can occur.
4. Asynchronous computer conferencing and e-mail. There is also the possibility for voice mail and file attachments, with easy linkages to the multimedia platform.

The evaluation of CO-LEARN focuses on how easy it is for users to learn to use the systems; the time required to use the various tools; the speed of task execution; cross-cultural issues, and the flexibility of use of the tools (Workshop on DELTA Evaluation projects, London, June, 1994).

Various models for group work are being tested within CO-LEARN eg user expertise model; organisational model; information model. Care is being taken to take account of the relevant organisational and social aspects, so as to avoid some of the traditional pitfalls of CSCW developments. A major focus of this project is to establish how to support the *processes* of learning in these virtual environments (Derycke and Kaye, 1993).

Acknowledgement

I would like to acknowledge the work of the MECPOL team in helping to carry out the evaluation of the Internet courses discussed in this Chapter, especially my colleague Celia Graebner, who carried out much of the work on the tutor evaluation, and Maggie McPherson, who assisted in the initial preparation of the student questionnaires. The MECPOL Project was supported by a grant from the European Union Socrates ODL Programme, project number 35318-CP-2-96-1-NO-ODL-ODL. The project Web site is: www.idb.hist.no/mecpol

Note

1. Abstracts of the conference papers can be found at: www.shef.ac.uk/uni/projects/csnl/

8 | Researching CSCL

Introduction

In this final chapter I will look at ways of researching group-work in CSCL environments, and propose a plan of research aimed at addressing some important questions concerning the role of CSCL in learning and training.

In carrying out research into computer supported cooperative learning, what sort of questions would we be trying to answer? What research focus would be appropriate, considering the learning purposes of CSCL? Where would we start looking for complementary research, and what kinds of complementary research have already been carried out?

CSCL, as described in this book, relies heavily on the use of computers and electronic communication networks to mediate the work of cooperative learning groups. The use of computers and networks for general communication is often referred to as computer-mediated communications (CMC). The introduction of CMC into organisational and educational life not only broadens the possibility for enhancing the goals of any endeavour, but also introduces a change in the social behaviour of those involved of a kind that has possibly never been experienced before.

Within education, the introduction of CMC into the educational process is partly based on the premis that computer conferencing will support and facilitate *group work* in ways that are not achievable face to face (see Harasim, 1990; Mason and Kaye, 1989; Verdejo *et al.*, 1994; Harasim *et al.*, 1995; Collis, 1996; Mason and Bacsich, 1998). The possibility to mediate educational activities through advanced learning technologies such as CMC begins to question many aspects of our educational practice to date. At the core of the use of this technology is the suggestion that tutors and learners need not *physically* meet in order to take part in group activities (such as seminars and tutorials) where 'presence' and active social participation through discussion is required. This in turn begins to question many of the current assumptions about 'effective' teaching and learning practices.

But to what extent does CMC support educational group work

(JCAL, 1997)? The medium is currently being used as a tool at various levels of education, on the assumption that it does support groups working together. The purpose of this chapter is to describe a possible research agenda concerned with ways of researching group-work in CSCL. I think it is important to research this area because there is a need to:

a) understand the nature of group-work as it occurs online, so that we can evaluate the possible position and 'worthwhileness' of CSCL technologies and processes within the wider educational context. This should help us address questions to do with the role of CSCL in supporting any activity in which a group of learners comes together for a shared purpose (eg, lectures; seminars; tutorials; problem solving; project work, and so on). Given the increasing demand for open and distance education, and the rise in student numbers in higher education, we can anticipate an increased demand for the use of CSCL

b) understand the ways in which groups work online in comparison to the ways in which they work in face-to-face meetings (by 'ways in which groups work' I mean such things as the processes, social relations and products of group meetings).

CSCL researchers are posing a new set of questions concerning learning. These questions often derive from a socio-cultural perspective on learning (Koschmann, 1996). Some important research questions that require answering include:

- How do groups with shared educational goals work cooperatively/ collaboratively using CSCL?
- What are the problems in working in this way?
- What are the benefits?
- How does CSCL group-work differ from what we know about group-work in face-to-face meetings?
- What are the unique characteristics of this medium for groups in education wishing to work together?
- What implications do teaching and learning in this way have for those involved?
- What would a future educational system that uses CSCL as a core medium of activity 'look like'?
- How do social factors enter into the process of learning?

Previous Relevant Research

Research looking at group-work supported by technology has largely focused on technologies that support group *decision making* (eg, in business). With a few exceptions, the research has been experimental and laboratory-based.

Group Decision and Support Systems (GDSS)

Research into GDSS has largely focused on the impact of these systems on the ways in which groups *make decisions* (Beaudouin-Lafon, 1998; Eom and Lee, 1990; Gray *et al.*, 1990; Greif, 1988; Johansen, 1988). The methodology has largely been experimental laboratory work. None of these studies has focused on the role of GDSS in educational settings, other than to look at their use for administrative and managerial purposes.

Group Communication Support Systems (GCSS)

Research into GCSS (eg, computer conferencing; e-mail) can be divided into two groups.

First, empirical experimental laboratory studies looking at decision making in GCSS environments. In a recent assessment of empirical research into the effects of electronic meetings on group processes and outcomes (Kraemer and Pinsonneault, 1990; Pinsonneault and Kraemer, 1990) it was concluded that GCSS affect group process in four ways:

- they increase the total effort of the group
- depth of analysis is increased
- there is a decrease in cooperation amongst members
- decision time is increased.

GCSS have two major effects on group outcomes: the quality of decisions is increased, but the confidence of the group members in those decisions is decreased (it is suggested that this is due to the decrease in cooperation).

With some notable exceptions (see Sproull and Keisler, 1991, for example), most of the research into GCSS has been conducted in laboratory settings, with consequent limitations on the meaning of the results. For example, the selection of participants may have been biased; the use of students recruited for the experiments may have consequences on the results; the experiments were carried out with small (three or four members) groups – no work was carried out with larger groups; the stage of development of the groups does not feature in the context setting of the work; most of the subjects in these experiments were working in largely non-meaningful contexts. McGrath (1990) indicates the need to be clear about this last point when making judgements about the results of such experiments. Whether these research findings have validity for conducting group work via GCSS in educational settings is not established.

Pinsonneault *et al.* conclude that we now need field research looking at the use of GCSS in *real* settings, and we need to study the *processes* of group-work mediated by GCSS. This is also a concern articulated by those interested in socio-cultural approaches to learning (eg Salomon and Perkins, 1998). The research agenda outlined below aims to address these concerns.

Second, studies concerned with the role and potential of GCSS in education: most of these studies have been concerned with establishing the place of GCSS in education, and with describing the experience of students and tutors involved in using computer conferencing (eg, Boshier, 1990; Emms and McConnell, 1988; Hiltz, 1986a and b; McConnell, 1990; Mason, 1989a). To date, little systematic work has been carried out into the ways in which groups function online and, to my knowledge, there has been no research to date on group processes in educational settings using these media.

More recently, an interest in computer supported collaborative argumentation (CSCA) has emerged. The interest here is in:

- methods for studying CSCA
- conditions for argumentative dialogue
- synchronous and asynchronous argumentation
- support for argumentative discourse (Veerman *et al.*, 1999).

A good review of this domain is offered by Kanselaar *et al.*, 1999.

The Context of CSCL Research

In researching CSCL, we have to bear in mind that we are working in a context where the focus is on group-work mediated by a CSCL technology which is asynchronous, time-bridging and distance-spanning, and which is characterised by the following attributes:

- communication is in a written form only

- group participants receive and send at various times
- there may be extensive and unpredictable lags in feedback
- the medium eliminates all non-verbal and para-verbal channels, and indeed all other sensory modes of communication (Hodgson and McConnell, 1991; McGrath, 1990).

Unlike most previous research into group work using GCSS, it will be important to carry out the research in *real* settings where participants use the medium for important, meaningful and purposeful reasons (eg, where they cannot complete their studies without constant and active use of the medium). It will also be important to address issues of group function and process as they occur in meaningful settings, rather than their occurrence in experimental laboratory settings.

Much of this research has to be seen as exploratory at this stage. This is a new medium for educational group-work. Although we can be guided by existing knowledge and practice of group-work, we cannot assume that our understanding extrapolates directly to working in CSCL. Most researchers in the field take pains to point this out (see, for example, Hardy *et al.*, 1991; Kling, 1991; Kraemer and Pinsonneault, 1990; McGrath, 1990; Pinsonneault and Kraemer, 1990). Hence the need for a new kind of research.

Koschman describes CSCL as a new learning paradigm, one that is still in its formative stages. However, he suggests a general analytic framework of research in this area:

> First, driven by the types of research question being asked, work in CSCL tends to focus on process rather than outcomes. Second, there is a central concern with grounding theories in observational data (Glaser and Strauss, 1968) and in the construction of thick descriptions (Lincoln and Guba, 1985) of the phenomenon under study. As a consequence, CSCL studies tend to be descriptive rather than experimental. A third and final aspect of this emerging body of research is that there is an expressed interest in understanding the process from the participant's viewpoint (Koschman, 1996, p.15).

We will have to be concerned with the relationship between the espoused educational purposes of any CSCL programme and the ways in which these are manifest in the work of the cooperative, online groups. For example, CSCL programmes are run in a cooperative mode where learners and tutors take equal responsibility for design and decision making. This requires considerable group-work involving, for example, sharing, supporting, challenging, and self/peer/tutor assessment. In addition, decision-making processes, planning, resolving conflicts of interest, and choice-making are issues which learners and tutors are all concerned with. One needs to understand the context in which the tutors and learners are working in order to begin to understand what is happening, and why. The CSCL epistemological culture is one in which learners and tutors alike work collectively to arrive at personal knowledge about the area of learning in which they are engaged. The situatedness of learning and the emphasis on communities of practice (Lave and Wenger, 1991; Lave, 1996) are important concerns. Just how this occurs and is 'worked-out' in this online environment is a major focus of CSCL research.

Researching Group-work in CSCL

What would an agenda for researching group-work in CSCL look like? What follows here is an attempt to answer this question.[1] The research perspective adopted tries to be sensitive to the purposes and methods of CSCL.

An Agenda for Action

In this agenda for action, there are three separate but closely interlinked parts to the research design, each one addressing an important question about the nature of educational group-work in a CSCL environment. Taken overall, it is imagined that this research agenda will provide a general understanding of 'online' group work.

Let me stress that the research has to be exploratory. Working with CSCL has led me to believe that group work is different in some respects when carried out in CSCL environments compared with face-to-face ones. Some of these differences have been elaborated in Chapter 3. A research programme would try to develop a picture of what it is like for people to work as learners and tutors in CSCL environments. Our interest would be in the ways in which the groups communicate online, and the ways in which knowledge is negotiated, presented, received, shared, controlled, understood and misunderstood by tutors and learners in the online environment. We would use research methods that would allow us to explore issues rather than methods which would impose a certain kind of highly structured framework on the research. We would be disinclined to use models of group-work and processes which might define *how* we look at the research data in advance of carrying out the research. It would, however, be possible to use these as ways of comparing group-work online with that in face-to-face groups.

But the overriding ambition would be to 'make sense' from a naturalistic research perspective (Lincoln and Guba, 1985).

The methodology therefore would depend to some extent on our expertise in facilitation methods. The research would be carried out in open learning environments, with the learners and tutors who make up the online groups taking part in the research. We would be working with their phenomena and helping them develop their ideas, perceptions and understandings of what it is like to learn in groups via CSCL. It is likely that audio or audio-visual recordings of these sessions would form the data for analysis of these parts of the research. Additionally, transcripts of the CSCL work would be analysed from our own (researchers') perspectives. At times we would want to relate our analysis to that of the groups' own analyses, and to that of the judges' (see below) interpretations of the groups' work online. But we would also be analysing the transcripts in order to examine the ways in which knowledge is negotiated, controlled, understood, etc. by the learners and tutors. Such a research plan is shown in Figure 8.1.

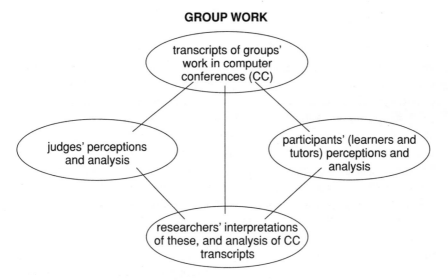

GROUP WORK

Figure 8.1 *A CSCL research plan*

Areas of Research

The following is a proposal for researching group-work in CSCL (mainly computer conferencing) environments. There are three broad areas of research, each of which will be discussed in turn:

1. What happens in CSCL group-work?
2. Using 'judges' to assess group-work.
3. Phenomenological case-studies.

1.   What happens in CSCL group-work?

This part of the research focuses on the processes that take place in CSCL group-work mediated by computer conferencing. This is achieved through an in-depth analysis of user participation rates in the groups, and an analysis of the group dynamics.

a)   Participation in the CSCL groups is assessed by measures of:

- how often (in real terms and as a percentage of the total) each participant joins the group
- how often (in real terms and as a percentage of the total) each participant enters items and/or responses to the groups' work
- entries made in terms of the number of words/sentences/phrases entered per participant.

The purpose of these measures is to indicate the various patterns of participation in the groups. Issues such as turn-taking, participant dominance and so on are considered here. The concern is to see if this medium supports individual participation in group-work in ways that are not possible in face-to-face meetings (eg, does the medium provide for a more egalitarian regime; is the democratic process 'widened'/facilitated). It can also be anticipated that the medium will support (to varying degrees) some individuals' ways of working, but not others'. For example, in using CSCL, it is our experience that some people who are very able and relaxed talkers in face-to-face groups are 'unable' to function online to the same degree; conversely, some people who find face-to-face meetings difficult, find online meetings more amenable to their way of interacting.

b)   Group dynamics

Group dynamics are researched by carrying out a qualitative content analysis of what happens in the groups. Transcripts from group conferences would be analysed, and a typology of group dynamics developed. Our purpose here is to illuminate and describe the process of group-work as seen from the perspective of the researcher. In doing this we bear in mind existing models and theories of group dynamics and group development (eg, Bales, 1950; Bales and Strodtbeck, 1951; Bion, 1961; McGrath, 1990; Rackham and Morgan, 1977; Tuckman, 1965) and the literature on group processes (Colman and Bexton, 1975; Colman and Geller, 1985; Gillette and McCollom, 1990; Smith, 1980; Smith and Berg, 1987), but the research does not seek specifically to use any of these models in the analysis of the data. In the research we would explore the relevance of such models and frameworks in CSCL. Since we hypothesise that this medium offers the opportunity for groups to work in ways that are not possible face-to-face, our analysis would indicate these new group processes.

The working hypothesis, developed through personal experience in using the medium, is that group-work mediated by CSCL is distinct in some features from group-work face to face. For example, discussions online often stop for periods of time, and are later picked up again. It is not uncommon for participants to lose their sense of 'where they are' in the discussion over time. Neither of these attributes seems likely to happen in face-to-face groups. An examination of group-work in CSCL would help us to determine recurring patterns and dynamics, and to see if groups go through stages of development. Our guiding theoretical basis here would be our present understanding of group-work as it occurs in face-to-face meetings, and we would intuitively use this as a constant comparison with our findings of what occurs in group-work online.

In this research, we would be working from a natural research paradigm (Carr and Kemmis, 1986; Hlynka and Belland, 1991; Lincoln and Guba, 1985; Reason and Rowan, 1981). The groups' online activities would be examined from the view point of ethnographers (Hammersley and Atkinson, 1983; Hughes *et al.*, 1993). We would seek to develop a 'grounded' theory perspective (Glaser and Strauss, 1968) of the dynamics of the groups, allowing as far as possible categories to be developed from the data themselves. This approach can be seen as complementing some of the experimental, hypothetico-deductive laboratory research already conducted in this area.

Some guiding questions in the research analysis include:

- What is the nature of the group-work – what are people trying to achieve?
- How do they go about organising themselves as a group and start their work?
- What roles do different people play in the groups, eg information giver; leader; supporter; questioner?
- What group norms seem to be in force? How do these arise and how are they maintained or challenged?
- How cohesive is the group – what is its culture, and how do different groups compare with each other?

- What is the role of the tutor in the groups? How does the tutor function in the group?
- Do groups go through stages of development online – and do these resemble developmental stages described by other authors and researchers?

2. Using 'judges' to assess group work

The focus here is on making judgements about the educational processes taking place in the groups. Professional people experienced in group-work (eg, university tutors, organisational training officers) act as 'judges' to examine transcripts of the group conferences in order to 'assess' the educational processes going on in them. The purpose here is to determine to what extent the groups are engaging in 'group-work' ie, work that involves collaboration and cooperation.

The assumption here is that the judges will provide their own frameworks (based on their professional practice and experience) for analysing the conference transcripts, rather than their being offered a framework to work to by the researchers. Important questions are:

- How does the group-work online compare with that of face-to-face meetings?
- What are the differences?
- How do the judges perceive the dynamics of the online group-work?
- What seem to be the unique qualities of online group-work?
- What implications for those involved (tutors and learners) does this suggest?

The 'judges'' meetings would be tape-recorded, and qualitatively analysed. We would be looking at:

- What sort of criteria do judges use (ie, what evidence do they look for) when making judgements about the nature of the group's online work?
- How are these criteria applied to the online group-work?
- What outcomes do judges arrive at?
- Do they think group-work is happening in the online conferences?
- What do they say about:
  the quality of that work
  the processes taking place
  the dynamics involved
- How do they measure these against their experience of similar group-work face to face?

The purpose is to facilitate the judges' meetings, but not to impose a predefined process or structure. Rather we would help judges understand the purpose of the meetings (ie, to analyse CSCL meetings and discuss the nature of the participants' activities in them) and facilitate discussion around this. We would be interested in the views of judges concerning the ways in which the groups communicate online, and the ways in which knowledge is negotiated, presented, received, shared, controlled, understood and misunderstood by tutors and learners in the online environment. In so far as we would 'structure' these meetings, it is primarily around these issues. The audio recordings of these meetings would be used to compare and contrast the various views of the judges, and we would look for recurring themes, judgements, views and opinions which could help structure a typology of views on the topic.

3.   *Phenomenological case studies*
The focus here is on the CSCL groups' defined purposes and their experience of working cooperatively online. This part of the research would be concerned with developing an understanding of the ways in which groups 'function' in CSCL environments, from the perspective of the participants in the groups. It might be sufficient to involve three or four groups in this part of the research.

These are essentially a series of phenomenological case studies aimed at being open to the concerns, constructs, assumptions and logic of the participants in the groups. This cooperative research design would allow us to match the groups' defined purposes with their own analysis of the groups' functions, processes and longitudinal development. In addition we (researchers, learners and tutors alike) would be in a position to develop an understanding of the process of learning (experiential and propositional) as it occurs online.

This would be carried out by gathering the groups together for such occasions. We would focus on why the groups work in the way they do, using transcripts of the CSCL meetings to stimulate recall of the group-work where necessary. The ways in which participants perceive the group processes and what sense they make of working in this way; their views on the 'benefits' of online group-work, gender issues, group development over time, roles people adopt online, and so on, would be examined. All of this would be underpinned by our major interest in the ways in which the groups communicate online, and the ways in which knowledge is negotiated.

The role of the researcher here is to help facilitate the process of the groups' self-analyses, and afterwards to help explain the thinking underlying the participants' actions in the group conferences. This design should help minimise the influence of the researcher's preconceptions. The audio-recordings of these meetings would be the basis for the researcher's analysis.

Conclusion

This chapter has outlined an agenda for researching group-work in CSCL environments. The approach suggested involves small-scale ethnographic and phenomenological case studies. The emphasis is on researching real uses of CSCL, in natural and meaningful contexts where tutors and learners are obliged to use the medium in order to complete their work.

Note

1. There are of course many other ways of researching CSCL (see eg Articulate, 1995, which lists a variety of evaluation tools; Mason, 1992, who discusses evaluation methods in computer conferences; Jones, 1998, who examines ethnographic approaches; Jones, 1999, who examines the whole issue of researching the Internet).

Bibliography

Akselsen, S and Lillehaug, S I (1993) Teaching and learning aspects of remote medical consultations, in Davies and Samways (1993)

Andriessen, J et al (1996) *Using Complex Information in Argumentation for Collaborative Text Production.* Paper presented at UCIS 1996 Conference, Poitier, France

Anttila, K M and Eriksen, M (1993) Schools in network, in Davies and Samways (1993)

Argyle, M (1991) *Cooperation: The basis of sociability*, Routledge, London

Aries, E (1976) Interaction patterns and themes of male, female, and mixed sex groups, *Small Group Behaviour*, **7** (1) 7–18

ARTICULATE (1995) *Evaluation Guidelines Handbook. Deliverable 17*, European Union DELTA Programme

Avril, C (1989) Personal presentation on Athena, MIT, March 1989

Axelrod, R (1990) *The Evolution of Cooperation*, Penguin Books, London

Bales, R F (1950) *Interaction Process Analysis: A method for the study of small groups*, Addison Wesley, Reading, Mass

Bales, R F and Strodtbeck, F L (1951) Phases in group problem solving, *Journal of Abnormal and Social Psychology*, **46** (4), pp 485–95

Banks, S, Graebner, C and McConnell, D (1998) *Proceedings of the International Conference on Networked Lifelong Learning: Innovative approaches to education and training through the Internet*, University of Sheffield, DACE. Abstracts published at: www.shef.ac.uk/uni/projects/csnl/nll

Barnes, D et al (1969) *Language, the Learner and the School*, Penguin, Middlesex

Barnes, D and Todd, F (1977) *Communication and Learning in Small Groups*, Routledge and Kegan Paul, London

Bastick, T (1999) *An Alternative Method of Measuring Teacher Quality.* Paper presented at 1999 EARLI Conference, Gothenburg

Bates, A W (1993) Educational aspects of the telecommunications revolution, in Davies and Samways (1993)

Beaudouin-Lafon, M (ed) (1998) *Computer Supported Cooperative Work (CSCW)*, John Wiley & Sons, London

Becker, H S, Geer, B and Hughes, E C (1968) *Making the Grade: The academic side of academic life*, John Wiley, NY

Beitelspacher, K and Neubert, K (1993) LINGO – an ISDN-based foreign language service, in Davies and Samways (1993)

Bion, W R (1961) *Experience in Groups and Other Papers*, Tavistock, London

Bischoping, K (1993) Gender differences in conversation topics, 1922–1990, *Sex Roles,* **28** (1/2), pp 1–18

Bodendorf, F and Seitz, R (1993) Teamwork training by use of innovative computer-supported technologies, *Proceedings of the AEESEAP/FEISEAP/IACEE International Conference on Engineering Education '93, November 10–12 1993*, Singapore

Bodendorf, F and Seitz, R (1994) Learning flexible task management by computer supported tele- and teamwork, *Proceedings of the 1994 ACM SIGCPR Conference, March 24–26 1994,* Alexandria, Virginia

Boder, A (1992) The process of knowledge reification in human–human interaction, *Journal of Computer Assisted Learning,* **8** (3), pp 177–85

Boder, A and Gardiol, C (1995) Building an evolving knowledge base from computer teleconferencing, in Verdijo and Cerri (1994)

Bonamy, J and Haugluslaine-Charlier, B (1995) Supporting professional learning: beyond technological support, *Journal of Computer Assisted Learning,* **11** (4), pp 196–202

Boot, R and Reynolds, M (1984) Rethinking experience based events, in Cox, C and Beck, J (1984)

Boot, R and Hodgson, V (1987) Open learning: meaning and experience, in Hodgson, V, Mann, S and Snell, R (eds) (1987)

Boot, R and Hodgson, V (1988) Open learning: philosophy or expediency?, *Programmed Learning and Educational Technology,* **25** (3)

Boshier, R (1990) Socio-psychological factors in electronic networking, I*nternational Journal of Lifelong Education,* **9** (1)

Boud, D (1988) Moving toward autonomy, in Boud, D (ed) (1988) *Developing Student Autonomy in Learning,* Kogan Page, London

Boud, D (1994) The move to self-assessment: liberating or a new mechanism for oppression?, in *Reflecting on changing practices, contexts and identities, Papers from the 24th Annual SCUTREA Conference, University of Hull,* published by Department of Adult Continuing Education, Leeds University, UK

Boud, D and Walker, D (1998) Promoting reflection in professional courses: the challenge of context, *Studies in Higher Education,* **23** (2), pp 191–206

Boyd, G (1987) Emancipative educational technology, *Canadian Journal of Educational Communication,* **16** (2), pp 167–92

Boyd, H and Cowan, J (1985) A case for self-assessment based on recent studies of student learning, *Assessment and Evaluation in Higher Education,* **10** (3), pp 225–35

Boydell, T and Pedler, M (1991) *Management Self-development,* Gower, UK

Brochet, M (1985) Computer conferencing as a seminar tool: a case study, *Workshop on Computer Conferencing,* University of Guelph, Canada

Brochet, M (1985) *Effective Moderation of Computer Conferences: Notes and suggestions,* University of Guelph Computing Support Service, Guelph, Canada

Brooks, V R (1982) Sex differences in student dominance behaviour in female and male professors' classrooms, *Sex Roles,* **8** (7), pp 683–90

Bryson, M (1994) Entry in a Caucus computer conference at Lancaster University, *Canadian Journal of Educational Communication,* **16** (2), Spring 1987. Special Issue, Computer Mediated Communication

Carr, W and Kemmis, S (1986) *Becoming Critical: Education, knowledge and action research,* Falmer Press, Brighton

Chandler, D (1990) The educational ideology of the computer, *British Journal of Educational Technology,* **21** (3), pp 165–74

Chesebro, J W and Bonsall, D G (1989) *Computer Mediated Communication – Human relationships in a computerized world,* University of Alabama Press, Tuscalosa and London

Coiro, S *et al* (1993) Design and experimental monitoring of an ISDN-based multimedia distance learning service, in Davies and Samways (1993)

Collaborative Group Work (1998) www.collaborate.shef.ac.uk

Collins, M and Berge, Z L (1998) *The Moderators Page: Resources for moderators and facilitators of online discussion*, Northern Arizona University. Available from: http://star.ucc.nau.edu/~mauri/moderators.html

Collis, B (1995) Networking and distance learning for teachers: a classification of possibilities, *Journal of Information Technology for Teacher Education*, **4** (2), pp 117–35

Collis, B (1996) *Tele-learning in a Digital World: The future of distance learning*, Int. Thomson Computer Press, London

Colman, D and Harold Bexton, W (eds) (1975) *Group Relations Reader*, Grex, California

Colman, D and Geller, M H (1985) *Group Relations Reader 2*, A K Rice Institute, Washington

COSMOS (1988) *A Research Programme into Group Working over Computer Networks*, British Telecom, Martlesham Heath, Ipswich

Cowie, H and Ruddick, J (1988) *Co-operative Group Work: An overview,* BP Educational Service, Sheffield University

Cox, C and Beck, J (1984) *Management Development: Advances in practice and theory*, J Wiley & Sons, London

Cox, S and Gibbs, G (1994) *Course Design for Resource Based Learning*, The Oxford Centre for Staff Development, Oxford

Crosby, C and Hunter, C S (1987) *A Partial Bibliography of References Related to Computer Conferencing,* University of Guelph, Guelph, Canada

Crowston, K and Malone, T W (1988) Intelligent software agents, *BYTE*, **13** (13)

Cunningham, I (1981) Self-managed learning in independent study, in Boydell, T and Pedler, M (eds) (1991)

Cunningham, I (1987) Openness and learning to learn, in Hodgson, V, Mann, S and Snell, R (eds) (1987)

Davie, L E (1989) Facilitation techniques for the online tutor, in Mason and Kaye (1989)

Davies, D, Davies, G and Jennings, C (1992) The ELNET final report, CECOMM, Southampton

Davies, G and Samways, B (eds) (1993) *Teleteaching: Proceedings of the IFIP third teleteaching conference,* IFIP, North Holland

Dearing Report into Higher Education (1997), HMSO, London

Derycke, A C and Kaye, A R (1993) Participative modelling and design of collaborative distance learning tools in the COLEARN project, in Davies and Samways (1993)

Deutsch, M (1949) A theory of cooperation and competition, *Human Relations*, **2**, pp 129–52

Dubois, B L and Crouch, I (eds) (1978) *Papers in Southwest English IV: Proceedings of the conference on the sociology of the languages of American women*, Trinity University, San Antonio, Texas

Dunlop, C and Kling, R (eds) (1991) *Computerisation and Controversy: Value conflicts and social change*, Academic Press Inc, Boston

Eakins, B and Eakins, G (1978) Verbal turn taking and exchanges in faculty dialogue, in Dubois, B L and Crouch, I (eds) (1978)

Elden, M and Chisholm, R F (1993) Emerging varieties of action research, H*uman Relations*, **46** (2), pp 121–42

Emms, J and McConnell, D (1988) An evaluation of tutorial support provided by electronic mail and computer conferencing, *Aspects of Educational Technology XXI*, Kogan Page, London

Engelbart, D and Lehtman, H (1988) Working together, *BYTE*, **13** (13)

Entwistle, N J and Ramsden, P (1983) *Understanding Student Learning*, Croom Helm, London

Eom, H B and Lee, S M (1990) Decision support systems applications research: a bibliography, *European Journal of Operational Research*, **46**, pp 333–42

Falchikov, N and Boud, D (1989) Student self assessment in higher education: a meta-analysis, *Review of Educational Research*, **59** (4), pp 395–430

Feenberg, A (1982) *Moderating an Educational Teleconference*, Western Behavioral Sciences Institute, La Jolla, California

Feenberg, A (1986) Network design: an operating manual for computer conferencing, *IEEE Transactions on Professional Communications*, **29** (1)

Feenberg, A (1989) The written world, in Mason, R and Kaye, A R (eds) (1989)

Fernback, J (1999) There is a there: notes towards a definition of cybercommunity, in Jones, S (ed) (1999)

Fisser, P and de Boer, W (1998) Implementing tele-learning: decision support for instructors, the TeleTOP Project, in Banks *et al* (1998)

Freire, P (1972) *Pedagogy of the Oppressed*, Penguin Education, Middlesex

Freire, P (1985) *The Politics of Education: Culture, power and liberation,* MacMillan, Basingstoke

French, J and French, P (1984) Gender imbalances in the primary classroom: an interactional account, *Educational Research,* **26** (2), pp 127–36

Gailson, P and Thompson, E (eds) (1999) *The Architecture of Science,* MIT Press, Cambridge, Mass

Galegher, J, Kraut, R E and Egido, C (eds) (1990) *Intellectual Teamwork: Social and technological foundations of cooperative work*, Lawrence Erlbaum Assoc, Hillsdale, NJ

Gardiol, C, Boder, A, and Peraya, D (1993) The JITOL project and model, in Davies, G and Samways, G (eds) (1993)

Gillette, J and McCollom, M (eds) (1990) *Groups in Context: A new perspective on group dynamics*, Addison Wesley, Reading, Mass

Giroux, H A (1983) *Theory and Resistance in Education: A pedagogy for the opposition*, Heinemann, London

Glaser, B G and Strauss, A L (1968) *The Discovery of Grounded Theory*, Weidenfield & Nicholson, London

Goodyear, P (1995) Situated action and distributed knowledge, *Educational Training Technology International*, **32** (1), pp 45–55

Goodyear, P and Steeples, C (1998) Creating shareable representations of practice, *Association for Learning Technology Journal*, **6** (3), pp 16–23

Graddol, D (1989) Some CMC discourse properties and their educational significance, in Mason, R and Kaye, A (eds) (1989)

Graddol, D and Swann, J (1989) *Gender Voices,* Blackwell, Oxford

Gray, P, Vogel, D and Beauclair, R (1990) Assessing GDSS empirical research, *European Journal of Operational Research*, **46**, pp 162–76

Green, L (1998) *Playing Croquet with Flamingos: A guide to moderating online conferences*, Office of Learning Technologies, Ontario, Canada. Available at: http://star.ucc.nau.edu/~mauri/moderate/flamingoe.html

Greeno, J G (1997) Response: on claims that answer the wrong question, *Educational Researcher*, **20** (1), pp 5–17

Greif, I (ed) (1988) *Computer Supported Cooperative Work: A book of readings*, Morgan Kaufmann, California

Grudin, J (1988) Perils and pitfalls, *BYTE,* **13** (13)

Gundry, J (1992) Understanding collaborative learning in networked organisations, in Kaye, A R (ed) (1992)

Haas, A (1979) Male and female spoken language differences: stereotypes and evidence, *Psychological Bulletin*, **86** (3), pp 616–26

Habermas, J (1972) *Knowledge and Human Interests*, Heinemann, London

Hammersley, M and Atkinson, P (1983) *Ethnography: Principles and practice*, Tavistock, London

Harasim, L (1987) *Computer Mediated Cooperation in Education: Group learning networks, second Guelph symposium on computer conferencing, June 1987,* University of Guelph, Ontario

Harasim, L (1987) Teaching and learning on-line: issues in computer mediated graduate courses, *Canadian Journal of Educational Communication*, **16** (2), pp 117–35

Harasim, L (1989) On-line education: a new domain, in Mason and Kaye (eds) (1989)

Harasim, L (ed) (1990) *Online Education: Perspectives on a new environment*, Praeger, NY

Harasim, L (ed) (1993) *Global Networks – Computers and international communication,* MIT Press, Cambridge, Mass

Harasim, L *et al* (1995) *Learning Networks: A field guide to teaching and learning online*, MIT Press, Cambridge, Mass

Hardy, G *et al* (1991) *Computer Mediated Communication for Management Training and Development: A research report*, CSML, Lancaster University, Lancaster

Hardy, G and Hodgson, V (1991) *Gender and Knowledge: An exploration*. Paper presented at the Women In Management Learning Conference, Lancaster University, 1991

Harris, D (1987) *Openness and Closure in Distance Education*, Falmer Press, Brighton

Harris, D (ed) (1988) *World Yearbook of Education 1988: Education for the new technologies*, Kogan Page, London

Haugen, H (1993) Just in time open learning – a European project from a Norwegian point of view, in Davies and Samways (1993)

Heron, J (1981) Self and peer assessment, in Boydell, T and Pedler, M (1991)

Hilkaa, A *et al* (1998) New media in the University of Helsinki: information and communication strategy and its implementation, in Banks *et al* (1998)

Hiltz, S R (1984) *Online Communities: A case study of the office of the future,* Ablex Pub, Norwood, NJ

Hiltz, S R (1986) The virtual classroom: using computer mediated communication for university teaching, *Journal of Communication*, **36** (2), pp 95–104

Hiltz, S R (1986) Collaborative learning in a virtual classroom, in *Proceedings of the Conference on Computer Supported Cooperative Work*, Portland, Oregon

Hiltz, S R and Turoff, M (1978) *The Network Nation: Human communication via computers*, Addison Wesley, Reading, Mass

Hiltz, S R and Turoff, M (1985) Structuring computer-mediated communication systems to avoid information overload, *Communications of the ACM*, **28** (7)

Hiltz, S R and Turoff, M (1987) *Workshop on CMC*, University of Guelph, Guelph, Ontario

Hiltz, S R and Wellman, B (1997) Asynchronous learning networks as a virtual classroom, *Communications of the ACM*, **40** (9), pp 44–49

Hlynka, D and Belland, J C (1991) *Paradigms Regained: The uses of illuminative, semiotic and post modern criticism as modes of inquiry in educational technology*, Educational Technology Pubs, Engelwood Cliffs

Hodgson, V, Mann, S and Snell, R (eds) (1987) *Beyond Distance Teaching – Towards open learning*, SRHE/OU Press, Milton Keynes

Hodgson, V, Lewis, R and McConnell, D (1989) *Information Technology-based Open Learning: A study report, Occasional Paper: InTER/12/89*, Lancaster University, UK

Hodgson, V and McConnell, D (1991) Online education and development, in Prior, J K (ed) (1991)

Hodgson, V and McConnell, D (1992) IT-based open learning: a case study in management learning, *Journal of Computer Assisted Learning*, **8** (3), pp 136–50

Holden, C (1993) Giving girls a chance: patterns of talk in co-operative group work, *Gender and Education*, **5** (2), pp 179–89

Hughes, J *et al* (1993) Ethnography for system design: a guide, in *Interdisciplinarity in Cooperation Technology*, Lancaster CSCW Research Centre, Lancaster University, Lancaster

Jameson, A L (1991) *Using Computer Mediated Communications (CMC) as a Tool to Support Group Development in a Distance Education Context: Is it beneficial?* MPhil Dissertation, Henley Management College, Brunel University

JCAL (1997) *Journal of Computer Supported Learning.* Special issue on computer mediated communications in higher education

Johansen, R (1988) *Groupware: Computer support for business teams,* The Free Press, NY

Johansen, R, Valle, J and Spangles, K (1979) *Electronic Meetings: Technical alternatives and social choices*, Addison Wesley, Reading, Mass

Johnson, D W and Johnson, R T (1990) Cooperative learning and achievement, in Sharan, S (1990)

Jones, A and Mercer, N (1993) Theories of learning and information technology, in Scrimshaw, P (ed) (1990)

Jones, C R (1998) *Context, Content and Cooperation: An ethnographic study of collaborative learning online.* PhD thesis, Manchester Metropolitan University, Manchester

Jones, D (1980) Gossip: notes on women's oral culture, *Women's Studies International Quarterly*, **3**, pp 193–98

Jones, S (ed) (1999) *Doing Internet Research: Critical issues and methods for examining the net,* Sage, Thousand Oaks

Josefowitz, N (1984) Teaching managerial skills to women: the issue of all-female vs mixed sex groups, in *Women and Men in Organizations: Teacher strategies*, ed D M Hai, The Organizational Behaviour Teaching Society, Washington, DC

Journal of Computer Assisted Learning, **11** (4). Special Issue: Support for Professional Learning

Kanselaar, G, Veerman, A L and Andriessen, J (1999) *Software for Problem Solving Through Collaborative Argumentation.* Paper presented at the biannual conference of the European Association for Research on Learning and Instruction (EARLI), Gothenburg, August 24–28 1999

Kaye, A R (1987a) Computer conferencing for distance education, *Nuove technologia e vita quotidiana in Europa,* Bologna, November 1987

Kaye, A R (1987b) Introducing computer-mediated communications into a distance education system, *Canadian Journal of Educational Communications,* **16** (2), pp 153–66

Kaye, A R (ed) (1992) *Collaborative Learning Through Computer Conferencing: The Najaden Papers,* (NATO ASI Series F: Computer and Systems Sciences, Vol. 90), Springer-Verlag, Berlin

Kelly, J (1991) A study of gender differential linguistic interaction in the adult classroom, *Gender and Education,* **3** (2) 137–43

Kerr, E B (1986) Electronic leadership: a guide to moderating conferences, *IEEE Transactions on Professional Communications,* **29** (1), pp 12–18

Kiesler, S, Siegel, J and McGuire, T W (1984) Social psychological aspects of computer mediated communication, *American Psychologist,* October 1984

Kling, R (1991) Computerization and social transformation, *Science, Technology and Human Values,* **16** (3)

Knight, G P and Bohlmeyer, E M (1990) Cooperative learning and achievement: methods for assessing causal mechanisms, in Sharan, S (1990)

Knowles, M (1975) *Self-directed Learning: A guide for learners and teachers,* Association Press, Chicago

Kolb, D A (1984) *Experiential Learning: Experience as the source of learning and development,* Prentice Hall, Englewood Cliffs, NJ

Koschmann, T (1996) Paradigm shifts and instructional technology: an introduction, in Koschmann, T (ed) (1996)

Koschmann, T (ed) (1996) *CSCL: Theory and practice of an emerging paradigm,* Lawrence Erlbaum Assoc, Malwah, NJ

Kraemer, K L and Pinsonneault, A (1990) Technology and groups: assessment of the empirical research, in Galegher, J, Kraut, R E and Egido, C (eds) (1990)

Krol, E (1994) *The Whole Internet: User's guide and catalog,* 2nd edn, O'Reilly & Associates, Inc., Sebastopol, California

Lally, V and Barrett, E (1999) Gender differences in an online learning environment: a case study, *Journal of Computer Assisted Learning,* **15**

Laurillard, D (1993) *Rethinking University Teaching: A framework for the effective use of educational technology,* Routledge, London

Lave, J (1996) Teaching, as learning, in practice, *Mind, Culture and Activity,* **3** (3), pp 149–64

Lave, J and Wenger, E (1991) *Situated Learning: Legitimate peripheral participation,* Cambridge University Press, Cambridge

Learning Research and Development Center (1996) *Advanced Cognitive Tools for Learning,* University of Pittsburgh. Available from: http://advlearn.lrdc.pitt.edu/belvedere/index.html

Levinson, P (1984) *Marshall McLuhan and Computer Conferencing.* Available from the author

Levy, P (1998) Networked professional development for library and information staff: a constructivist approach, in Banks *et al* (1998)

Lewis, R (1995) Editorial: Professional Learning, *Journal of Computer Assisted Learning,* **11** (4), pp 193–95

Lewis, R and Goodyear, P (1992) *Just in Time Open Learning – A DELTA project outline,* NL/1/92, Neuropelab, Archamps, France

Light, P, Colbourn, C and Light, V (1997) Computer mediated tutorial support for conventional university courses, *Journal of Computer Assisted Learning,* **13**, pp 228–35

Lincoln, Y and Guba, E (1985) *Naturalistic Inquiry,* Sage, London

Luft, J (1963) *Group Processes,* National Press, Palo Alto, California

McAteer, E *et al* (1997) Computer mediated communications as a learning resource, *Journal of Computer Assisted Learning,* **13**, pp 219–27

McCollom, M and Gillette, J (1990) The emergence of a new experiential tradition, in Gillette, J and McCollom, M (eds) (1990)

McConnell, D (1988) Computer conferencing in teacher inservice education: a case study, in Harris, D (ed) (1988)

McConnell, D (1988) Group learning in computer conferences, in Smith, D (ed) (1988)

McConnell, D (1990) A case study: the educational use of computer conferencing, *Educational and Training Technology International,* **27** (2), pp 211–23

McConnell, D (1991) Computers, electronic networking and education: some American experiences, *Educational and Training Technology International,* **28** (3)

McConnell, D (1992) Computer mediated communication for management learning, in Kaye, A R (ed) (1992)

McConnell, D (1994) Managing open learning in computer supported collaborative learning environments, *Studies in Higher Education,* **19** (3), pp 341–58

McConnell, D (1996) *Working with Students to Learn About Networked Learning: A phenomenological case study.* Paper presented at the Asynchronous Networked Learning Conference, New York. Available from: www.aln.org

McConnell, D (1997) Interaction patterns of mixed sex groups in educational computer conferences: part 1 – empirical findings, *Gender and Education,* **9** (3), pp 345–64

McConnell, D (1998) Developing networked learning professionals: a critical perspective, in Banks *et al* (1998)

McConnell, D (1999) Examining a collaborative assessment process in networked lifelong learning, *Journal of Computer Assisted Learning,* **15**, pp 232–43

McConnell, D and Hodgson, V (1990) Computer mediated communications systems – electronic networking and education, *Management Education and Development,* **21** (1), pp 51–58

McConnell, D, Hardy, V and Hodgson, V (1996) *Groupwork in Educational Computer Conferences: Final Report to the ESRC No R/000/23/4531,* DACE, University of Sheffield. Available from: www.shef.ac.uk/uni/projects/csnl/ and www.regard.ac.uk/

McCreary, E and Van Duren, J (1987) Educational applications of computer conferencing, *Canadian Journal of Educational Communication,* **16** (2), pp 107–15

McDowell, L and Sambell, K (1999) *Students' Experience of Self Evaluation in Higher Education: Preparation for lifelong learning?* Paper presented at the Bi-annual conference of the European Association for Research on Learning and Instruction (EARLI), Gothenburg, August 24–28, 1999

McGrath, J E (1990) Time matters in groups, in Galegher, J, Kraut, R E and Egido, C (eds) (1990)

Malm, P S (1993) *Groupware Applications, Experimental Systems and Models*, Mimeo, Norwegian Telecom Research, P.O.B. 1156, N-9001, Tromso, Norway

Mantovani, G (1994) Is computer-mediated communication intrinsically apt to enhance democracy in organizations?, *Human Relations*, **47** (1), pp 45–62

Margolis, H (1982) *Selfishness, Altruism and Rationality*, Cambridge University Press, Cambridge

Mason, R (1987) Computer conferencing: its contribution to self directed learning, *British Journal of Educational Technology*, **19** (1), pp 28–42

Mason, R (1989) The use of computer-mediated communication for distance education at the Open University, in Mason, R and Kaye, A R (eds) (1989)

Mason, R (1989) *The Use of Computer Networks for Education and Training*, Training Agency, Sheffield

Mason, R (1991) Moderating educational computer conferencing, *DEOSNEWS,* **1** (19). Available from: http://star.ucc.nau.edu/~mauri/papers/mason.html

Mason, R (1992) Evaluation methods for computer conferencing applications, in Kaye, A R (ed) (1992)

Mason, R (1993) Computer conferencing and the new Europe, in Harasim, L M (ed) (1993)

Mason, R (1993) Designing collaborative work for online courses, in Davies, G and Samway, B (eds) (1993)

Mason, R (1998) Models of online courses, in Banks, S, Graebner, C and McConnell, D (1998)

Mason, R and Bacsich, P (1998) Embedding computer conferencing into university teaching, *Computers Educ,* **30** (3/4), pp 249–58

Mason, R and Kaye, A R (1989) *Mindweave: Communication, computers and distance education*, Pergamon, Oxford

Mason, R and Kaye, T (1990) Towards a new paradigm for distance education, in Harasim, L (ed) (1990)

Meeks, B N (1985) An overview of conferencing systems, *BYTE*, 1985, pp 169–85

Michard, C and Viollet, C (1991) Sex and gender in linguistics: fifteen years of feminist research in the United States and Germany, *Feminist Issues,* Spring, pp 53–88

Miller, C M L and Parlett, M (1974) *Up to the Mark: A study of the examination game,* Society for Research into Higher Education, London

Morrison, T R (1989) Beyond legitimacy: facing the future in distance education, *International Journal of Lifelong Education*, (8), pp 3–24

NL/2/92 (1992) *JITOL Evaluation Toolset – Version 1*, (Occasional Paper), Nuropelab, International Business Park, Le Forum, 74166 Archamps, France

NL/6/93 (1993) *JITOL Evaluation Toolset – Version 2*, (Occasional Paper), Nuropelab, International Business Park, Le Forum, 74166 Archamps, France

Opper, S (1988) A groupware toolbox, *BYTE*, **13** (13), pp 275ff

Osgood, D (1987) The difference in higher education, *BYTE,* **12** (2), pp 165–78

Paquette, G, Bergeron, G and Bourdeau, J (1993) The virtual classroom revisited, in Davies and Samways (1993)

Paulsen, M (1989) EKKO: A virtual school, in Mason, R and Kaye, A R (1989)

Paulsen, M F (1995) *Moderating Educational Computer Conferences*, NKI Electronic College of Computer Science. Available from: http://star.ucc.nau.edu/ ~mauri/moderate/morten.html

Paulsen, M F (1995) *The Online Report on Pedagogical Techniques for Computer-Mediated Communication*, NKI Electronic College of Computer Science. Available from www.hs.nki.no/~Emorten/cmcped.htm

Pedler, M (1981) Developing the learning community, in Boydell, T and Pedler, M (eds) (1991)

Pedler, M (ed) (1991) *Action Learning in Practice*, 2nd edn, Gower, Aldershot, England

Pedler, M, Burgoyne, J and Boydell, T (1986) *A Manager's Guide to Self Development,* 2nd edn, McGraw-Hill

Pinnsonneault, A and Kraemer, K L (1990) The effects of electronic meetings on group processes and outcomes: an assessment of the empirical research, *European Journal of Operational Research*, **46**, pp 143–61

Polanji, M (1958) *Personal Knowledge: Towards a postcritical philosophy*, Routledge & Kegan Paul, London

Prior, J K (ed) (1991) *Gower Handbook of Training and Development*, Gower, Aldershot

Rackham, N and Morgan, T (1977) *Behaviour Analysis in Training*, McGraw-Hill

Reason, P and Rowan, J (eds) (1981) *Human Inquiry: A sourcebook of new paradigm research*, John Wiley, Chichester

Reynolds, M (1994) Decision-making using computer conferencing: a case study, *Behaviour & Information Technology*, **13** (3), pp 239–52

Rheingold, H (1993) *Virtual Community: Homesteading on the electronic frontier*, Addison-Wesley, New York

Rodden, T (1991) A survey of CSCW systems, *Interacting With Computers*, **3** (3), pp 319–53

Rodriguez-Rosello, L (1993) Existing and future technology for teleteaching, in Davies and Samways (1993)

Rogers, C (1969) *Freedom to Learn*, Charles E Merrill, Columbus, Ohio

Rohfeld, R W and Hiemstra, R (1995) *Moderating Discussions in the Electronic Classroom*, Syracuse University. Available from: http://star.ucc.nau.edu/~mauri/moderate/rohfeld.html

Rowan, R (1986) T*he Intuitive Manager*, Little, New York

Rueda, J (1992) Collaborative learning in a large-scale computer conferencing system, in Kaye, A R (ed) (1992)

Salomon, G (1997) *Novel Constructivist Learning Environments and Novel Technologies: Some issues to be concerned*. Invited Keynote Address at the EARLI Conference, 23–26 August, 1997

Salomon, G and Perkins, D N (1998) Individual and social aspects of learning, *Review of Educational Research*, **23**, pp 1–24

Saunders, M and Machell, J (1994) *Report on the Evaluation of the User-Trials, DELTA Deliverable, JITOL Project D2015*, CSET, Lancaster University, UK

Scardamalia, M (1999) *Engaging Students in a Knowledge Society*. Paper presented at the Bi-annual conference of the European Association for Research on Learning and Instruction (EARLI), Gothenburg, August 24–28 1999

Scardamalia, M *et al* (1989) Computer supported intentional learning environments, *Journal of Educational Computing Research*, **5**, pp 51–68

Scardamalia, M and Bereiter, C (1996) Computer support for knowledge building communities, in T Koschman (ed) (1996)

Scrimshaw, P (ed) (1990) *Language, Classrooms and Computers*, Routledge, London

Seitz, R and Bodendorf, F (1994) Innovative support technologies for tele- and teamwork at universities, in Verdijo, M F and Cerri, S A (eds) (1994)

Shafriri, N (1999) *Learning as a Reflective Activity: Linkage between the concept of learning and the concept of alternative assessment.* Paper presented at the Bi-annual conference of the European Association for Research on Learning and Instruction (EARLI), Gothenburg, August 24–28 1999

Sharan, S (1990) *Cooperative Learning: Theory and research,* Praeger, NY

Sharan, S and Shachar, H (1988) *Language and Learning in the Cooperative Class-room*, Springer-Verlag, NY

Sharpe, R and Bailey, P (1998) Networked learning for professional development: technologies to meet learning outcomes, in Banks *et al* (1998)

Simons, R (1999) *CL-NET: Computer supported collaborative learning networks in primary and secondary education.* Paper presented at the Bi-annual conference of the European Association for Research on Learning and Instruction (EARLI), Gothenburg, August 24–28 1999

Singleton, J (ed) (1998) *Learning in Likely Places: Varieties of apprenticeship in Japan,* Cambridge University Press, Cambridge

Slavin, R E (1990) *Cooperative Learning: Theory, research and practice,* Prentice Hall, Englewood Cliffs, NJ

Smith, D (ed) (1988) *New Technologies and Professional Communications in Education*, NCET, London

Smith, K K and Berg, D N (1987) *Paradoxes of Group Life,* Jossey-Bass, San Francisco

Smith, M and Kollock, P (1998) *Communities in Cyberspace,* Routledge, London

Smith, P (1980) *Group Processes and Personal Change*, Harper and Row, London

Snell, R (1989) Graduating from the school of hard knocks, *Journal of Management Development*, **8** (5)

Snell, R (1989) *Learning to Work in a Peer Learning Community*, Group Relations Training Association Bulletin, Lancaster University, UK

Spender, D (1995) *Nattering on the Net: Women, power and cyberspace*, Spinifex, Melbourne

Sproull, L and Keisler, S (1991) *Connections – New ways of working in the networked organization*, MIT Press, Cambridge, Mass

Stefani, L (1998) Assessment in partnership with learners, *Assessment and Evaluation in Higher Education,* **23**, pp 339–50

Stephenson, J and Weil, S (eds) (1992) *Quality in Learning: A capability approach to higher education*, Kogan Page, London

Swann, J and Graddol, D (1988) Gender inequalities in classroom talk, *English in Education*, **22**, pp 48–65

Thorne, B and Henley, N (1975) Difference and dominance: an overview of language, gender, and society, in Thorne, B and Henley, N (eds) (1975)

Thorne, B and Henley, N (eds) (1975) *Language and Sex: Difference and dominance*, Newbury House, Rowley, Mass

Topping, K (1992) Cooperative learning and peer tutoring: an overview, *The Psychologist*, **5**, pp 151–61

Tuckman, B W (1965) Developmental sequence in small groups, *Psychological Bulletin*, **63** (6), pp 384–400

Turkle, S (1995) *Life on the Screen: Identity in the age of the Internet,* Phoenix, London

Turoff, M (1987) Seminar on CMCS in education, University of Guelph, Guelph, Ontario, Canada

Turoff, M (1989) The anatomy of a computer application innovation: computer mediated communications (CMC), *Technological Forecasting and Social Change,* **36**, pp 107–22

Van den Brande, L (1993) *Flexible and Distance Learning,* John Wiley & Son, Chichester

Van Gelder, L (1991) The strange case of the electronic lover, in Dunlop *et al* (1991)

Veerman, A, Andriessen, J and Kanselaar, G (1999) *Collaborative Problem Solving through Diagram-mediated Argumentative Discussion.* Available from: a.veerman@fss.uu.nl

Verdejo, M F and Cerri, S A (eds) (1994) *Collaborative Dialogue Technologies in Distance Learning,* Springer Verlag, Berlin

Vivian, V (1986) Electronic mail in a children's distance course: trial and evaluation, *Distance Education,* **7** (2)

Vygotsky, L S (1978) *Mind in Society: The development of higher psychological processes,* Harvard University Press, Cambridge, Mass

Wenger, E (1998) *Communities of Practice,* Cambridge University Press, Cambridge

Wexelblat, A (1993) The reality of cooperation: virtual reality and CSCW, in Wexelblat, A (ed) (1993)

Wexelblat, A (ed) (1993) *Virtual Reality: Applications and explorations,* Academic Press, Boston

Wheelan, S A and Verdi, A F (1992) Differences in male and female patterns of communication in groups: a methodological artefact? *Sex Roles,* **27** (1/2), pp 1–15

Whitehead, J (1989) How do we improve research-based professionalism in education? A question that includes action research, educational theory and the politics of educational knowledge, *British Educational Research Journal,* **15** (1)

Winograd, T (1988) Where the action is, *BYTE,* **13** (13), pp 256ff

Witman, D F, Colman, R W and Katzman, S L (1999) From paper-and-pencil to screen-and-keyboard: toward a methodology for survey research on the Internet, in S Jones (ed) (1999)

Wood, D and Wood, H (1996) Vygotsky, tutoring and learning, *Oxford Review of Education,* **22** (1), pp 5–16

Yates, S J (1997) Gender, identity and CMC, *Journal of Computer Assisted Learning,* **13**, pp 281–90

Yates, S J (1999) *The Medium and the Construction of Knowledge and Identity in Computer Mediated Communications.* Paper presented at CSNL Seminar, University of Sheffield. Available from the author: s.j.yates@open.ac.uk

Young, M F D (1971) *Knowledge and Control: New directions for the sociology of education,* Macmillan, London

Young, R E (ed) (1988) *Interim Report on the Cosmos Project, Report No: 45.5EXT,* Cosmos Coordinator's Office, Queen Mary College, London

Zimmerman, D H and West, C (1975) Sex roles, interruptions and silences in conversation, in Thorne, B and Henley, N (eds) (1975)

Index